Gandhi

Under Cross-Examination

by G. B. Singh & Tim Watson

Foreword by Prof. Lewis Baldwin

Sovereign Star Publishing, Inc
Lathrop, CA, USA

Published 2009 by Sovereign Star Publishing, Inc.

Gandhi Under Cross-Examination. 2nd Edition. Copyright © 2009 by G. B. Singh and Tim Watson. All rights reserved. No part of this publication may be reproduced, stored in a retrieval system, or transmitted in any form or by any means, digital, electronic, mechanical, photocopying, recording, or otherwise or conveyed via the internet or a web site without prior written permission of the publisher, except in the case of brief quotations embodied in critical articles and reviews.

Cover illustration by Serious Imaging (seriousimaging.com).

Inquiries should be addressed to:

Sovereign Star Publishing, Inc
PO Box 392
Lathrop, CA 95330
United States of America

www.sovstar.com

ISBN 978-0-9814992-2-2; 0-9814992-2-8

Also by G. B. Singh:

Gandhi: Behind the Mask of Divinity (Prometheus Books, 2004)

Also by Tim Watson:

"The Ethics of Timelessness" (Mellen University Press, 1994)

Contents

~

Foreword

By Prof. Lewis V. Baldwin

~

Thousands of books have been written on the significance of Mahatma Gandhi as a man of faith and as an exemplary voice, active presence, and source of influence in the struggle for justice, peace, and human dignity. Gandhi is also among Hinduism's most celebrated saints and sages, and his place in the pantheon of great religious thinkers and activists is well established. In *Gandhi Under Cross-Examination*, G. B. Singh and Tim Watson challenge these images of Gandhi while suggesting the need for a re-examination of his importance as an historical figure.

Gandhi's experiences with the racial train and coach incidents in South Africa in 1893, which coursed through parts of his *Autobiography*, are commonly viewed as the critical turning point in his march toward greatness as a *satyagrahi* [a nonviolent resister], but Singh and Watson question the credibility of Gandhi's account through a process of skeptical inquiry and cross-examination. They essentially conclude, unequivocally and by implication, that the Indian leader's account of the incidents in South Africa was fabricated. Clearly, such a conclusion strikes at the heart of Gandhi's reputation as a man of integrity, and as one who devoted his life to the search for truth.

Gandhi Under Cross-Examination will undoubtedly evoke a range of responses from people worldwide. Admirers of Gandhi will dismiss the work as a blatant effort to tarnish the image and reputation of one of the world's great leaders. Many critics of Gandhi may well view it as a noble attempt to set the historical record straight. Still others will greet the book in the spirit of ambivalence, and conclude that it merely exposes certain deficiencies in Gandhi's capacity to recall experiences and events with specificity years after they occurred. After all, memory does not always serve us well as a guide to accurate historical reporting. In any case, *Gandhi Under Cross-Examination* should not be casually dismissed or ignored in our continuing quest for the historical Gandhi.

My primary interest, as a Martin Luther King, Jr. scholar, is in what this book means for African Americans who have long held Gandhi in the highest esteem. Gandhi remains for the African American community a paragon of Godly devotion, a powerful prophetic voice, and a model of spirituality and religiously based social praxis, and the authors understand that all too well. Their purpose in part is to present another side of Gandhi which they feel deserves careful consideration and scrutiny. In short, this work should be viewed as a call to conversation around the claims and conclusions made regarding Gandhi by Singh and Watson.

Since the assassination of King in April 1968, there has been virtually no serious debate, especially in the public square, about Gandhi's meaning and significance for black America. Scholars like this author and Greg Moses have suggested the need to reconsider and perhaps redefine Gandhi's influence on King, particularly in view of King's indebtedness to Christian pacifism and to the Christian stoicism and nonviolent tradition forged by the black church and African American intellectuals from Frederick Douglass to Howard Thurman and Benjamin E. Mays. But the dialogue needs to be revived and significantly expanded to cover the larger connections between Gandhi and African Americans for two reasons. First, because Gandhi's links to blacks in this country go back as far as George Washington Carver, and are as recent as King, Thurman, and Mays. Second, because violence, much of which is intra-communal in nature, is tearing at the moral fiber of the black community, and we need to know if we should still look to figures like Gandhi for answers and/or solutions.

Singh and Watson challenge us to take a new and more serious and critical look at Gandhi's personality and values, and to come to conclusions based on the evidence in Gandhi's own accounts of his struggle with racism. Only then can we, as Singh and Watson suggest, intelligently distinguish between Gandhi the historical figure and Gandhi the iconic symbol. This is a challenge that no human being should ignore in this age of cynicism, violence, and terror.

Dr. Lewis Baldwin teaches in the Religious Studies Department at Vanderbilt University in Nashville, Tennessee. He is the author of five books and numerous articles on the life and work of Martin Luther King, Jr. He also teaches courses on King and Gandhi.

Introduction

~

For decades, Mahatma Gandhi managed to escape attentive scrutiny and skeptical inquiry in spite of the many questions surrounding the mysterious life that he led. As the individual responsible for starting "modern Gandhian scholarship," I hope the reader will agree after reading this book that the Gandhi case has to be reopened and subjected to rigorous scholarly investigation.

While stationed at Fort Sill, Oklahoma in 1983, circumstances convinced me to thoroughly research Gandhi. In 1993, I first had doubts about Gandhi's official account of the racial incidents he encountered while traveling by train in 1893 South Africa. One issue I could not reconcile was Gandhi's well-documented behavior in Durban, South Africa. In 1893, Gandhi was allegedly the victim of racial hatred when he was thrown off a train at Pietermaritzburg. In 1895, however, he was promoting racial segregation in Durban. How did the alleged victim of racism become a perpetrator of prejudice himself in the short space of two years?

After sharing my doubts with some Gandhian scholars, I realized they too were baffled but had never dared to question the account. I was stationed in South Korea in 2001-02 as part of the U.S. Army's contingency force. It was in Seoul that I first met Dr. Tim Watson, the co-author of this book. Our friendship grew and we developed a mutual interest in Gandhi, particularly concerning the racial incidents Gandhi suffered. Our lively debates helped me conclude that Dr. Watson displayed unique talents and shared my approach to the Gandhi subject. In the months that followed, I invited him to join me in evaluating the racial train incidents through the process of skeptical inquiry.

One

Coming to Natal

~

What...is Truth? A difficult question; but I have solved it for myself by saying that it is what the voice within tells you. How then, you ask, different people think of different and contrary truths? Well, seeing that the human mind works through innumerable media and that the evolution of the human mind is not the same for all, it follows that what may be truth for one may be untruth for another, and hence those who have made these experiments have come to the conclusion that there are certain conditions to be observed in making those experiments....

~ Mahatma Gandhi
Oct. 27, 1921

Before the advent of the "Union of South Africa" in 1910, the region went through a momentous period of colonial history. During that time, the year 1893 was a significant watershed in developing the colonial nation-building process for the Natal colony located in southern Africa. In May 1893, the white settlers of the colony celebrated the fiftieth anniversary of the annexation of Natal by the British as part of the Cape Colony. This was a significant event to commemorate because in 1856, Natal had become a separate colony with its own "representative government." Then, in May 1893, the Legislative Council of Natal passed a bill for a more audacious "responsible government" and by July it had finalized the process, in which the monarch in England gave his final assent. In August 1893, Pietermaritzburg (also called Maritzburg), the capital city of Natal, marked the fiftieth anniversary of the British occupation, which was an important milestone in the social and economic development of the city. In September 1893, new elections were held there for and by the white settlers to form a new Legislative Assembly under the constitution of Natal's newly enacted responsible government.[1]

While Natal was experiencing such breathtaking historic events in 1893, equally profound was another event in the making: Mahatma Gandhi was hired in India by Dada Abdulla and Co. to assist in a legal case, Dada Abdulla and Co. versus T.H.K. Mohamed and Co., and Mosa Amod and Co. located in southern Africa. His job was to instruct council, dispose of English correspondences and translate the Gujarati documents - Gujarati being Gandhi's mother tongue.[2] Gandhi landed at the port city of Durban on May 23, 1893.[3] After a stay of only a few days in Durban, his employer sent him to Pretoria in the neighboring Transvaal colony to assist in the legal case for which he was hired earlier. What transpired for Gandhi, we are told, while he was traveling on this journey, changed the entire course of his life and had many long-term consequences following several appalling episodes of racial discrimination. This will be explored in greater depth later in our investigation.

In those days, there was no direct railway line between Durban and Pretoria (see plate 1). Therefore, travel entailed three separate phases: (1) Durban to Charlestown by train, a distance of 304 miles, (2) Charlestown to Johannesburg by stagecoach pulled by a team of horses, a distance of 135 miles. This section had no rail lines and only a dirt road existed, and (3) Johannesburg to Pretoria, again by train, a distance of 37 miles. The timetable[4] for the journey to Charlestown appears below:

No. #44
Durban - Pietermaritzburg
Dep: 3.30 p.m. Arr: 8.42 p.m.

No. #112
Pietermaritzburg - Mooi River

Dep: 9.00 p.m. Arr: 12.27 a.m.

Mooi River - Estcourt
Dep: 12.37 a.m. Arr: 1.27 a.m.

Estcourt - Ladysmith
Dep: 1.58 a.m. Arr: 4.23 a.m.

No. #120
Ladysmith - Waschbank
Dep: 4.33 a.m. Arr: 6.03 a.m.

Waschbank - Glencoe Jet
Dep: 6.04 a.m. Arr: 6.52 a.m.

Glencoe Jet - Newcastle
Dep: 6.58 a.m. Arr: 8.54 a.m.

Newcastle - Ingogo
Dep: 9.14 a.m. Arr: 9.59 a.m.

Ingogo - Charlestown
Dep: 10.02 a.m. Arr: 11.50 a.m.

On this particular train route, the engine carried the following passenger cars: one 8-wheeled 3rd class car, one 8-wheeled 1st class car with toilet facilities, one 8-wheeled 2nd class car, and one van.

The stagecoach route from Charlestown to Johannesburg followed the schedule given below:[5]

Charlestown - Dep: 12.00 p.m.
Paardekop - Arr: 4.00 p.m.
Standerton - Arr: 7.00 p.m.
(Sleep overnight)
Heidelberg - Arr: 2.00 p.m.
Johannesburg - Arr: 6.00 p.m.

In short, less than some six hours into the rail journey from Durban, the train reached Pietermaritzburg after a journey of some 70 miles. At this location, on June 7, 1893, Gandhi experienced a racial incident, in which he was humiliated after being thrown off the train and left to reflect on his sorry condition the whole night on the platform.[6] He was to face further humiliations, especially the assault that took place during the coach journey. Mahatma Gandhi has himself elaborated on how the incident that transpired at the Pietermaritzburg train station changed his life irrevocably (see plate 2). He vowed from thereon to fight racial injustice and thereby devoted the rest of his life to the pursuit of that lofty goal. This life-transforming event had many consequences down the line, and is summed up by Allister Sparks in his well-acclaimed 1990 book, *The Mind of South Africa*:

> By such small twists of fate is history made. The decision taken in the waiting room of the Pietermaritzburg train station that winter's night not only affected the course of events in South Africa but led to the founding of a strategic philosophy which began the great groundswell of postwar decolonization that may be seen in retrospect to have been the most important event of the twentieth century, which inspired the American civil rights movement, and which still permeates nationalist, dissident, and humanist movements three-quarters of a century later.[7]

Today, Mahatma Gandhi hardly needs an introduction. Almost everyone is familiar with him. The literature on Gandhi is already voluminous beyond reckoning and new books are being added to the list everyday. Despite the burgeoning nature of Gandhian literature, Gandhi's autobiography, written in the 1920s, continues to hold a special place as the most widely read book of its kind, no other subsequent title displacing it to date. Those who have studied his autobiography can easily point out that Gandhi himself has placed a special emphasis on the 1893 historical encounters on the train in South Africa that dramatically altered the future course of his life. Moreover, no Gandhi biography would be considered complete if the train incident were not mentioned. When Bertrand Russell, a master skeptic, read Gandhi's autobiography, even he couldn't help but conclude, "I should therefore judge that it was this journey which was the turning point in Gandhi's life."[8] More recently, Dr. Xavier, a psychiatrist in the State of Alabama, by virtue of his special training, had this to say about Gandhi's life-transforming experience:

> In South Africa, Gandhi experienced extreme racial discrimination. Once when he was traveling in first class he was thrown off the train because he refused to travel in third class, meant for colored people. This was Gandhi's moment of truth. He could either put up with such injustice, go back to India, or stay and fight against it. He chose to stay and fight against the injustices. Whether or not Sartre's argument holds good in general - that when an individual makes an important choice for himself/herself, he/she is making a choice for the whole of humanity - here was an instance where it was dramatically true. The courage of his convictions about the truth of his cause transformed the shy, retiring Gandhi into an able political leader almost over night.[9]

What we find so significant about the series of racial train incidents is the life-altering effect they purportedly had. Gandhi tells us that the events that unfolded in those early days in South Africa were the deciding factor in altering the entire course of his life. To use a train analogy, it was precisely the racial train incidents that rerouted Gandhi's life. Had these events not occurred, there is every likelihood he would have stayed on the main line from Durban to Pretoria, where he would have taken up his job in the legal firm without the least consideration of altering his destination. As it happens, the racial train and coach incidents appear to have sidetracked the aspiring lawyer if not to have derailed his ambitions in the legal field altogether. Posterity being the judge, it appears in hindsight to have been a blessing. The day Gandhi was sidetracked and his career rerouted is regarded as one of the pivotal events altering the entire course of the speeding juggernaut known as the twentieth century.

Richard Attenborough, after many years of exhaustive research, directed the Oscar-winning 1982 film *Gandhi*. While normally regarded as historical dramas, screen and stage plays have one drawback in terms of mimesis in that they are required to entertain, very often at the expense of verisimilitude. "Historical drama" may be a misnomer. "Historical fiction" would be a more accurate genre designation, since true historicity is difficult, in fact nearly impossible to achieve. This is as true of Shakespeare's treatment of Henry IV or V as it is of Richard Attenborough's portrait of Archie Grey Owl or Mahatma Gandhi. There is no denying the painstaking nature of Attenborough's exhaustive research or the rigor he attempted to invoke in his historical portrayal of Gandhi; the problem lies in the film medium's need to embellish and dramatize in order to entertain. Reading from Gandhi's autobiographical prose in voiceover narrative does not entertain and is far from dramatic. The screenwriter is therefore forced to invent dialogue often absent from the autobiographical and historical narrative. The director is also compelled to add violence and action in order to enhance the film's dramatic qualities and entertainment value. For example, moviegoers quite early in the movie witnessed on screen how Gandhi, while traveling, was evicted from the train, followed by several shockingly heartbreaking scenes as captured here in the screenplay:

> It is the young Gandhi - a full head of hair, a somewhat sensuous face.... He is lost in his book.... He grins suddenly at some insight, then looks out of the window, weighing the idea.

> As he does the European passes the compartment and stops dead on seeing an Indian face in the First Class section.... Gandhi pivots to the porter, holding his place in the book, missing the European.... We see the cover of the book: The Kingdom of God is Within You, by Leo Tolstoy.

GANDHI: Tell me - do you think about hell?

PORTER: (stares at him blankly): "Hell!"

GANDHI: No - neither do I. But ... (he points abruptly to the book) but this man is a Christian and he has written -

The porter has glanced down the corridor, where from his point of view we can just glimpse the European talking with the conductor.

PORTER: Excuse me, baas, but how long have you been in South Africa?

GANDHI: (puzzled): A - a week.

PORTER: Well, I don't know how you got a ticket for -

He looks up suddenly then turns back quickly to his work....

CONDUCTOR: Here - coolie, just what are you doing in this car?

Gandhi is incredulous that he is being addressed in such a manner.

GANDHI: Why - I - I have a ticket. A First Class ticket.

CONDUCTOR: How did you get hold of it?

GANDHI: I sent for it in the post. I'm an attorney, and I didn't have time to -

He's taken out the ticket but there is a bit of bluster in his attitude and it is cut off by a cold rebuff from the European.

EUROPEAN: There are no colored attorneys in South Africa. Go and sit where you belong.

He gestures to the back of the train. Gandhi is nonplussed and beginning to feel a little less sure of himself....

PORTER: I'll take your luggage back, baas.

GANDHI: No, no - just a moment, please.

He reaches into this waistcoat and produces a card which he presents to the conductor.

GANDHI: You see, Mohandas K. Gandhi, Attorney at Law. I am going to Pretoria to conduct a case for an Indian trading firm.

EUROPEAN: Didn't you hear me? There are no colored attorneys in South Africa!

Gandhi is still puzzled by his belligerence, but is beginning to react to it, this time with a touch of irony.

GANDHI: Sir, I was called to the bar in London and enrolled in the High Court of Chancery - I am therefore an attorney, and since I am - in your eyes - colored - I think we can deduce that there is at least one colored attorney in South Africa....

EUROPEAN: Smart bloody kaffir - throw him out!

He turns and walks out of the compartment.

CONDUCTOR: You move your damn sammy carcass back to third class or I'll have you thrown off at the next station.

GANDHI (anger, a touch of panic): I always go First Class! I have traveled all over England and I've never....[10]

The preceding racial humiliations that Gandhi faced were experienced by large segments of the population. Today, the people of the city of Pietermaritzburg carry a sense of guilt, for had it not been for the injustices perpetrated by their forefathers, Mahatma Gandhi might have escaped these incidents of gross racial discrimination.[11] While Mark Twain has no direct relevance to Gandhi, the Gandhi incident is considered relevant to Twain scholarship because on May 14, 1896 Mark Twain boarded a train from Durban and proceeded to the city of Pietermaritzburg, reaching there at 9 p.m. This journey was uneventful and would never have been explored or delved into further were it not for author Robert Cooper, who would have us believe that this journey of Mark Twain's carried with it an underlying symbolic significance and a "mysterious" connection to Gandhi.[12] Because of the extreme nature of Gandhi's racial experiences, and the transformations it brought forth, Mahatma Gandhi has been elevated to the spiritual ranks of Apostle Paul, Abraham, Moses, Jesus, etc.[13]

<u>NOTES</u>

[1] Bill Guest. "Indians in Natal and Southern Africa in the 1890s" in *Gandhi and South Africa: Principles and Politics*, ed. by Judith M. Brown and Martin Prezesky. Pietermaritzburg: University of Natal Press, 1996.

[2] Hassim Seedat. "Gandhi in South Africa 1893-1894" in *The South African Gandhi: An Abstract of the Speeches and Writings of M. K. Gandhi 1893-1914*. Natal: Madiba Publishers, 1996.

[3] The date is quoted by Hassim Seedat in "Confrontation with Colour" on page 109 in a book "*The South African Gandhi: An Abstract of the Speeches and Writings of M. K. Gandhi, 1893-1914*. Durban: Madiba Publishers, 1996.

---

[4] Edward Donald Campbell. *The Birth and Development of the Natal Railways.* Pietermaritzburg: Shuter and Shooter, 1951, page 124. Numbers #44, 112, and 120 represent the respective train engines.

[5] Ibid., page 130. The departure time for the stagecoach is based upon the train arriving at Charlestown at 11.30 a.m. There was a 30 minutes stopover at Charlestown. Since Gandhi's train reached Charlestown at 11.50 a.m., most likely the stagecoach did not leave Charlestown before 12.20 p.m.

[6] The date is quoted by Hassim Seedat on page 201 in "Gandhi: The Pietermaritzburg Experience" in *Pietermaritzburg 1838-1988: A New Portrait of an African City* by J. Laband and R. Haswell (eds), Pietermaritzburg: University of Natal Press and Shuter & Shooter, 1988.

[7] Allister Sparks. *The Mind of South Africa.* New York: Alfred A. Knopf, 1990, p. 89.

[8] Bertrand Russell. "Mahatma Gandhi." *Atlantic Monthly*, December 1952, p. 36.

[9] N. S. Xavier. *Two Faces of Religion: A Psychiatrist's View.* Tuscaloosa, Alabama: Portals Press, 1987, pp. 155-56.

[10] John Briley. *Gandhi: The Screenplay.* New York: Grove Press, 1982, pp. 21-24. The Gandhi National Memorial in conjunction with the government of India, while celebrating Gandhi's birth centenary, released a movie, *Mahatma - Life of Gandhi 1869-1948*, on October 2, 1968. Amazingly and for unknown reasons this long movie failed to depict the famous train incident at Pietermaritzburg. Mr. Vithalbhai Jhaveri (1916-1985), a famous Gandhian, wrote the screenplay and directed the movie.

[11] Personal Communications with Professor James D. Hunt in 1999. He is a well-known Gandhian scholar and had been to Maritzburg a number of times and had witnessed this historical guilt complex among the residents.

[12] Robert Cooper. *Around The World With Mark Twain.* New York: Arcade Publishing, 2000, pp. 269-72.

[13] Teresa De Bertodano. *Soul Searchers: An Anthology of Spiritual Journeys.* Grand Rapids, Michigan: William B. Eerdmans Publishing Company, 2002, pp. 112-13.

Two

Gandhi's Calling

~

My mind is narrow. I have not read much literature. I have not seen much of the world. I have concentrated upon certain things in life and beyond that I have no other interest.

~ Mahatma Gandhi
Sept. 28, 1944

The racial humiliation Gandhi faced in 1893 completely changed his life. This was Gandhi's "moment of truth"[1] and "the turning point in Gandhi's life"[2] Anand Sharma, India's Minister of State for External Affairs in 2008, described the importance of the incident, saying, "If Gandhi was not thrown off the train in Pietermaritzburg on June 7, 1893, then maybe we would not have had a Gandhi who introduced active passive resistance to fight for freedom and democracy in South Africa and India."[3] Gandhi himself described the incident as "an experience that changed the course of life."[4]

According to Gandhi's official accounts, the Pietermaritzburg train incident directly inspired his calling to war against racism on behalf of all oppressed peoples. His sense of social justice was aroused by his own humiliation, resulting in the momentous decision to battle color discrimination even at the cost of altering his original plan to return to India after a one year stint in South Africa. This prompted the development of *Satyagraha*, the "weapon of truth" used to fight injustice. It is fair to say that the world's Mahatma was born in a cold, dark waiting room, almost like baby Jesus in a Bethlehem manger.

Gandhi Under Cross-Examination

Because the train incident was so influential in Gandhi's life, it is important to analyze how it affected him by examining his actions in the years following the incident. That is the reason for this chapter, which discusses how Gandhi, a victim of racial abuse, chose to approach racial issues after the train incident and throughout his 21-year stay in South Africa.

The reactions of the racially abused and morally enraged Gandhi can be gauged by his work through the Natal Indian Congress (NIC). Within a short span of time after the life-changing train incident, Gandhi gathered the Indian community to form the NIC, the core of which was composed of rich, upper-caste Indians. As secretary of the group, Gandhi recorded the NIC's constitution on August 22, 1894. The first of seven primary objectives detailed by the group was: "To promote concord and harmony among the Indians and Europeans residing in the colony."[5]

This objective should raise the curiosity of any attentive reader. What motivated Gandhi to seek cordial relations with the very people who threw him off the train in Pietermaritzburg? Why did he want harmony with a racist civilization which relegated him to such a low rung? Why would Gandhi pursue intimacy with the society responsible for promoting the racism he had sworn to war against? These are the answers we will search for in our examination of Gandhi.

In August 1895, just one year after establishing the NIC, Secretary Gandhi reported the progress of his organization in "Report of the Natal Indian Congress." Only one actual accomplishment was listed, which was the solution to the "problem" of the Durban Post Office. The post office had two entrances, one for whites and the other for blacks. The Indians were required to share an entrance with the blacks, which Gandhi considered unacceptable. He successfully petitioned the Natal authorities to open a third entrance into the post office. Gandhi first documented this campaign for a separate door in August 1895. Writing in "Report of the Natal Indian Congress," he said:

A correspondence was carried on by the late President with the Government in connection with the separate entrances for the Europeans and Natives and Asiatics at the Post Office.... The result has not been altogether unsatisfactory. Separate entrances will now be provided for the three communities.[6]

On a visit to India in the summer of 1896, Gandhi further explained his post office victory in a speech given to an upper-caste audience in Rajkot, Gujarat:

I may further illustrate the proposition that the Indian is put on the same level with the native in many other ways also. Lavatories are marked 'native and Asiatics' at the railway stations. In the Durban Post and telegraph offices there were separate entrances for natives and Asiatics and Europeans. We felt the indignity too much and many respectable Indians were insulted and called all sorts of names by the clerks at the counter. We petitioned the authorities to do away with the invidious distinction and they have now provided three separate entrances for natives, Asiatics, and Europeans.[7]

This is truly bewildering. Are we to believe that the very same Gandhi who was tossed unceremoniously from a train simply for being the wrong color was now promoting segregation himself? The popular history books have completely ignored this aspect of Gandhi's life in South Africa, yet it is a sad reality well-documented by primary sources. Rather than using his training as a lawyer to help the vulnerable natives of South Africa, the far reaching consequences of which might have toppled apartheid much sooner, Gandhi chose a bigoted path.

Rudimentary excavation beneath the surface soil of Gandhi's life quickly reveals strange contradictions of his official account of the train incident. The resolution to the Durban Post Office "problem" is certainly one of the strangest, yet this unfortunate accomplishment can be understood as an extension of Gandhi's goal of achieving concord with whites. In Gandhi's mind, an integral part of achieving this goal included convincing the whites that upper-caste Indians were superior to blacks. The makings of the long, painful oppression of South African blacks seem interwoven with Gandhi's history in that country.

His strategy was to segregate the two communities and extensively disseminate anti-black propaganda designed to portray native blacks as savage Neanderthals and upper-caste Indians as refined devotees of the British Empire. Gandhi's tactics were simple: petitions, delegations to government officials, letters to the press and prominent public figures, court cases, official notification to the government of resolutions passed at party meetings, and later editorials in the *Indian Opinion*. Gandhi devoted his time, education, and talents to achieving legal superiority over the black natives; equality was only on his agenda when it included an opportunity to suppress the blacks. The various documents produced by these efforts and carefully collected and preserved within *The Collected Works of Mahatma Gandhi* (CWMG) provide undeniable proof of Gandhi's bizarre South African pursuits.

The Collected Works is the official collection of Gandhi's writings, which has been approved by the Gandhi family and validated by countless Gandhi scholars and researchers. The one hundred volume work, which is approximately 50,000 pages long, is published by the Indian government. The first volume was released in 1958 and the last in 1994. The *Indian Opinion* was a newspaper Gandhi founded to promote his various causes. While *Indian Opinion* articles have been cited from the *Collected Works*, the newspapers Gandhi published still exist independently of CWMG and are archived in both South Africa and India.

In a September 24, 1903 report on the doings of the Colonial British Government, Gandhi wrote: "We believe as much in the purity of race as we think they do, only we believe that they would best serve the interest, which is as dear to us as it is to them, by advocating the purity of all the races and not one alone. We believe also that the white race in South Africa should be the predominating race."[8] This simultaneous demand for segregation and celebration of white dominance sheds light on Gandhi's previous talk of "concord" with the Europeans.

Gandhi's brief stint in South Africa, which Gandhi officially said was increased so he could stay to combat racism, became an extended tour of duty to promote segregation. At the NIC's expense, Gandhi returned to India in June 1896 to fetch his wife and children. He stayed there for five months in order to mobilize support among upper-caste Indians for their peers living in South Africa. Public lectures throughout India occupied much of his time.

His comments during a public speech at Bombay's Framji Cowasji Institute on September 26, 1896 reveal his devotion to reframing South African public opinion so that upper-caste Indians were viewed as completely different from the blacks:

> Ours is one continual struggle against a degradation sought to be inflicted upon us by the Europeans, who desire to degrade us to the level of the raw Kaffir whose occupation is hunting, and whose sole ambition is to collect a certain number of cattle to buy a wife with and, then, pass his life in indolence and nakedness. The aim of the Christian Governments, so we read, is to raise people whom they come in contact with or whom they control. It is otherwise in South Africa. There, the deliberately expressed object is not to allow the Indian to rise higher in the scale of civilization but to lower him to the position of the Kaffir; in the words of the Attorney-General of Natal... The struggle against such degradation is so severe that our whole energy is spent in resistance.[9]

Several times we have mentioned that Gandhi protested this "degradation" particularly because it was meted out against upper-caste Indians. In the same speech, he cast the discrimination suffered by South African Indians in terms his Bombay audience could understand, saying, "Statute-books describe the Indians as belonging to the 'aboriginal or semi-barbarous races of Asia,' while, as a matter of fact, there is hardly one Indian in South Africa belonging to the aboriginal stock." Of the races inhabiting India, he knew at least one example comparable to South Africa's blacks, suggesting: "The Santhals of Assam will be as useless in South Africa as the natives of that country."[10]

The Santhals are Indian tribals considered by Hindus as members of the untouchable community. In this speech Gandhi clearly exercises his Hindu ideology in order to appease his audience, who from the context are obviously upper-caste Hindus. Gandhi's implication is painfully clear. Not only is he offended by classification with the supposedly inferior "aboriginal stock," but he would consider anti-Indian discrimination in South Africa perfectly acceptable if suffered by a low-caste Indian equivalent to the South African blacks.

Gandhi continued his lecture circuit for several months. In Madras, he delivered another speech, essentially repeating what he had said in Bombay. One specific example of discrimination he mentioned was a Durban bylaw which "requires registration of colored servants." Gandhi was adamantly opposed to this bylaw because, "This rule may be, and perhaps is, necessary for the Kaffirs who would not work, but absolutely useless with regard to the Indians. But the policy is to class the Indian with the Kaffir whenever possible."[11]

Why was it that the blacks "would not work"? After the British Empire had seized their land and virtually enslaved them, why should they work? Could not the refusal of the black natives to work be viewed as a nonviolent work stoppage? Why did Gandhi so inexplicably oppose this act of civil disobedience as practiced by the blacks?

From his home state of Gujarat, he published a lengthy document titled: "The Grievances of the British Indians in South Africa: An Appeal to the Indian Public." This document, also called the "Green Pamphlet," brought to the attention of Gandhi's Indian readers that "We are classed with the natives of South Africa - Kaffir races." Addressing a Durban bylaw, Gandhi wrote:

There is... a bye-law in Durban which provides for the registration of native servants and 'others belonging to the uncivilized races of Asia.' This presupposes that the Indian is a barbarian. There is a very good reason for requiring registration of a native in that he is yet being taught the dignity and necessity of labour. The Indian knows it and he is imported because he knows it. Yet, to have the pleasure of classifying him with the natives, he too is required to be registered. The Superintendent of the Borough Police has never, so far as I know, put the law in motion. Once I raised an objection, in defending an Indian servant, that he was not registered. The Superintendent resented the objection and said he never applied the law to Indians and asked me if I wanted to see them degraded.[12]

This quotation exposes several aspects of Gandhi's mindset. Despite his passionate objection to this law, Gandhi admits it was not applied to Indians. Not only does he endorse the discrimination against blacks while explicitly calling them lazy, but Gandhi himself presupposes that the black native is a "barbarian." Furthermore, while the unaware reader might incorrectly render the phrase "classed with" the black natives as "treated like" the blacks, Gandhi's anger is actually sparked not by any practical discrimination, but merely by the equation of South African blacks and Indians. By "Indians" we mean upper-caste Indians - as in the case of the Santhals, Gandhi was all too eager to equate the blacks with lower-caste Indians.

Gandhi was not content with simple statutory superiority over the black natives. He appears to have desired not just a stark legal distinction between the blacks and the upper class Indians, but also physical distance. In 1904, for instance, he addressed a letter to Johannesburg's Medical Officer of Health, saying:

Why, of all places in Johannesburg, the Indian Location should be chosen for dumping down all the kaffirs of the town passes my comprehension.... Of course, under my suggestion, the Town Council must withdraw the Kaffirs from the Location. About this mixing of the Kaffirs with the Indians, I must confess I feel most strongly. I think it is very unfair to the Indian population and it is an undue tax on even the proverbial patience of my countrymen.[13]

Although Gandhi devoted far more effort to achieving superiority over the blacks, various letters from 1894 show him making some attempts to convince British authorities that "both the English and the Indians spring from a common stock."[14] In June 1894, he wrote:

> We beg to point out that both the Anglo-Saxon and the Indian races belong to the same stock... Max Muller, Morris, Greene and a host of other writers with one voice seem to show very clearly that both the races have sprung from the same Aryan stock, or rather the Indo-European as many call it. We have no wish whatever to thrust ourselves as members of a brother nation on a nation that would be unwilling to receive us as such, but we may be pardoned if we state the real facts.[15]

This equality of the races doctrine is commendable and certainly appropriately enlightened for the Mahatma we know. However, a deeper examination of a similar letter from December 1894 reveals a disturbing method for making his point:

> I venture to point out that both the English and the Indians spring from a common stock, called the Indo-Aryan.

> A general belief seems to prevail in the Colony that the Indians are little better, if at all, than savages or the Natives of Africa. Even the children are taught to believe in that manner, with the result that the Indian is being dragged down to the position of a raw Kaffir. Such a state of things, which the Christian legislators of the Colony would not, I firmly believe, wittingly allow to exist and remain, must be my excuse for the following copious extracts, which will show at once that the Indians were, and are, in no way inferior to their Anglo-Saxon brethren.[16]

An inextricable aspect of Gandhi's argument for equality was Indian superiority over black Africans. Rather than pursuing a vision of "all men created equal," Gandhi made it very clear he would be satisfied with a society where upper-caste Indians and whites were considered equal while blacks were forced to the lowest rung by both racial groups. Gandhi pushed this distorted view of equality without any regard for the damage he did to the black community in the process.

In May 1895, Gandhi penned another long petition, this time to Lord Ripon, secretary of state for the colonies. The petition particularly stressed Gandhi's belief that the Indian was being degraded to the level of a "raw Kaffir." He concluded the letter with an extraordinary prediction about the fate of upper-caste Indians if they continued to be subjected to racial pressure from the whites:

> By persistent ill-treatment they cannot but degenerate, so much so that from their civilized habits they would be degraded to the habits of the aboriginal Natives, and a generation hence, between the progeny of the Indians thus in course of degeneration and the Natives, there will be very little difference in habits, and customs, and thought. The very object of immigration will be frustrated, and a large portion of Her Majesty's subjects, instead of being raised in the scale of civilization, will be actually lowered. The results of such a state of things cannot but be disastrous. No self-respecting Indian can dare even visit South Africa. All Indian enterprise will be stifled.[17]

The evidence shows beyond a doubt that Gandhi's scathingly racist view of black Africans, derived from his Hindu caste ideology, was deep-rooted and unquestioning. We would remind the reader that Gandhi was advocating the very ideology of prejudice he swore to defeat. His association with the upper-caste Indians in South Africa reinforced his anti-black sentiments; his perpetual habit of viewing white society as the pinnacle of the "civilization scale" generated greater prejudice against the black natives forcibly relegated to the bottom of the scale. It's easy to believe that there was not a single time during Gandhi's nearly 21 years in South Africa that he took time to meet with leaders of the black community.

His loyalty to British imperialism was also unwavering. All Gandhi could say in the midst of the Boer War was: "It was the Indians' proudest boast that they were British subjects. If they were not, they would not have had a footing in South Africa."[18] He seemed to harbor a vision of upper-caste Indians joining hands with the white British to rule the South African colonies. It is not difficult to picture the consequences for black Africans under such domination. Perhaps low-caste Indians would fare a degree better than black natives, but they too would suffer on a low rung in Gandhi's Vedic civilization scale.

In 1914, Gandhi's time came to bid farewell to South Africa forever. The historical record specifically shows Gandhi paying his respects to both the Indians and the whites, but nowhere is there the slightest mention of the black natives. During the several going-away parties held in his honor, he recalled his past 21 years of struggle in South Africa. Proudly he mentioned his heroism during the Boer War, but not a single word crossed his lips about his participation in the war on blacks (this is the topic of Chapter Nine). There was no soul-searching, no inner turmoil, and no rigorous introspection. Instead, Gandhi's departing words were of praise for the British Empire:

> Rightly or wrongly, for good or for evil, Englishmen and Indians have been knit together, and it behooves both races so to mould themselves as to leave a splendid legacy to the generations yet to be born, and to show that though Empires have gone and fallen, this Empire perhaps may be an exception and that this is an Empire not founded on material but on spiritual foundations.[19]

The blacks of South Africa were in a precarious predicament. They faced not one, but two masters. First, the formal master, the whites who slowly and steadily took over the land, turning blacks into serfs. Second, Gandhi-style Indians who came to South

Africa, piggybacking on whites and extolling themselves as brothers to the oppressive Empire, which they claimed was conceived on "spiritual foundations."

Gandhi's actions after the 1893 train incident simply do not agree with his own historical accounts of that same "life-changing" incident. In his autobiography, Gandhi offered a reason for staying in Africa past the originally planned date, writing: "The hardship to which I was subjected was superficial - only a symptom of the deep disease of colour prejudice. I should try, if possible, to root out the disease."[20] Despite this supposed resolution of "rooting out" racism, he immediately became an unapologetic carrier of it himself, spreading the disease throughout South Africa. How can a man, upon facing severe racial humiliation and beatings, commit his life to battling racial injustice and then turn around to mete out worse discrimination on those of an even lower social stratum?

Whatever the answers, it seems that the practical effect of Gandhi's racial train incident, which he cites as his turning point, was to shape him for the worst. This makes understanding what really happened in Pietermaritzburg all the more pertinent, which is why we are now going to examine that incident in depth.

NOTES

[1] N. S. Xavier. *Two Faces of Religion: A Psychiatrist's View.* Tuscaloosa, Alabama: Portals Press, 1987, pp. 155-56.

[2] Bertrand Russell. "Mahatma Gandhi." *Atlantic Monthly*, December 1952, p. 36.

[3] "Gandhi's Philosophy Must Permeate Throughout the World," *The Hindu*, September 19, 2008.

[4] Collected Works of Mahatma Gandhi, Vol. 74, p. 275. (This reference can also be represented as CWMG.)

[5] CWMG, Vol. 1, pp. 178-79.

[6] Ibid., p. 266.

[7] Ibid., pp. 367-68.

[8] CWMG, Vol. 3, pp. 255-56.

[9] CWMG, Vol. 1, p. 410.

[10] Ibid., p. 408.

[11] Ibid., p. 435.

[12] Ibid., p. 367.

[13] CWMG, Vol. 3, p. 429.

[14] CWMG, Vol. 1, p. 192.

[15] Ibid., p. 149.

[16] Ibid., p. 192.

[17] Ibid., p. 229-30.

[18] CWMG, Vol. 2, p. 342.

[19] CWMG, Vol. 14, p. 261.

[20] Mohandas K. Gandhi. *An Autobiography or The Story of My Experiments With Truth.* (1927, 1929); reprint, Boston: Beacon Press, 1957, pp. 111 to 117.

Three

Celebrating The Incident

~

Truth is the first thing to be sought for, and Beauty and Goodness will then be added unto you. That is what Christ really taught in the Sermon on the Mount. Jesus was, to my mind, a supreme artist because he saw and expressed Truth; and so was Muhammad, the Koran being the most perfect composition in all Arabic literature - at any rate.... It is because both of them strove first for Truth that the grace of expression naturally came in and yet neither Jesus nor Muhammad wrote on Art. That is the Truth and Beauty I crave for, live for, and would die for.

~ Mahatma Gandhi
Nov. 20, 1924

C ircumstances following the Second World War brought about dramatic changes in the European colonial powers and their impact on the subject peoples. In August 1947, the British Indian Empire was to withdraw altogether from mother India, leaving in its wake the two separate political entities of Hindu India and Islamic Pakistan. One consequence of this partition was the largest forced mass migration of people in history, with the resulting number of lives lost estimated at up to one million.

In Hindu India, political power was transferred from the British Raj into the hands of Gandhi and his close followers. Shortly after these events, Gandhi himself was assassinated leaving his followers to continue running the operations of the Gandhi propaganda machine - designed to spread Gandhi's good name and reputation all over the world - except in South Africa.[1]

Gandhi Under Cross-Examination

The official reason South Africa was immune to Gandhi's propaganda machine was because of its history of racial discrimination. Concurrent with Gandhi's death, South Africa turned further inward when it started to take formal measures by institutionalizing apartheid laws to further subjugate and segregate the people of color, especially the blacks. Under such politically repressive circumstances, the Gandhi propaganda machine couldn't promote its messiah, unlike in other places. However oppressive the situation was in South Africa, the Gandhi propaganda machine went underground and functioned quite effectively once it took root. At times it surfaced only to be squelched by the state security apparatus.

Largely as a result of political and economic pressures brought to bear upon official South Africa, the world witnessed the dismantling of apartheid laws with the advent of 1990 and consequently the African National Congress and Nelson Mandela came to the forefront of democratic South Africa. These dramatic changes also changed the fortunes for the Gandhi propaganda machine and set the stage for openly exploiting Mahatma Gandhi as a phenomenon for the new generation. Nelson Mandela extended his hand of friendship toward official India and this was reciprocated. In January 1991, under the leadership of Dr. Mahomed M. Motala in South Africa, the Gandhi Memorial Committee was formed, a committee comprising prominent Indians living in South Africa and an integral part of the Gandhi propaganda machine. The first task the committee set for itself was to map out a strategy for promoting Gandhi under programs such as the "Gandhi Education Foundation," the "Gandhi Bursary Trust," and the "Gandhi Memorial Institute."

The timing was perfect: The year 1993 was on the horizon - a pivotal year for Gandhi's propaganda machine to take full advantage of the centenary celebrations of the racial train incident at Pietermaritzburg. 1993 marked the centenary of June 1893, when the young M. K. Gandhi had faced a series of racial humiliations during his journey to Pretoria, particularly those events that transpired at Pietermaritzburg railway station, the hallmark of all of his humiliations and the pivotal incident that led Gandhi to undertake a protracted battle against racial discrimination. New democratic South Africa made it possible to openly commemorate the one hundredth anniversary of the incident on South African soil.

On June 6, 1993, a large statue of Mahatma Gandhi was erected in Pietermaritzburg in front of the busy Church Street Mall (also called "Maritzburg Mall"), just opposite the colonial building with the City Hall and Tatham Art Gallery. The statue was a gift of the government of India unveiled by Archbishop Desmond Tutu. Karan Singh, a member of India's cabinet, represented the Indian government at this solemn ceremony attended by many dignitaries as well as ordinary citizens. The inscription at the base of the statue read: "This statue marks the centenary of the event on the night of June 7, 1893 when M. K. Gandhi was forcibly removed from a train compartment at Pietermaritzburg station because of discrimination based on race." To mark the occasion, Nelson Mandela issued the appropriate remarks:

> It is an honor for me to be here to unveil the very first statue of hope.... This event is also very significant because we are unveiling here the very first statue of an anti colonial figure and a hero of millions of people worldwide. Gandhiji influenced the activities of liberation movements, civil rights movements and religious organizations in all five continents of the world. He impacted on men and women who have achieved significant historical changes in their countries not least amongst whom are Martin Luther King.... The Mahatma is an integral part of our history because it is here that he first experimented with truth; here that he demonstrated his characteristic firmness in pursuit of justice; here that he developed Satyagraha as a philosophy and a method of struggle.[2]

The Gandhi Memorial Committee published a souvenir book - a "memorial edition" - in June 1993. The day after the statue was unveiled, there was a conference held on "Gandhi and his Significance" organized by the Arts Faculty of the University of Natal on the occasion of the centenary of Gandhi's racial experience.[3] A plaque commemorating the 1893 event was unveiled in the railway station's foyer in 1995.[4]

The year 1997 brought about another wave of support for Gandhi. At a moving ceremony on April 25 at Pietermaritzburg railway station, Nelson Mandela, the president of South Africa, conferred the "Freedom of Pietermaritzburg" award on Mahatma Gandhi posthumously. Gopalkrishna Gandhi, Mahatma Gandhi's grandson, and at the time India's High Commissioner (Ambassador) to South Africa, accepted the award on behalf of his grandfather and noted that Gandhi's experience at the railway station was something like a second birth: "When Gandhi was evicted from the train, an Indian visiting South Africa fell but when Gandhi rose, an Indian South African rose."[5] Mandela, at the conclusion of the ceremonies, clearly defined the importance of Gandhi, "It is a token of our appreciation of Mahatma Gandhi's enormous contribution to the birth of a New Pietermaritzburg and a New South Africa."[6]

Apparently, this ceremony was not dignified enough to satisfy India. They had hoped for something more fitting and evidently worked out a deal with Nelson Mandela. Carefully laid plans called for I. K. Gujral (India's prime minister at the time) to pay a week-long visit from October 4-12, 1997 to Egypt, Uganda, and South Africa and to carry with him plans for promoting Gandhi.[7] On the scheduled day, Mr. Gujral and his team arrived at Pietermaritzburg railway station and waited for Nelson Mandela. Together, they were to rename this railway station after Mahatma Gandhi. Mandela failed to attend and the renaming ceremony didn't go as planned.[8] What could have happened? No one knows. The Indian media reported that Mandela showed his displeasure at Gujral because, according to the news, Mandela did not approve of the Indian premier taking three years to pay homage to Nelson on South African soil in spite of Mandela's two earlier invitations.[9] How accurate that news is we simply do not know. Gujral had described his African visit as a "pilgrimage." As part of his itinerary, he paid homage to Mahatma Gandhi's important sites in South Africa, including a wreath laying ceremony on the grave of Reverend

John Dube (1871-1946), a famous South African black leader and a contemporary of Gandhi's.[10]

October 2002 brought a number of Indian beauties to South Africa to compete in the first Miss India pageant, participants being limited to the Indian Diaspora. The beauties undertook a historic train journey, retracing the steps of Mahatma Gandhi and other important Indians associated with him. The final stop on this whistle stop journey was Pietermaritzburg, where a white conductor symbolically kicked an individual off the train, just as Gandhi had experienced in June 1893.[11]

February 2003 brought the Indian cricket team to Maritzburg in order to participate in the World Cup Group-A league against Namibia. Amazingly, the team boarded a train for a ten-minute ride from nearby Pentrich railway station to Pietermaritzburg in the "Gandhi Memorial Train," a replica of the carriage that Mahatma Gandhi had boarded back in 1893. The band welcomed the team at the Maritzburg railway platform, where they attended the unveiling of a stone plaque at the spot where Gandhi fell on the platform. The mayor of Maritzburg, in his speech, confirmed, "Gandhi's decision on the fateful night of June 1893, to stay in South Africa and launch a campaign of resistance against racial oppression, was to reverberate around the world, particularly in India and South Africa...."[12] To mark the occasion, Sourav Ganguly, the Indian team captain said, "We get very little time outside cricket and it is great to visit such a place which has great historic value. We all have heard and read about Mahatma Gandhi, but to understand from close quarters how difficult his struggle was is simply mind-boggling. As Indians, we are all proud of the great man."

If the immediate past provides any sense of what is likely to take shape on the site, altering the landscape of Pietermaritzburg forever, then the plan to set up statues of Nelson Mandela and Gandhi side by side at the City Hall Park is the most likely scenario.[13] Recently, we learned that India has dispatched a bust of Gandhi scheduled to be erected in the near future at the railway station at Pietermaritzburg or in close proximity.

As evidenced by the historical events over the last hundred years or so of what Gandhi experienced on his journey to Pretoria in June 1893, these events have never elicited the slightest doubt. The idea of raising even a question concerning these incidents has never been considered or even dared. Given the availability of a wide spectrum of Gandhi apologists, a few Gandhi haters, a large cadre of Gandhi historians and other professional historians occupying the prestigious chairs of academia, one would think someone might have questioned the veracity of these accounts. Yet, there is not a single instance of anyone questioning the authenticity of these racial incidents. We decided to be the first to question the authenticity of these accounts. We have developed suspicions that perhaps the world has been duped into believing these racial episodes actually took place. This book is intended to provide the reader with the entire story. In order to unfold the mystery on an historical basis, we decided to place Gandhi's entire train and coach journey of 1893 under the microscope through a process of skeptical inquiry. In applying this methodology of skeptical inquiry, we opened the pages of Paul Kurtz's book, *"The New Skepticism: Inquiry and Reliable Knowledge."*[14] We decided to apply the knowledge, principles and art of skeptical inquiry as discussed by Dr. Kurtz in his monumental work to the racial incidents that Gandhi is said to have encountered in June 1893. To unveil the mystery in a systematic fashion, this book is laid out in such a format as to make the process of inquiry interesting, educational, and provocative.

In Chapter Four, we delve into the "authentic evidence" that scholars and historians have always relied on. Surrounding this "evidence," the context under which it is brought forth is elaborated briefly. In Chapter Five, we subject the four "historical accounts" to comparative analysis, looking for patterns of marked inconsistency and profound contradiction. In addition, we decided on something dramatically different by calling Gandhi to the witness stand, subjecting his testimony to cross-examination. In Chapter Six, we take a close look at the contemporary historical documents, a simple process that has never been attempted before. Chapter Seven is no less unique in the literature. This chapter analyzes the first "testimony," in which Gandhi's racial encounters were brought before the world jury in the book by Reverend J. J.

Doke, author of a 97-page book published in 1909. Chapter Eight intensely scrutinizes the burgeoning relationship between Gandhi and Rev. Doke - a topic that has been overlooked all along. Chapter Nine examines the origins of Gandhi's *Brahmacharya* vow of poverty and celibacy. Chapter Ten provides a summary of Gandhi's politics of victimization and discusses lessons we can learn from the story of Gandhi's racial train and coach incidents. The conclusion offers a final interpretation of the information discussed throughout this book.

NOTES

[1] For details on the Gandhi propaganda machine, read part 1 of *Gandhi: Behind the Mask of Divinity*. Amherst, N.Y.: Prometheus Books, 2004.

[2] This speech by Nelson Mandela is available on http://www.anc.org.za/ancdocs/history/mandela.

[3] The proceedings of the conference in a revised form appeared in *Gandhi and South Africa: Principles and Politics*. Pietermaritzburg: University of Natal Press, 1996, edited by Judith M. Brown and Martin Prozesky. The Gandhi Memorial Committee comprising a group of some prominent Indians in South Africa was established to promote Gandhi and it published a souvenir book marking the occasion.

[4] Ibid.: mentioned on the back cover of the book

[5] Quoted in the article titled "Pietermaritzburg: The Beginning of Gandhi's Odyssey." This article is available on http://www.sscnet.ucla.edu/southasia/History/Gandhi/Pieter.html.

[6] This speech by Nelson Mandela is available on http://www.anc.org.za/ancdocs/history/mandela. The touching ceremony inspired Dr. Y.P. Anand, director of National Gandhi Museum, to write a monograph of seventeen pages titled, *Pietermaritzburg Railway Station: The Start of the Journey from Mohandas Karamchand Gandhi to Mahatma Gandhi*. New Delhi: National Gandhi Museum, 1998.

[7] *India Today International*, November 10, 1997, p. 17.

[8] "Gujral's Bungled S. Africa Visit: Disappointments and Rhetoric Prevail" in *Times-India* October 17, 1997, p. 1.

[9] "African Safari" *India Today International*, October 20, 1997, pp. 25-27.

[10] To learn about John L. Dube, we recommend chapter 16 of *"Natal and Zulu-land: From Earliest Times to 1910 A new History"* edited by Andrew Duminy and Bill Guest. Pietermaritzburg: University of Natal Press, 1989. Gandhi had no meaningful connection with Rev. Dube.

[11] "Indian beauties to follow Gandhi trail in S. Africa" located at http://in.news.yahoo.com/021023/43/1wqzy.html.

[12] Quoted in "Gandhi's kin says thank you to Indian players" and located at http://www.cricketnext.com/news1/next/joshi/tap726.htm. In September 2004, Abdul Kalam, the President of India, while on an official visit to South Africa, boarded the same train to commemorate the event of 1893. On September 30, 2006, while on a four-day official visit to South Africa, the Indian Prime Minister Manmohan Singh boarded the same train at Pentrich Station traveling to Pietermaritzburg train station. Upon reaching there, he remarked, "It's a soul-stirring experience" and "I came to breathe some of the air that transformed Gandhi."

[13] *Times of India* (Times News Network) February 24, 2003. According to this news Dasareth Bundhoo, secretary of the Gandhi Memorial Committee in South Africa complains of Gandhi's statue as being a target of disrespect by some local citizens. The City of Johannesburg, who set up Gandhi's statue in October 2003 in central Johannesburg made sure that it was immune to contempt: They installed sensors, alarms and sirens on the statue.

[14] Paul Kurtz. *The New Skepticism: Inquiry and Reliable Knowledge.* Buffalo, N.Y.: Prometheus Books, 1992.

Four

What Is The Evidence?

~

I am surrounded by exaggeration and untruth. In spite of my best efforts to find it, I do not know where Truth lies. But it seems to me that I have come nearer to God and Truth. It has cost me old friendships but I am not sorry for it.... Sixty years of striving have at last enabled me to realize the ideal of truth and purity which I have ever set before myself.

~ Mahatma Gandhi
Apr. 1947

Mahatma Gandhi's literature is vast. Based upon in depth study of his literature, we have compiled Gandhi's own words relating to the racial incidents. Only four times in his life did Mahatma Gandhi mention the series of incidents. Therefore, it is only through Gandhi's eyewitness reports made long after the alleged incidents that we have any record of them at all. It was not until 1909 that the first account of the racial train and coach incidents appeared. From 1893 to 1909, Gandhi remains silent on the matter. In fact, it is not until 1923 that he begins to even contemplate writing about the incident. We do not wish to impute any motives or to offer any reasons for his long silence at this juncture. We simply wish to state the facts and these are the facts. The why and wherefore will be addressed in a later chapter.

1. <u>M. K. Gandhi: An Indian Patriot in South Africa</u>, by J. J. Doke (1909)

This is the first Gandhi biography covering his life from October 2, 1869, to October 28, 1909. In this sense it is truly historic. Rev. Joseph J. Doke (1861-1913) came to Johannesburg in 1907 and worked there as a minister of the Central Baptist Church. As fate would have it, the ongoing Indian Passive Resistance Movement and other events led him to meet Gandhi in person. Further events set the stage for Reverend Doke to write the biography as explained by Bishop James K. Mathews in his dissertation at Columbia University:

> He was really "tricked" into allowing this to be done. Mr. Doke came to his office one day in about 1908, asking Gandhi if he were ready to be a martyr. The ready reply was, "I am nothing. I am willing to die at any time or to do anything for the cause." The "martyrdom" consisted in allowing the biography to be written, for the minister felt that it would help the cause of the Indians for their leader to be known in England.[1]

Keep in mind that no written or oral biographical information on Gandhi existed before this book was written. It was the first ever biography of Gandhi, who largely dictated the account himself. Gandhi then took the manuscript with him on his way to London for the second deputation, as part of his ongoing Satyagraha campaigns, in June 1909. He somehow convinced Lord Ampthill (senior British official as former governor of Madras and governor-general of India, who had Indian sympathies) to write the introduction. By October 1909, Nasarwanji M. Cooper, editor of the *Indian Chronicle*, published the book. While in London, Gandhi tried his best to extract any mileage he could out of his biography. He had with him about seven hundred copies for distribution; out of the targeted distributions, he mailed one copy to Leo Tolstoy in Russia, emphasizing the uniqueness of his Satyagraha struggle depicted in the book.[2] Remember, this is the first book that explained Gandhi's historical encounter with the racial incidents as he was traveling in 1893. Considering that the revelation should coincide with the campaign to disseminate the Doke biography that turned

Gandhi into a martyr for the cause of Indians of Transvaal, the timing could not have been more auspicious. The reader's view on the subject may be influenced by the following passage from the Doke biography:

> The case for which he [Gandhi] was engaged needed his presence in Pretoria. The train could only take him as far as Charlestown. His clients had advised him to take bed-ticket for the journey. This he neglected to do, having his own rugs with him. At Pietermaritzburg, before starting, a fellow-passenger called the guard, and to his surprise, Mr. Gandhi was ordered to "come out and go into the van-compartment." As he held a first class ticket, and knew that the carriage went through to Charlestown, he refused. The guard insisted. The train was ready to start. He refused again. A constable was brought, and the Indian stranger was forcibly ejected, his bundles pitched out after him, and, with the train gone, he was left to shiver in the waiting room all night.
>
> When at length he reached the Transvaal, and began his coach-journey, he again felt the disadvantage of being an Indian. The coach was about to leave Paardeberg with Mr. Gandhi seated on the box when the guard, a big Dutchman, wishing to smoke, laid claim to this place, telling the Indian passenger to sit down at his feet. "No," said Mr. Gandhi, quietly, "I shall not do so." The result was a brutal blow in the face. The victim held on to the rail, when another blow nearly knocked him down. Then the passengers interfered, much to the guard's disgust. "Let the poor beggar alone," they said, and the man threatening to "do for him" at the next stage desisted. But at Standerton the coach was changed, and the rest of the journey was accomplished without incident.

It is almost amusing now, to anyone acquainted with colonial prejudice, if it were not so pitiful, to note how utterly ignorant the new-comer was of it all. He even drove to the Grand National Hotel on reaching Johannesburg, where, of course, there was "no room" for him. Everywhere it was the same. The colour-bar was a terrible disadvantage, and experiences like these so disheartened and disgusted him, that, but for his contract with the Indians, he would have left South Africa at once.[3]

2. <u>Satyagraha in South Africa</u> by M. K. Gandhi (1923)

Convicted of sedition (for inciting crowds against the government) in 1922 and sentenced to six years in prison, Gandhi actually served only two years at Yeravda Central Jail, India. There in 1923, he commenced writing a book, dictated to another inmate in his native tongue. By November 22, 1925, the newspaper *Navajivan* completed the serial publication of this work titled *Satyagraha in South Africa*. The English translation appeared in 1928, though it was never published serially or published in the United States during this time period.[4] Chapter 6 of the book titled "A Review of the Early Struggle" must be reproduced here at length to show what Gandhi himself would like us to believe concerning what happened in 1893:

> I will not describe my bitter experience in the courts within a fortnight of my arrival, the hardships I encountered on railway trains, the thrashings I received on the way and the difficulty in and the practical impossibility of securing accommodation in hotels.... I saw that from the standpoint of self-interest South Africa was no good to me. Not only did I not desire but I had a positive aversion to earning money or sojourning in a country where I was insulted. I was on the horns of a dilemma. Two courses were open to me. I might either free myself from the contract with Messrs Dada Abdulla on the ground that circumstances had come to my knowledge which had not been disclosed to me before, and run back to India. Or, I might bear all hardships and fulfill my engagement. I was pushed out of the train by

a police constable at Maritzburg, and the train having left, was sitting in the waiting room, shivering in the bitter cold. I did not know where my luggage was, nor did I dare to inquire of anybody, lest I might be insulted and assaulted once again. Sleep was out of the question. Doubt took possession of my mind. Late at night, I came to the conclusion that to run back to India would be cowardly. I must accomplish what I had undertaken. I must reach Pretoria, without minding insults and even assaults. Pretoria was my goal. The case was being fought out there. I made up my mind to take some steps, if that was possible, side by side with my work. This resolution somewhat pacified and strengthened me but I did not get any sleep.

Next morning I wired to the firm of Dada Abdulla and to the General Manager of the Railway. Replies were received from both. Dada Abdulla and his partner Sheth Abdulla Haji Adam Jhaveri who was then in Natal took strong measures. They wired to their Indian agents in various places to look after me. They likewise saw the General Manager. The Indian traders of Maritzburg came to see me in response to the telegram received by the local agent. They tried to comfort me and told me that all of them had had the same bitter experiences as myself, but they did not mind such things, being habituated to them. Trade and sensitiveness could ill go together. They had therefore made it a principle to pocket insults as they might pocket cash. They told me how Indians could not enter the railway station by the main gate and how difficult it was for them to purchase tickets. I left for Pretoria the same night. The Almighty Searcher of all hearts put my determination to a full test. I suffered further insults and received more beatings on my way to Pretoria. But all this only confirmed me in my determination.[5]

3. <u>An Autobiography or The Story of My Experiments With Truth</u> by M. K. Gandhi (1925)

Gandhi's autobiography has another strange facet. Amazingly, it is not intended to be a bona fide autobiography as the title above implies. He even apprises us of his intentions in the introduction:

> [It] is not my purpose to attempt a real autobiography. I simply want to tell the story of my numerous experiments with truth, and as my life consists of nothing but those experiments,.... But I should certainly like to narrate my experiments in the spiritual field which are known only to myself, and from which I have derived such power as I possess for working in the political field."[6]

In this chapter, we are only presenting the facts pertaining to the accounts Gandhi gives of what happened in the racial incidents of 1893 and the facts in this case are that this book, by Gandhi's own admission, was never intended to be factual. Why would Gandhi make such a confession? We would like to introduce a hypothesis at this juncture that we intend to explore in a later chapter. Could it be that Gandhi felt pressured into doing something against his own conscience? Could it be that he was encouraged by a means-ends relationship to distort the truth in order to promote the independence movement? Could it also be that he wished to come clean about such political opportunism in an attempt to exonerate himself?

Though the "vision" originated somewhat earlier, the roots of the idea to write an autobiography came while he was in prison and he continued to work on it after his release. He wrote weekly narratives in his native Gujarati language, which were then published in weekly installments in Gandhi's paper, Navajivan, from November 29, 1925 to February 3, 1929. A carefully revised English translation (done by his close disciples: Mahadev Desai, Pyarelal Nayar, and Miss Slade) appeared later, simultaneously, in *Indian Opinion* in South Africa and *Young India* in India beginning on December 3, 1925. Four months later, *Unity* in the United States began to serially publish the "autobiography" for 135 weeks, beginning on April 5, 1926. Gandhi himself was an active participant in decisions, making sure that his weekly installments received widespread publicity. It is no accident that his autobiography received instant exposure virtually all over the world. In 1927 and 1929, Macmillan published the autobiography in two volumes. The second edition, published in 1940, came out in one big volume. This book has been translated into numerous languages, including Hindi, Kannada, Malayalam, Marathi, Oriya, Punjabi, Tamil, Telugu, Urdu, Sanskrit, Spanish, Portuguese, French, German, Polish, Russian, Swedish, Arabic, Turkish, Serbo-Croatian, Japanese, Korean, Nepalese, Tibetan, and Swahili. The autobiography, though it covers Gandhi's life only until December 1920, is definitely the most widely read of his works.[7] Concerning the 1893 incident, Gandhi begins his narrative in the middle of chapter 8 titled - "On the Way to Pretoria" - and continues to devote the entire next chapter titled "More Hardships" and part of the following chapter to the incident. In these chapters, he explores these events in some detail as in the passage that follows:

On the seventh or eighth day after my arrival, I left Durban. A first class seat was booked for me. It was usual there to pay five shillings extra, if one needed a bedding. Abdulla Sheth insisted that I should book one bedding but, out of obstinacy and pride and with a view to saving five shillings, I declined. Abdulla Sheth warned me. "Look, now," said he "this is a different country from India. Thank God, we have enough and to spare. Please do not stint yourself in anything that you may need."

I thanked him and asked him not to be anxious.

The train reached Maritzburg, the capital of Natal, at about 9 p.m. Beddings used to be provided at this station. A railway servant came and asked me if I wanted one. "No," said I, "I have one with me." He went away. But a passenger came next, and looked me up and down. He saw that I was a "coloured" man. This disturbed him. Out he went and came in again with one or two officials. They all kept quiet, when another official came to me and said, "Come along, you must go to the van compartment."

"But I have a first class ticket," said I.

"That doesn't matter," rejoined the other. "I tell you, you must go to the van compartment."

"I tell you, I was permitted to travel in this compartment at Durban, and I insist on going on in it."

"No, you won't," said the official. "You must leave this compartment, or else I shall have to call a police constable to push you out."

"Yes, you may. I refuse to get out voluntarily."

The constable came. He took me by the hand and pushed me out. My luggage was also taken out. I refused to go to the other compartment and the train steamed away. I went and sat in the waiting room, keeping my hand-bag with me, and leaving the other luggage where it was. The railway authorities had taken charge of it.

It was winter, and winter in the higher regions of South Africa is severely cold. Maritzburg being at a high altitude, the cold was extremely bitter. My overcoat was in my luggage, but I did not dare to ask for it lest I should be insulted again, so I sat and shivered. There was no light in the room. A passenger came in at about mid-night and possibly wanted to talk to me. But I was in no mood to talk.

I began to think of my duty. Should I fight for my rights or go back to India, or should I go on to Pretoria without minding the insults, and return to India after finishing the case? It would be cowardice to run back to India without fulfilling my obligation. The hardship to which I was subjected was superficial - only a symptom of the deep disease of colour prejudice. I should try, if possible, to root out the disease and suffer hardships in the process. Redress for wrongs I should seek only to the extent that would be necessary for the removal of the colour prejudice.

So I decided to take the next available train to Pretoria.

The following morning I sent a long telegram to the General Manager of the Railway and also informed Abdulla Sheth, who immediately met the General Manager. The Manager justified the conduct of the railway authorities, but informed him that he had already instructed the Station Master to see that I reached my destination safely. Abdulla Sheth wired to the Indian merchants in Maritzburg and to friends in other places to meet me and look after me. The merchants came to see me at the station and tried to comfort me by narrating their own hardships and explaining that what had happened to me was nothing unusual. They also said that Indians travelling first or second class had to expect trouble from railway officials and white passengers. The day was thus spent in listening to these tales of woe. The evening train arrived. There was a reserved berth for me. I now purchased at Maritzburg the bedding ticket I had refused to book at Durban.

The train took me to Charlestown.

MORE HARDSHIPS

The train reached Charlestown in the morning. There was no railway, in those days, between Charlestown and Johannesburg, but only a stage-coach, which halted at Standerton for the night *en route*. I possessed a ticket for the coach, which was not cancelled by the break of the journey at Maritzburg for a day; besides, Abdulla Sheth had sent a wire to the coach agent at Charlestown.

But the agent only needed a pretext for putting me off, and so, when he discovered me to be a stranger, he said, "Your ticket is cancelled." I gave him the proper reply. The reason at the back of his mind was not want of accommodation, but quite another. Passengers had to be accommodated inside the coach, but as I was regarded as a "coolie" and looked a stranger, it would be proper, thought the "leader," as the white man in charge of the coach was called, not to seat me with the white passengers. There were seats on either side of the coachbox. The leader sat on one of these as a rule. Today he sat inside and gave me his seat. I knew it was sheer injustice and an insult, but I thought it better to pocket it. I could not have forced myself inside, and if I had raised a protest, the coach would have gone off without me. This would have meant the loss of another day, and Heaven only knows what would have happened the next day. So, much as I fretted within myself, I prudently sat next to the coachman.

At about three o'clock the coach reached Pardekoph. Now the leader desired to sit where I was seated, as he wanted to smoke and possibly to have some fresh air. So he took a piece of dirty sack-cloth from the driver, spread it on the footboard and, addressing me, said, "*Sami*, you sit on this, I want to sit near the driver." The insult was more than I could bear. In fear and trembling I said to him, "It was you who seated me here, though I should have been accommodated inside. I put up with the insult. Now that you want to sit outside and smoke, you would have me sit at your feet. I will not do so, but I am prepared to sit inside."

As I was struggling through these sentences, the man came down upon me and began heavily to box my ears. He seized me by the arm and tried to drag me down. I clung to the brass rails of the coachbox and was determined to keep my hold even at the risk of breaking my wristbones. The passengers were witnessing the scene, - the man swearing at me, dragging and belabouring me, and I remaining still. He was strong and I was weak. Some of the passengers were moved to pity and exclaimed: "Man, let him alone. Don't beat him. He is not to blame. He is right. If he can't stay there, let him come and sit with us." "No fear," cried the man, but he seemed somewhat crestfallen and stopped beating me. He let go my arm, swore at me a little more, and asking the Hottentot servant who was sitting on the other side of the coachbox to sit on the footboard, took the seat so vacated.

The passengers took their seats and, the whistle given, the coach rattled away. My heart was beating fast within my breast and I was wondering whether I should ever reach my destination alive. The man cast an angry look at me now and then and, pointing his finger at me, growled: "Take care, let me once get to Standerton and I shall show you what I do." I sat speechless and prayed to God to help me.

After dark we reached Standerton and I heaved a sigh of relief on seeing some Indian faces. As soon as I got down, these friends said: "We are here to receive you and take you to Isa Sheth's shop. We have had a telegram from Dada Abdulla." I was very glad, and we went to Sheth Isa Haji Sumar's shop. The Sheth and his clerks gathered round me. I told them all that I had gone through. They were very sorry to hear it and comforted me by relating to me their own bitter experiences.

I wanted to inform the agent of the Coach Company of the whole affair. So I wrote him a letter, narrating everything that had happened, and drawing his attention to the threat his man had held out. I also asked for an assurance that he would accommodate me with the other passengers inside the coach when we started the next morning. To which the agent replied to this effect: "From Standerton we have a bigger coach with different men in charge. The man complained of will not be there tomorrow, and you will have a seat with the other passengers." This somewhat relieved me. I had, of course no intention of proceeding against the man who had assaulted me, and so the chapter of the assault closed there.

In the morning Isa Sheth's man took me to the coach, I got a good seat and reached Johannesburg quite safely that night.

Standerton is a small village and Johannesburg a big city. Abdulla Sheth had wired to Johannesburg also, and given me the name and address of Muhammad Kasam Kamruddin's firm there. Their man had come to receive me at the stage, but neither did I see him nor did he recognize me. So I decided to go to a hotel. I knew the names of several. Taking a cab I asked to be driven to the Grand National Hotel. I saw the manager and asked for a room. He eyed me for a moment, and politely saying, "I am very sorry, we are full up," bade me good-bye. So I asked the cabman to drive to Muhammad Kasam Kamruddin's shop. Here I found Abdul Gani Sheth expecting me, and he gave me a cordial greeting. He had a hearty laugh over the story of my experience at the hotel. "How ever did you expect to be admitted to a hotel?" he said.

"Why not?" I asked.

"You will come to know after you have stayed here a few days," said he. "Only *we* can live in a land like this, because, for making money, we do not mind pocketing insults, and here we are." With this he narrated to me the story of the hardships of Indians in South Africa.

Of Sheth Abdul Gani we shall know more as we proceed.

Singh & Watson

He said: "This country is not for men like you. Look now, you have to go to Pretoria tomorrow. You will have to travel third class. Conditions in the Transvaal are worse than in Natal. First and second class tickets are never issued to Indians."

"You cannot have made persistent efforts in this direction."

"We have sent representations, but I confess our own men too do not want as a rule to travel first or second."

I sent for the railway regulations and read them. There was a loophole. The language of the old Transvaal enactments was not very exact or precise; that of the railway regulations was even less so.

I said to the Sheth: "I wish to go first class, and if I cannot, I shall prefer to take a cab to Pretoria, a matter of only thirty-seven miles."

Sheth Abdul Gani drew my attention to the extra time and money this would mean, but agreed to my proposal to travel first, and accordingly we sent a note to the Station Master. I mentioned in my note that I was a barrister and that I always travelled first, I also stated in the letter that I needed to reach Pretoria as early as possible, that as there was no time to await his reply I would receive it in person at the station, and that I should expect to get a first class ticket. There was of course a purpose behind asking for the reply in person. I thought that, if the Station Master gave a written reply, he would certainly say "no," especially because he would have his own notion of a "coolie" barrister. I would therefore appear before him in faultless English dress, talk to him and possibly persuade him to issue a first class ticket. So I went to the station in a frock-coat and necktie, placed a sovereign for my fare on the counter and asked for a first class ticket.

"You sent me that note?" he asked.

"That is so. I shall be much obliged if you will give me a ticket. I must reach Pretoria today."

He smiled and, moved to pity, said: "I am not a Transvaaler. I am a Hollander. I appreciate your feelings, and you have my sympathy. I do want to give you a ticket - on one condition, however, that, if the guard should ask you to shift to the third class, you will not involve me in the affair, by which I mean that you should not proceed against the railway company. I wish you a safe journey, I can see you are a gentleman."

With these words he booked the ticket. I thanked him and gave him the necessary assurance.

Sheth Abdul Gani had come to see me off at the station. The incident gave him an agreeable surprise, but he warned me saying: "I shall be thankful if you reach Pretoria all right. I am afraid the guard will not leave you in peace in the first class, and even if he does, the passengers will not."

I took my seat in a first class compartment and the train started. At Germiston the guard came to examine the tickets. He was angry to find me there, and signalled to me with his finger to go to the third class. I showed him my first class ticket. "That doesn't matter," said he, "remove to the third class."

There was only one English passenger in the compartment. He took the guard to task. "What do you mean by troubling the gentleman?" he said. "Don't you see he has a first class ticket? I do not mind in the least his travelling with me." Addressing me, he said, "You should make yourself comfortable where you are."

The guard muttered: "If you want to travel with a coolie, what do I care?" and went away.

At about eight o'clock in the evening the train reached Pretoria.

FIRST DAY IN PRETORIA

I had expected someone on behalf of Dada Abdulla's attorney to meet me at Pretoria station. I knew that no Indian would be there to receive me, since I had particularly promised not to put up at an Indian house. But the attorney had sent no one. I understood later that, as I had arrived on Sunday, he could not have sent anyone without inconvenience. I was perplexed, and wondered where to go, as I feared that no hotel would accept me.

Pretoria station in 1893 was quite different from what it was in 1914. The lights were burning dimly. The travelers were few. I let all the other passengers go and thought that, as soon as the ticket collector was fairly free, I would hand him my ticket and ask him if he could direct me to some small hotel or any other such place where I might go; otherwise I would spend the night at the station. I must confess I shrank from asking him even this, for I was afraid of being insulted.

The station became clear of all passengers. I gave my ticket to the ticket collector and began my enquiries. He replied to me courteously, but I saw that he could not be of any considerable help. But an American Negro who was standing near by broke into the conversation.

"I see," said he, "that you are an utter stranger here, without any friends. If you will come with me, I will take you to a small hotel, of which the proprietor is an American who is very well known to me. I think he will accept you."

I had my own doubts about the offer, but I thanked him and accepted his suggestion. He took me to Johnston's Family Hotel. He drew Mr. Johnston aside to speak to him, and the latter agreed to accommodate me for the night, on condition that I should have my dinner served in my room.

"I assure you," said he, "that I have no colour prejudice. But I have only European custom, and, if I allowed you to eat in the dinning room, my guests might be offended and even go away."

"Thank you," said I, "even for accommodating me for the night, I am now more or less acquainted with the conditions here, and I understand your difficulty. I do not mind you serving the dinner in my room. I hope to be able to make some other arrangement tomorrow."

I was shown into a room, where I now sat waiting for the dinner and musing, as I was quite alone. There were not many guests in the hotel, and I had expected the waiter to come very shortly with the dinner. Instead Mr. Johnston appeared. He said: "I was ashamed of having asked you to have your dinner here. So I spoke to the other guests about you, and asked them if they would mind your having your dinner in the dinning-room. They said that they had no objection, and that they did not mind your staying here as long as you liked. Please, therefore, come to the dinning-room, if you will, and stay here as long as you wish."

I thanked him again, went to the dining room and had a hearty dinner.[8]

4. Interview with Rev. John R. Mott (1938)

Singh & Watson

Reverend John R. Mott (1865-1955) was a highly respected church leader. His life achievements ranged from his chairmanship of the World Student Christian Federation, chairman of the International Missionary Council, leader of the World YMCA and the World Council of Churches, and finally culminated in his being a recipient of the Nobel Peace Prize in 1946, which he shared with Emily Greene Balch. He was known to have had some discussions and correspondences with Gandhi. However, in 1938, Mott presided over the International Missionary Conference in Tambaram, near Madras in south India. While in India, he paid a visit to Gandhi and the record shows that Mott asked extensive questions, one of which appears below:

Mott: What have been the most creative experiences in your life? As you look back on your past, what, do you think, led you to believe in God when everything seemed to point to the contrary, when life, so to say, sprang from the ground, although it all looked impossible?

Gandhi: Such experiences are a multitude. But as you put the question to me, I recalled particularly one experience that changed the course of my life. That fell to my lot seven days after I had arrived in South Africa. I had gone there on a purely mundane and selfish mission. I was just a boy returned from England wanting to make some money. Suddenly the client who had taken me there asked me to go to Pretoria from Durban. It was not an easy journey. There was the railway journey as far as Charlestown and the coach to Johannesburg. On the train I had a first-class ticket, but not a bed ticket. At Maritzburg where the beddings were issued the guard came and turned me out and asked me to go to the van compartment. I would not go and the train steamed away leaving me shivering in the cold. Now the creative experience comes there. I was afraid for my very life. I entered the dark waiting-room. There was a white man in the room. I was afraid of him. What was my duty, I asked myself. Should I go back to India, or should I go forward, with God as my helper, and face whatever was in store for me? I decided to stay and suffer. My active non-violence began from that date. And God put me through the test during that very journey. I was severely assaulted by the coachman for my moving from the seat he had given me.[9]

Of the four times that Gandhi mentioned the incidents, there is no question that the account as enumerated in his autobiography had a far-reaching impact on readers and commentators. It is an inescapable fact that some apologists and scholars using Gandhi's autobiography have twisted the narrative somewhat to provide more credence and validity to the racial sufferings of Gandhi.[10] We have only presented the facts as we know them at this juncture. What we have said about the four accounts of the racial incident is beyond dispute. These are the facts pertaining to the events influencing the writing of the accounts and to the accounts themselves. We have added nothing that the accounts themselves cannot vouch for.

NOTES

[1] James K. Mathews. *The Matchless Weapon: Satyagraha.* Bombay: Bharatiya Vidya Bhavan, 1989, page 12.

[2] G. B. Singh. *Gandhi: Behind the Mask of Divinity.* Amherst, NY: Prometheus Books, 2004, page 30.

[3] Joseph J. Doke. *M. K. Gandhi: An Indian Patriot in South Africa.* London: Indian Chronicle, 1909, chapter 11. G. A. Natesan published the first Indian edition in 1919 with 111 pages. Akhil Bharat Seva Sangh published a new edition in 1959 with 156 pages. The Publications Division of the Government of India published another edition in 1967 with 116 pages. Obscure Press in London republished this book with 180 pages in 2006.

[4] G. B. Singh. *Gandhi: Behind the Mask of Divinity.* Amherst, NY: Prometheus Books, 2004, page 35.

[5] Mohandas K. Gandhi. *Satyagraha in South Africa.* 1928; reprint, Navajivan Publishing House, 1972, pp. 38-39. This book is also contained in Volume 34 of the Collected Works of Mahatma Gandhi.

[6] Mohandas K. Gandhi. *An Autobiography or The Story of My Experiments With Truth.* (1927, 1929); reprint, Boston: Beacon Press, 1957, p. xii. This autobiography is also contained in Volume 44 of the Collected Works of Mahatma Gandhi.

[7] G. B. Singh. *Gandhi: Behind the Mask of Divinity.* Amherst, NY: Prometheus Books, 2004, page 37.

[8] Mohandas K. Gandhi. *An Autobiography or The Story of My Experiments With Truth.* (1927, 1929); reprint, Boston: Beacon Press, 1957, pp. 111 to 117.

[9] CWMG, Vol. 74, page 275.

[10] See the following: Burnett Britton. *Gandhi Arrives in South Africa.* Canton, Maine: Greenleaf Books, 1999, pages 20-21. Arun and Sunanda Gandhi. *The Forgotten Woman: The Untold Story of Kastur, Wife of Mahatma Gandhi.* Hunstville, Arkansas: Ozark Mountain Publishers, 1998, pages 61-64. Frederick B. Fisher. *That Strange Little Brown Man Gandhi.* New Delhi: Orient Longmans Ltd., 1970 (reprint) Check Mrs. Fisher's statement on pages 236-37. Chandran D. S. Devanesen. *The Making of the Mahatma.* New Delhi: Orient Longmans Ltd., 1969, pages 233-239. Chester Bowles. "What Negroes Can Learn From Gandhi." This article was originally published in March 1, 1958 issue of *The Saturday Evening Post.* Also "What Negroes Can Learn from Gandhi" is available in the author's *The Conscience of a Liberal: Selected writings and speeches.* New York: Harper & Row, 1962, pp. 333-39.

Five

Gandhi Under Cross-Examination

~

I am devoted to none but Truth and I owe no discipline to anybody but Truth.

> ~ Mahatma Gandhi
> May 25, 1935

Who can say how much I must give and how much omit in the interests of truth? And what would be the value in a court of law of the inadequate ex parte evidence being tendered by me of certain events in my life? If some busybody were to cross-examine me on the chapters already written, he would probably shed more light on them, and if it were a hostile critic's cross-examination, he might even flatter himself for having shown up "the hollowness of many of my pretensions."

> ~ Mahatma Gandhi
> *An Autobiography*

Part One

M ahatma Gandhi was a fully trained lawyer. Considering the time period of the very tail end of the nineteenth century when only a handful of Indians left their homes to go overseas in pursuit of higher education, Gandhi happens to fall within the rarest of categories. He received his law degree from the Inner Temple in London. The million-dollar question we need to ask is: How good a lawyer was he? We hardly know anything of substance about his legal skills and the details of his legal practice. What kind of clients did he represent? What kind of cases did he take on? We know that in India after his graduation, he failed to establish a law practice more than once. While in South Africa, it is reported several times in the literature that he had a flourishing legal practice in Johannesburg (see plate 3). We have not been able to verify any evidence that attests to the above fact. Only recently, Burnett Britton, in his work *Gandhi Arrives in South Africa*, was an investigation undertaken into Gandhi's performance and effectiveness in the first four years in South Africa as an attorney.[1] It seems from the evidence gathered that his skills as a lawyer were far from adequate. In fact, it is questionable whether he ever had the flourishing legal practice he is claimed to have had while living in South Africa. Even judging from the defense cases for the non-violent resisters (called the S*atyagrahis*) that he represented in the court of law, his skills as a defense lawyer leave much to be desired especially from a professional of his educational background and training.

We also know from the historical documents that Gandhi himself had been convicted of offenses a number of times which landed him in prison. From the documents available, he pleaded guilty every time he faced prosecution. As a result, there was never an opportunity to put Gandhi through the third degree of cross-examination, since he never remained on the hot seat long enough. We decided that the time had finally come to place Gandhi the lawyer on the witness stand and put him through the rigors of a cross-examination with respect to the racial train and coach incidents. The fact remains that the accounts are so riddled with chronological and factual inconsistency as to call their authenticity into question. On the sheer grounds of chronological, logical and factual inconsistency, Gandhi's accounts of the racial train incidents can safely be discounted. As a lawyer trained in the law, he would know better than anyone that, as an eyewitness of his own experiences, his testimony would not stand up in court. The academic court should be no more forgiving. In light of the evidence, the sworn testimony of the one and only witness in the case, the plaintiff, is so riddled with chronological and factual inconsistency as to have the entire case thrown out of any legal or academic court in any land. It is not our intention to prejudice the jury. We simply wish to present the evidence. Naturally, as academics, we will, like lawyers, present our findings much as a lawyer would state his case. It is at that point that we will endeavor to sway the jury, not before. In the interim, we will simply present our findings before the world court and let the jury judge for itself. For now, the jury is still out on the issue, but we are confident that, by the time we present our case, the verdict will come in, making it an open and shut case.

Part Two

Day 1:

In order to prove that Gandhi has fabricated his own eyewitness testimony, let us begin by examining some of the contradictory accounts he gives in his own testimony. The first major contradiction occurs in the identity of the assailant he claims threw him off the train. In *Satyagraha in South Africa* written in 1924,[2] Gandhi writes: "I was pushed out of the train by a police constable at Maritzburg, and the train having left, was sitting in the waiting room, shivering in the bitter cold." Yet, in the interview with Rev. John R. Mott, Gandhi claims that it was a railroad employee who came to turn him out: "At Maritzburg where the beddings were issued the guard came and turned me out and asked me to go to the van compartment." This statement is immediately followed by a follow-up statement, which makes no mention of the presence or intervention of any other official but the guard: "I would not go and the train steamed away leaving me shivering in the cold." At no point does Gandhi mention the presence of a police constable. If anything, we are left with the impression that the guard who demanded that he leave for the van compartment was the same man to turn him out at the station. On the basis of this contradictory testimony alone, serious doubts are raised about the testimony of the plaintiff. Were Gandhi a witness on the witness stand, you can just imagine how he might be cross-examined. In an academic court, it should be no different. Let us then ask the witness the questions that would be posed by any lawyer under cross-examination.

Did you not, Mr. Gandhi, state in your *Satyagraha* account written in 1924, that you were in fact thrown off a train by a police constable? Let me just read the passage to remind you of your own words, for you did clearly state, "I was pushed out of the train by a police constable at Maritz-burg...." Yet, in testimony given in 1938, in an interview with Rev. Mott, you contradicted this statement by claiming that it was a railroad employee that personally removed you and I quote: "...The guard came and turned me out and asked me to go to the van compartment." You then added, "I would not go and the train steamed away leaving me shivering in the cold." As a lawyer, Mr. Gandhi, you must surely know that eyewitness testimony is only reliable when the eyewitness identifies one suspect, not two. To pick out two different suspects of different appearance, job description, and social position from a police lineup rather discredits both the eyewitness's testimony and the identification of the suspect concerned.

Here, we can safely discount both Mr. Gandhi's testimony and the identity of the suspect or assailant he has implicated in the racial train incident. What holds true in a court of law should hold true in an academic court. Disparate eyewitness accounts given by the same eyewitness must be corroborated. If contradictions emerge between two pieces of testimony and inconsistencies are found, the witnesses' sworn testimony becomes suspect. In terms of Gandhi's autobiography subtitled *The Story of My Experiments with the Truth* (as he so aptly calls it), it seems to have been very experimental and lacking in any real integrity. Take for example the account given of what took place on the train in the 1925[3] autobiographical account. He claims to have been approached by a railway servant while he was seated in first class. The railway servant, he alleges, asked him if he would require any bedding. Gandhi claims to have replied, "No, I have one with me." Then, Gandhi tells us, the man went away. Gandhi then recounts how a passenger came down the aisle, and noticing a "colored" man sitting in first class, proceeded to redress what appeared to him to be a wrong. Gandhi informs us, "Out he went and came in again with one or two officials." Under cross-examination, it is obvious what Gandhi might be asked:

> In your testimony, Mr. Gandhi, you clearly stated, "Out he went and came back in again with one or two officials." Did the passenger return accompanied by one, two or more officials, Mr. Gandhi? You see for a grievance by a plaintiff to be taken seriously, the identity and exact number of suspects must be identified before the suspects can be tried. You then go on to add, Mr. Gandhi, in the same autobiographical account that, "They all kept silent, when another official came to me and said, *Come along, you must go to the van compartment.*" Yet, in your 1938 interview with Reverend Mott, you clearly state that it was one guard who accosted you and threw you off the train. Who exactly were you confronted by, Mr. Gandhi, that day in Maritzburg? Was it two officials or more or merely one? Was it a railroad employee whom you refer to as a guard or was it a police constable who had you thrown off the train?

These are the very kinds of questions Mahatma Gandhi would be subjected to under cross-examination in a court of law, so the question is does the case of alleged racial discrimination on board a train in South Africa stand up in court? The answer is no, precisely because there are entirely different assailants identified and a different chronology of events given in each account. In the 1925 autobiographical account, we are told that Gandhi was approached by a total of what seems to be four railway employees though it is by no means certain: First, what Gandhi refers to as a railway servant appears on the scene, then "one or two" officials, and finally another official makes an appearance. When these railway employees fail to remove him to the van compartment, Gandhi informs us that a constable is summoned: "The constable came. He took me by the hand and pushed me out." All in all, Gandhi is confronted in the 1925 account by what appears to be four, possibly five different men, three or four railway officials followed by a police constable, whom he tells us threw him off the train. Yet, in the 1938 interview with Rev. Mott, Gandhi is accosted not by three or four railway officials but by one and the police constable is absent from the scene altogether suggesting that as a playwright, Gandhi has rewritten his script and replaced a one-man show involving one railway official in the 1938 account with a cast of five in the 1925 account, because it was at this time in his life that he required the most dramatic testament of the incident to be used in the cause of *Satyagraha*. In one account, it is a police constable who is involved, while in the other, it is a guard who is the one and only official to intervene in the affair and have him thrown off the train. To quote the passage again from the 1938 interview, we can see that the assailants have been reduced from the 1925 cast of five to a one-man show: "At Maritzburg where the beddings were issued the guard came and turned me out and asked me to go to the van compartment. I would not go and the train steamed away leaving me shivering in the cold."

Clearly, Gandhi is unreliable as a witness, since he cannot even pick the right suspect out of the police lineup. In fact, he is not even consistent about the exact number of suspects involved in his different historical accounts. It is clear from the inconsistent statements he has given that Gandhi's testimony is unreliable. As a plaintiff, the case he has brought before the world court has no merit and must be dismissed on the grounds of contradictory statements, inconsistent chronology, misidentification of both the identity and number of suspects involved, and many other anomalies and inconsistencies in his account not yet mentioned. We will come to these other inconsistencies forthwith.

Before embarking on his train journey from Durban - Pretoria being his ultimate destination - Gandhi was given due warning by his employer, Abdulla Sheth, about the racial conditions in South Africa, where a "colored" person was apt to be regarded as a "coolie," and however much his station in life made him a gentleman, would be treated accordingly. The 1925 account in *The Story of My*

Singh & Watson

Experiments With Truth makes it clear that Gandhi is once again being highly experimental with the truth. It is a revealing title that Gandhi has chosen for his autobiography, if indeed we can call it that, since "truth" is never an experiment or indeed experimental if it is to be an authentic and practiced discipline. What is clear from the account is that Abdulla Sheth not only advises Gandhi to seek a sleeping berth on board the train, but urges him to do so for the sake of safety:

> Abdulla Sheth insisted that I should book one bedding but, out of obstinacy and pride and with a view to saving five shillings, I declined. Abdulla Sheth warned me, *"Look, now,"* said he *"this is a different country from India. Thank God we have enough and to spare. Please do not stint yourself in anything that you may need."* [emphasis added]

What is implicit in the account is that Gandhi is being advised to seek a sleeping berth for the sake of safety. The words "this is a different country from India" make it perfectly clear that his advice is to be heeded as a warning. Gandhi even tells us, "Abdulla Sheth warned me," so it is obviously to be taken as a warning. Yet, in the 1924 account given just one year earlier in *Satyagraha in South Africa*, we see so dramatically disparate an account of these events, that we are left asking, after reading the 1925 account of one year later, if Gandhi is suffering from amnesia, Alzheimer's, or is simply making the story up as he goes along. In the 1924 account, Gandhi tells us that he considered leaving South Africa altogether on the grounds that his future employer did not adequately prepare him in advance for conditions in South Africa. In fact, Gandhi insists that his future employer was so far from circumspect in disclosing the facts about South Africa that Gandhi was left totally unprepared for what he found there:

> I was on the horns of a dilemma. Two courses were open to me. I might either free myself from the contract with Messrs Dada Abdulla on the grounds that circumstances had come to my knowledge which had not been disclosed

to me before, and run back to India. Or, I might bear all hardships and fulfill my engagement.

Seeing the disparity between the two accounts given only a year apart from one another, one is left wondering if Gandhi has experienced these life episodes in two different parallel universes. In truth, the anecdotal accounts are so mutually opposed, so utterly antithetical, it is as if they were given by two entirely different storytellers. It is reminiscent of a "broken telephone," in which a message is passed from one person to the next and in the process pieces of information are added and lost so that by the end of the circuit, the rumor has been so utterly altered as to be unrecognizable from the original. It seems then that Gandhi is not keeping his diary in order. As he fabricates his fanciful tales, he forgets previous accounts, so that after the mere passage of a single year, he has so utterly forgotten the previous fables he has concocted that in conjuring the same trick twice, he has forgotten the devices he used in the last magic show and has altered the trick altogether.

After the alleged incident of being thrown off the train, Gandhi tells us that he was left shivering in the cold, having with him only his handbag, but that he neglected to inquire after his luggage for fear of being insulted and assaulted again. The 1924 account is consistent with the 1925 version concerning the fate of his luggage. In the 1924 account, Gandhi says of his appropriated luggage, "I did not know where my luggage was, nor did I dare to inquire of anybody, lest I might be insulted and assaulted once again." In the account of a year later in the autobiography, Gandhi writes, "I went and sat in the waiting room, keeping my hand-bag with me, and leaving the other luggage where it was. The railway authorities had taken charge of it." There is no denying that the two accounts appear to match. Each makes reference to the luggage and the fact that it is not in his possession, having been in fact appropriated by the railway authorities. It is also clear from the two accounts that it is cold, and that he is left shivering in the cold. This implies freezing or near freezing temperatures. What is left out of the 1924 account is the fact that it was winter and bitterly cold. The 1925 account makes explicit the fact that Maritzburg, where the alleged incident took place, is in the high altitudes and is bitterly cold in winter, which he makes clear in his autobiography:

> It was winter, and winter in the higher regions of South Africa is severely cold. Maritzburg being at a high altitude, the cold was extremely bitter. My overcoat was in my luggage, but I did not dare to ask for it lest I should be insulted again, so I sat and shivered.

What is peculiar about the account is that Gandhi is informing us that "the cold was extremely bitter," but that he would prefer to endure the subzero temperatures to being "insulted again" as he puts it. How strange that a man, who, during the train journey put himself in mortal danger more than once, suffering alleged beatings and other humiliations, would prefer deathly cold to risking what he refers to as further insults by inquiring after his luggage. Under cross-examination, Gandhi might well be asked to answer for these inconsistencies. The interrogator's line of questioning might even center on this very issue.

> Now, Mr. Gandhi, you claim to have been thrown off the train without your luggage and coat, is that correct? You also claim that it was intensely cold in that region at that time of year. Yet, you insist that you preferred shivering in the intense cold throughout the night to inquiring after the luggage containing your overcoat for fear of risking further insult. What perplexes us, Mr. Gandhi, and the world court is the fact that before, during your train journey, you claim to have suffered repeated violence and other humiliations merely on account of your pride. Yet now, when faced with severe cold, you preferred being molested by biting winds that could have brought on pneumonia, than risk being upbraided or physically accosted for merely inquiring after your luggage. And how is it, Mr. Gandhi, that after braving this intense cold and shivering throughout the night, you did not come down with a severe cold or pneumonia, afflictions that you fail to mention and would certainly have elic-

ited more sympathy for you if you had? How is it that you managed to evade catching a severe cold, something you make no mention of in any of your testimony?

Is it not far more likely, Mr. Gandhi, that you have fabricated the entire fanciful tale on account of the fact that an Indian, whose blood chemistry is not used to such cold and who is dressed more for the Indian climate than South Africa's Natal winter, paints a very pathetic picture indeed and elicits greater sympathy? We put it to you, Mr. Gandhi, that you have invented the entire nonsensical tale to convince us that you had to endure humiliations beneath the dignity of a human being, which sheer logic tells us never happened. Who indeed would be so daft as to spend an entire night in sub-zero temperatures when one's personal luggage and overcoat are within easy reach and merely require asking after, risk of further insult or not? Is it not the cold a greater insult than a harsh word? Based on the sheer illogic and dubiousness of the Gandhian account, we can safely dismiss his testimony. First of all, there is the sheer illogic of preferring a night of intense cold to the fear of "pocketing" another insult from the Natal railway authorities. Then, there is the fact that the entire account appears fabricated because of its inherent illogic and also because it seems adapted to pricking our consciences. An Indian thrown from a train left to shiver in intense cold is a more pathetic spectacle than a passenger being ejected from a train. It lends greater drama and pathos to an event that escalates from mere insult to an incident life threatening in its injuriousness.

Another serious inconsistency occurs in the disparity between accounts given on what occurred that night in the waiting room at Maritzburg. In the 1925 account from *The Story of My Experiments with the Truth*, Gandhi appears to be getting exceedingly experimental with the truth. In this account, he informs us that he entered a vacant waiting room and that it was not until about mid-

Singh & Watson

night that a stranger intruded upon his solitude: "There was no light in the room. A passenger came in at about mid-night and possibly wanted to talk to me. But I was in no mood to talk." Since Gandhi makes explicit in the account that there was no light in the room, it being pitch black at this time, it is unlikely that he would be able to identify the stranger by race. It is unlikely that he would be able to see well enough to determine whether the stranger was white or a person of color. In addition, he makes it clear that the room was vacant when he first entered. Contrast this account of events in the waiting room with the 1938 account given in the interview with Reverend Mott: "I entered the dark waiting-room. There was a white man in the room. I was afraid of him."

What is clear beyond a shadow of a doubt is that the two accounts given in 1925 and 1938 of what occurred in the waiting room that fateful night could not be more at odds with one another. In the 1925 account, the room was vacant when Mr. Gandhi first entered it to escape the bitter cold and biting wind. In the account given thirteen years later, he entered the waiting room to find it occupied by a white man, whose presence made him feel fear immediately. The one consistent element in the two accounts is the fact that it was dark. This being the case how was he able to identify the man in the waiting room as white or even as a passenger? If it were the dead of night with no light in the room, how would he have been able to identify any of the stranger's characteristics? The other glaring disparity between the two accounts is that the stranger is presented as sociable and friendly in the first account, seeming anxious to communicate or talk with his fellow passenger, Gandhi, who tells us that he was in no mood to talk. If it were as dark as he alleges, how could he discern the mood of the individual in question if it were too dark to read his facial expressions? In addition, he fails to identify the race of the man in question in the 1925 account. In the account of some years later, Gandhi tells us that there was a white man in the room whose presence intimidated him. While it is true that Gandhi could have become confused over details related to the incident, i.e. mistaking the time in which he confronted the stranger in the waiting room, the fact remains that there are just too many glaring inconsistencies in the account.

The question is, if the man in the 1925 account, who appeared willing and even anxious to talk to Gandhi, were white, why would he be so anxious to talk to a "coolie"? In addition, in the 1925 account, Gandhi even admits to feeling unsociable at the time, so why would the stranger wish to talk to a man showing such apparent signs of unsociability? Oh yes, we remember now. It was dark. Additionally, why would Gandhi describe the stranger as so unthreatening in the first account and so utterly intimidating in the second? And why, additionally, would the stranger be described as sociable and seemingly anxious to talk in the first account and utterly intimidating in the second account, presumably because he is exhibiting an expression of disdain or dislike on his face? And finally and perhaps most absurdly, how would Gandhi be able to pick up on such subtle nuances as overtures of friendliness or disdain in a darkened room in the pitch black of night? Indeed, a lawyer would have a field day with testimony of this kind. So riddled with inconsistencies and improbabilities, and logical absurdities is this testimony that it is likely the case would be thrown out of court on the basis of these few short sentences from his autobiographical account and his interview with Rev. Mott, in which Gandhi relates what occurred in the waiting room that night.

As for two other accounts given in *Satyagraha in South Africa* (1924), and in the biography by Doke, *M. K. Gandhi: An Indian patriot in South Africa* (1909), Gandhi mentions only shivering in the waiting room all night. From these accounts, one would assume that Gandhi was alone all night in the waiting room. There is no mention of the presence of anyone else in the waiting room. In the account given by Doke in 1909, it states: "A constable was brought, and the Indian stranger was forcibly ejected, his bundles pitched after him, and, with the train gone, he was left to shiver in the waiting room all night." In the 1924 *Satyagraha* account, Gandhi informs us: "I was pushed out of the train by a police constable at Maritzburg, and the train having left, was sitting in the waiting room, shivering in the bitter cold." He further adds that, "Sleep was out of the question. Doubt took possession of the mind." One imagines him to be alone here and in a state of reflection or meditation upon his circumstances. There is nothing in either account to indicate the presence of another individual in the waiting room. For a lawyer trained in the law, his eyewitness testimony is inexcusably and inexplicable flawed. How could he have made such glaring oversights?

The only reasonable answer to this question is that when put on the spot in the interview with Rev. Mott, he was unable to refer back to an event that had taken place at a previous juncture in his life and had therefore forgotten what he had written at that time. What this suggests is that the event was not called upon from memory but from the inventive faculty known as the imagination. If he were called upon to remember an actual event from his life, he would rely on the memory of the event itself to recall details of the racial train incident, but as the evidence of flawed testimony would suggest, the story is probably not true and it would therefore be impossible to rely on memory to recall incidents that never happened. There does not appear to be any other conclusion to be drawn here. We are left with only one conclusion on the obvious disparities to be found in the four accounts: The testimony is either fabricated or due to its sheer inconsistency inadmissible in an academic or legal court.

In courtroom dramas, there is often a climax in which a witness is exposed for perjury through cross-examination, their entire testimony coming apart at the seams. While Gandhi appears to have committed perjury on a number of counts in the sworn testimony he has given in the four separate accounts of the racial train incident, perhaps no statement is more provably and scandalously false than his testimony of what occurred in the waiting room in Maritzburg on the night he was allegedly thrown off the train late at night in the bitter cold. By cross-examining Mr. Gandhi on the testimony he has given of what occurred that night in the waiting room in Maritzburg, we believe we can show that he has committed perjury. Should we succeed, we believe the case against the accused will be thrown out of court on the basis of perjury.

Let us begin our line of questioning:

Would you say that the testimony you have given is the truth, the whole truth and nothing but the truth, so help you

God? If so, would you care to explain why the four accounts of what occurred in the waiting room when you were thrown off the train at Maritzburg are so contradictory? Allow me to refresh your memory. In the 1925 account, you stated that: "There was no light in the room. A passenger came in about mid-night and possibly wanted to talk to me. But I was in no mood to talk." That's very interesting Mr. Gandhi because in your interview with Reverend Mott in 1938, you stated: "I entered the dark waiting-room. There was a white man in the room. I was afraid of him." Would you care to explain, Mr. Gandhi, it being pitch black and there being no light in the waiting room, how you were able to identify the occupant as a white man? Would you also care to explain why the same figure seems so innocuous and unthreatening, even sociable, in the 1925 account and so completely threatening in the 1938 account that you feared to be in the same room with him? How can you account for this discrepancy Mr. Gandhi? How additionally could you read such disparate emotions on the stranger's face when your own testimony assures us that it was too dark to make out his features let alone what was written on them?

In addition, in the 1925 account, you indicate that the room was initially vacant, but that a stranger intruded on your privacy somctimc around midnight. Yet, in the 1938 account, you indicate that a white man was already present in the waiting room when you first entered it. How would you account for the discrepancy in these two accounts Mr. Gandhi? For that matter how do you account for the fact that in the 1909 and 1924 accounts, you seem to be alone in the waiting room? You simply mention being unable to sleep and shivering in the cold all night. You make no mention whatsoever of there being any company present in the room with you. We put it to you Mr. Gandhi that your account of events simply does not ring true. How can the room be vacant in the 1925 account and already occupied by a white man according to the 1938 account? And how can the man with whom you shared the room be described in turns as sociable and willing to talk in the 1925 account and so utterly menacing a presence in the 1938 account that you were terrified to even be in the same room as him?

In the 1925 account, you even describe the man who entered the room around midnight as a fellow passenger. If indeed he was a passenger, how could you possibly distinguish him from a railway official if there was no light and the room was pitch black? In the 1938 account, you describe the same individual, who you claim was already in the room upon your arrival, as white. Again, how could you possibly see well enough to know whether he was white or a person of color? We put it to you, Mr. Gandhi, that this is a tale of your own invention no more real than a scene from any of the great fictions. We put it to you that you have invented the entire fanciful yarn and when put on the spot in interviews where you are called upon to recall events from that time, you have forgotten the stories you have so inventively spun and have been forced to *adlib ex tempore* and invent new ones.

Are you going to sit there and tell us that these stories are true Mr. Gandhi, when you have so obviously committed perjury? Are you going to tell us that the white man was there when you entered the room and at the same time was not there and only entered the room at about the stroke of midnight? Are you going to tell us that he was sociable and in the mood for company, but was at the same time, so menacing and threatening an individual that you were reluctant to even stay in the same room with him? Are you going to tell us that there was no light in that room, it being utterly dark, but that you were able to distinguish that the man you shared the room with was both white and a passenger? It's amazing that you can reconcile so many discrepancies, Mr. Gandhi. It's a talent rivaled only by those adepts proficient in talking out of both sides of their mouths. We congratulate you on your mastery of double talk. Being able to provide so many disparate accounts of a single event, it is rather a catch all for the gullible who are inclined to believe a story simply because it sounds good.

If only the scholars and men of peace that quote you took the time to read you they might see what monkeys they are making of themselves. If they saw that you had four different versions of the same event, they might be inclined to actually question the status of that event or wonder like us whether it ever really happened at all. In conclusion, we must thank you for entertaining us at least, Mr. Gandhi. You have certainly done that. Why, for nearly a century now your stories have entertained audiences all over the world rather as Kipling did before you. The only difference of course was that we knew Kipling's stories were fictions. Yours we took to be fact.

In the 1924 account from *Satyagraha in South Africa*, Gandhi adds that he suffered further humiliations in his journey including further "insults" and "beatings," yet he expands on none of these incidents. Is it likely that a man so stung by the indignity of racial discrimination and violence that he has chosen to write about it thirty-one years (from 1893 to 1924) after the alleged incident took place would not feel compelled to relate the entire episode in full in much earlier accounts more contemporaneous with the events themselves? In fact, the statement he makes at the close of the 1924 account renders the entire incident suspect by virtue of the sheer triteness of the statement: "I suffered further insults and received more beatings on my way to Pretoria. But all this only confirmed me in my determination." The statement lacks the sonorousness with which the ring of truth normally resonates. The account of further racial incidents during the rail journey appears fabricated because of its sheer triteness and brevity. Indeed, if Gandhi had suffered further beatings as he alleges, would it not be more consistent with logic for the plaintiff to bring all the testimony out?

Why hold back? If the plaintiff is going to win the case against the white supremacists and liberate people of color from oppression, would it not be more reasonable for him to recount all of the human rights abuses he has suffered on that occasion? In addition, it seems unlikely that a man who has suffered personal injuries of this kind would not feel motivated by sheer weight of passion to recount the entire episode from start to finish. And why wait for thirty-one years before mentioning the issue in India? Why did a lawyer of his standing not write about the incident immediately after the event?

In the 1925 *Autobiography* account, Gandhi informs us that in the morning he sent a long telegraph to the General Manager of the railway and also to Abdulla Sheth, who immediately went to meet the General Manager, who in turn informed him that he had already instructed the Station Master to ensure that Mr. Gandhi reached his destination safely:

> The following morning I sent a long telegram to the General Manager of the Railway and also informed Abdulla Sheth, who immediately met the General Manager. The Manager justified the conduct of the railway authorities, but instructed him that he had already instructed the Station Master to see that I reached my destination safely.

What is odd about the above account is that, firstly, he says, "The Manager justified the conduct of the railway authorities," but after justifying their conduct, he nevertheless took action by instructing the Station Master to see that Mr. Gandhi reached his destination safely. There is an inherent contradiction here. How can the General Manager "justify" the racial discrimination of the railway authorities, and then proceed to take steps to redress the wrong? Anyone living and working abroad in foreign countries would know that victims of racism find it exceedingly difficult to seek redress for discrimination as minorities by appealing to a racist caste that enjoys privilege. There is no reason whatsoever for the General Manager or Station Master of the railway to intervene on Gandhi's behalf. The entire account is illogical and inconsistent precisely because, if Gandhi's account of the racial train incident were true, he would confront the same endemic racism and discrimination at every level of appeal. The standard practice when wrongs of this kind are committed is to whitewash the affair by failing to acknowledge the problem. Indeed, it is doubtful that Gandhi experienced the kind of human rights victory he is claiming to have had because the standard reaction of officials belonging to such an organization is to close ranks to protect other officials and to operate on the basis of denial. Indeed, according to Gandhi's autobiography account, racial discrimination by railway officials was endemic since the Indian merchants who allegedly met Mr. Gandhi at the train station recounted their own tales of woe:

> The merchants came to see me at the station and tried to comfort me by narrating their own hardships and explaining that what had happened to me was nothing unusual. They also said that Indians travelling first or second class had to expect trouble from railway officials and white passengers.

The logical inconsistency of this account lies in the fact that, according to Gandhi's own words, racial discrimination was endemic on the railway and that "Indians traveling first or second class had to expect trouble from railway officials and white passengers," and yet the General Manager and Station Manager are alleged to have taken action to redress the wrong. Are we to believe that in a country where such racial discrimination was not only practiced but condoned by the white establishment at every level, white officials would actually take action to correct an injustice suffered by a member of a racial minority? What makes the entire account dubious is the fact that white officials connected with the railway should show any concern whatsoever for Gandhi's plight if their conduct is to be logically consistent with the widespread racism in practice on the railway system of South Africa at the time.

Under cross-examination Gandhi might be asked a number of questions about the disparity between the 1924 and 1925 accounts.

We can imagine the questions the plaintiff might be asked on this score.

> Why, Mr. Gandhi, would you provide so much more detail in the 1925 account than in the previous account of one year earlier? Would it not be more logical for a man who had suffered such injuries to wish to get the whole episode off his chest as quickly as possible, affording him a sense of relief? Indeed, someone suffering from the sting of racial injustice would feel motivated to write about the entire incident from start to finish with great urgency, certainly in the 1924 account, and one would have thought thirty-one years earlier. Why did it take you so long, Mr. Gandhi, to write about something for which you apparently still feel the sting of racial injustice several years on? And why is there so much more detail in your account of events in *The Story of My Experiments With the Truth* than in the previous account? Could it be that you felt compelled to add more to the story to lend greater authenticity to the tale? Is it not true that you fabricated the entire fable and embellished it to give it an air of authenticity that would have a cathartic effect upon your readers?

In light of the prosecution's questions and the logical contradiction this line of questioning exposes, the entire episode appears to be an instance of blatant hyperbole calculated to win sympathy. The series of embellishments given in the second account are so much more detailed and persuasive than that given in the account of one year previously that the question arises: Why was such important testimony absent from the first account? Could it be that Gandhi found a need to include greater detail in order to remove any doubts on the part of readers and to inoculate his story against skeptical inquiry? He seems to anticipate the objections of skeptics who might wish to subject him to such cross-examination. It is rather like the attempt of a social scientist to employ the dialectic to immunize himself against rhetorical attack by posing objections and then replying to objections. Unfortunately for Gandhi, it is precisely the inconsistencies and disparities in his accounts that encouraged us to launch this skeptical inquiry in the first place. Far from inoculating himself against further skeptical inquiry, he has invited a hornet's nest of skepticism by giving so many contradictory statements and inconsistent testimony on the alleged incident throughout his career.

In the 1925 account, Gandhi describes the treatment he received on the coach journey from Charlestown to Johannesburg, an account entirely absent from the one he had given one year previously. Here, he recounts how he suffered abuse by being treated as a "coolie" who did not have the right to travel inside the coach with other white passengers. The first of a long string of insults Gandhi details is of having his ticket cancelled as he is not considered fit to sit with the other white passengers. The consequence of this is that he is of course forced to sit without the coach on one of the seats provided outside the coachbox, as recorded in the autobiography:

> ...The agent only needed a pretext for putting me off, and so, when he discovered me to be a stranger, he said, "*Your ticket is cancelled.*" I gave him the proper reply. The reason at the back of his mind was not want of accommodation, but quite another. Passengers had to be accommodated inside the coach, but as I was regarded as a "coolie" and looked a stranger, it would be proper, thought the "leader," as the white man in charge of the coach was called, not to seat me with the white passengers. There were seats on either side of the coachbox... I knew it was sheer injustice and an insult, but I thought it better to pocket it. I could not have forced myself inside, and if I had raised a protest, the coach would have gone off without me. [emphasis added]

What is of course logically inconsistent in this account is the fact that the same man who had endured verbal and physical abuse simply to avoid the insult of being removed from first class to the van compartment would now stomach the intolerable injustice of being treated not like a gentleman but a "coolie," who instead of being allowed, as the purchased ticket entitled him, to sit within the coach, is forced to sit without as one who has been reduced to the status of a dog. It is not until Gandhi suffers the additional insult, according to his account of being asked by the "leader" to sit on a piece of dirty sack-cloth at his feet while he has a smoke that Gandhi in his autobiography erupts into self-righteous rage:

> The insult was more than I could bear. In fear and trembling I said to him, "It was you who seated me here, though I should have been accommodated inside. I put up with the insult. Now that you want to sit outside and smoke, you would have me sit at your feet. I will not do so, but I am prepared to sit inside."

Gandhi then proceeds to give account of how he is slapped, assaulted and cajoled by his assailant, the "leader," who tries to remove him from his seat repeatedly till the latter is compelled to relent and leave off by the white passengers sitting in the coach who are moved to pity:

> As I was struggling through these sentences, the man came down on me and began heavily to box my ears. He seized me by the arm and tried to drag me down. I clung to the brass rails of the coachbox and was determined to keep my hold at the risk of breaking my wristbones. The passengers were witnessing the scene, - the man swearing at me, dragging and belaboring me, and I remained still. He was strong and I was weak. Some of the passengers were moved to pity and exclaimed: *"Man let him alone. Don't blame him. He is not to blame. He is right. If he can't stay there, let him come and sit with us."* [emphasis added]

What makes the account so implausible is the hyperbolic nature of the scene, which is so utterly savage as to resemble a cartoon. One can imagine an assault in which a series of blows are administered, but this spectacle of Gandhi being so manhandled requires more suspension of disbelief than a horror film. Additionally, one would assume that someone suffering so injurious an insult would seek full redress for wrongs committed. Yet Gandhi appears to demand no such justice. He claims to have written a letter to the Coach Company about the whole affair. The agent who replied allegedly promised better treatment from Standerton, where the next coach would depart from: "From Standerton we have a bigger coach with different men in charge. The man complained of will not be there tomorrow, and you will have a seat with the other passengers." This appears to have placated Gandhi. How such a letter could possibly satisfy a man who had suffered so many insults and humiliations is hard to fathom. The patronizing tone of the letter seems only to add insult to injury. Not only is no apology given for the injurious slights Gandhi has suffered, but there is no promise made to take disciplinary action against the man in question. Gandhi is simply informed that the bully in question will not be on the coach, which is tantamount to dismissing the whole affair in the most patronizing fashion. Instead of feeling the sting constant injustices, Gandhi instead appears bewilderingly satisfied: "This somewhat relieved me. I had of course no intention of proceeding against the man who had assaulted me, and so the chapter of the assault closed there."

Are we to believe this? The chapter on the assault closed there? Are we to believe that a man who has just experienced the most appalling string of human rights abuses should decide to suddenly forget the whole thing after seemingly receiving satisfaction through a letter of reply, which far from redressing the wrong, simply dismisses the whole affair out of hand? And keep in mind that this is no ordinary man, but a lawyer and someone with access to the necessary legal apparatus to take action and seek redress. Indeed, Gandhi has not won the moral victory he purports to have won at all, but if we could even believe the account, seems to have suffered defeat after defeat. The fact that he should decide to forget a string of incidents of so violent and appalling a nature only to drag them up years later presumably because the sting of racial injustice is still with him is logically inconsistent to say the least.

Under cross-examination, the interrogator might ask several questions related to the absurdity of what Mr. Gandhi is expecting us to believe. Such questions would revolve around the logical inconsistency of closing a chapter so abruptly only to open it years later.

Mr. Gandhi, you stated in your testimony that upon receiving the letter, you were satisfied, "relieved" as you put it. You then add that, "the chapter of the assault closed there." You then went on to reopen said chapter years later, presumably because the sting of racial injustice was still with you and you felt the compulsion at that time to expunge such racism from South Africa and the world. Why not at the time, Mr. Gandhi? Does it not seem strange that, with the welts of injustice fresh on your back, you should not react to your plight at the time, but only years later? They say, Mr. Gandhi, that time heals old wounds, yet far from being healed, it would appear that, over time, your welts have developed into festering wounds such that you felt the injustice of past events more strongly years after the fact than you did at the actual time. Does this not seem strange to you, Mr. Gandhi? Forgive us if we sound skeptical. It is just that your account has none of the resonance we would normally associate with the ring of truth.

In addition to your apparent willingness to dismiss the whole affair, you add, "I had, of course no intention of proceeding against the man who had assaulted me...." Why pray not? It seems to us that as plaintiff in this case, you should wish to have the man who assaulted you prosecuted or at the very least disciplined for the indiscretion. Yet, you insist that you had no intention of proceeding against the man. You even insert the caveat "of course." You had *of course* no intention of proceeding against the man? Why use the phrase "of course," since logically, it shouldn't be taken for granted? We are sorry Mr. Gandhi, but your grievance seems to lack authenticity. Why would you not wish to proceed against the man who assaulted you? Logically, any man who had been subject to violence both physical and mental at the hands of some offending party would naturally wish to proceed against them. Yet, you insist that *of course* you did not wish to launch proceedings against the man in question. Is it because you did not have a case? Is it because the assailant did not exist? Is it because the entire fanciful tale is the invention of your own fertile imagination? Could it be, Mr. Gandhi, that you are attempting to exploit the politics of victimization to your own ends?

One can almost hear the objection ring out in the academic court at this point, as the prosecution rises to interject: Objection your Honor! The barrister is leading the witness. We will reply to this objection dialectically.

While some might object that our cross-examination is in some way leading the witness, the fact is that there is no logical consistency in Mr. Gandhi not wishing to launch proceedings against the man who assaulted him on the coach. If the incident offended and injured his mind sufficiently for him to write about it several years on and to recall so painful an incident throughout his career, how could he possibly not wish to prosecute the offending party or demand that the coach company at least discipline the offending party? Yet, far from insisting on such disciplinary action or court proceedings, Gandhi insists that he does not wish to proceed against the man who assaulted him, even adding the words "of course" to this bewildering assertion. In reply to the objection, we maintain that no man would neglect to prosecute the offending party in an incident that so deeply offended him that he was able to recall it years afterwards and to bring it up repeatedly as a *causus beli* for his own political movement against white oppression in his own homeland. It seems rather, and we affirm our contention in the strongest possible terms, that Mr. Gandhi is merely exploiting the politics of victimization in an effort to elicit greater sympathy for his campaign against British colonial rule, while at the same time using it as a locus to promote his own ascendancy as the proponent of a Nietzchian "slave morality" adapted to championing the cause of the oppressed.[4]

In keeping with Hegel's master/slave dialectic, Gandhi seems to be inventing the entire incident in an attempt to promote what Nietzsche calls "the slave morality," a morality designed by the oppressed class precisely with the aim of liberating them from the tyrannical yoke of the oppressor. Our aim in subjecting the racial train incidents to skeptical inquiry is not to debunk the politics of repression, conspiracy theory and the case for exploitation, but merely to show that intellectual counter-terrorism is very often invoked against oppressive regimes. Such tactics very often take the form of psychological warfare and black operations, which are specifically designed to confuse the opposition in an effort to seek certain political ends. If you can convince enough members of the imperial camp that their side has committed heinous wrongdoings, you deprive them so utterly of moral justification as to undermine their power structure.

What Gandhi is attempting to do with the story of the racial train incidents is to incite dissidence within the white establishment in order to subvert British white rule in India. By depriving the British of the moral justification for empire, the self-righteous conviction that they are civilizing the barbarians beyond their borders, by demonstrating that they themselves are barbarians, Gandhi has effectively denied them their position of self-justification and their *causus beli*. Our objection to Gandhi's tactics is neither ideological nor moral. We simply wish to expose through skeptical inquiry the truth about the four accounts. We have shown that there are enough inconsistencies and anomalies within the accounts themselves to warrant a closer examination of the four historical accounts. Our aim as historians is simply to expose the fact, through skeptical inquiry, that the incidents that allegedly took place on the trains and coaches are dubious at best, and in light of the evidence, highly unlikely to have occurred. To assign ideological motives for us doing so would be a gross misrepresentation of our intentions. We are simply historians, nothing more. Our aim is solely to ascertain the truth and expose it to the light of day, since it is our firm belief that nothing should be hidden from the people and if we are to uphold true democracy in our world, we should endeavor to eliminate all forms of deception, so that the citizens of this world will be better able to judge the authenticity of this world and its events with discerning eyes and not be blinded by the cataracts of manipulation.

Another troubling issue concerning the coach incident is the disparities between the 1909 account dictated to J.J. Doke and the 1925 account from the Gandhi autobiography and the subsequent account given in the interview with Reverend Mott. In the earliest account from 1909, the attack of the guard on board the coach is described as being most brutal. There is no doubt whatsoever that the blows being described are those of close-fisted punches. Upon Gandhi's refusal to give up his seat, we are told that the guard responded with a "brutal blow," followed by another that nearly knocked him down as Doke recounts:

> The coach was about to leave Paardeberg with Mr. Gandhi seated on the box when the guard, a big Dutchman, wishing to smoke, laid claim to this place, telling the Indian passenger to sit down at his feet. "No," said Mr. Gandhi, quietly, "I shall not do so." *The result was a brutal blow in the face. The victim held on to the rail, when another blow nearly knocked him down.* [emphasis added]

It is clear that the blows described are of sufficient force and of a particular kind. A "brutal blow," especially of the kind that nearly knocks the victim down, would be none other than a close-fisted punch. Yet, no mention is made in any of the narrative accounts to this blow causing any kind of bodily harm. Not only is no mention made of a bloody nose, bruising, or a black eye, but there does not appear to have been any cuts or abrasions either. It is perplexing indeed that Gandhi would fail to mention the nature of the resulting injuries, since these "brutal blows" would most definitely have resulted in some form of bruise, cut, or abrasion. It only makes sense that Gandhi would desire to elicit more sympathy by discussing the injuries resulting from this incident.

There is only one explanation for the absence of such testimony. If cause and effect analysis is invoked here, it is clear that the cause, namely a "brutal blow," would have resulted in the effect of a fat lip, bloody nose, swollen cheek, bruise, or black eye. Yet no mention is made of any of these effects. If the effects are absent, we can safely deduce that so too is the cause. The "brutal blows" that would have resulted in these effects never occurred. Had they occurred, the victim would have described the effects that would necessarily have resulted from the cause. In addition to the injurious effects, there would have been a further causal chain that is completely omitted from the narrative, namely, that of treatment. The victim would have most certainly required treatment at some stage. A "brutal blow" would have required medical treatment of some kind. A bruise or swelling would have required ice or a cold cloth to bring down the swelling. A cut would have required iodine or antiseptic crème to prevent infection. Yet, no mention is made of any treatment being administered for any such injury. By invoking causal analysis, we can see that, if the effects, namely injuries and treatment for injuries are absent from the narrative account, than by deduction, the cause, must also be logically absent and by deduction, the account itself fabricated.

While some might argue that the injurious "brutal blows" are all that need be mentioned, we would argue that the victim would naturally wish his audience to understand the seriousness of the blows by describing the seriousness of their effects, i.e. a bloody nose, a black eye, etc. and the form of treatment that would be undertaken as a result of such injuries. We can only deduce from the absence of such accounts that the cause, namely the "brutal blows," never in fact took place.

In addition, the violence described in the 1925 autobiography account is of an entirely different kind. In this account, the blows described are a "boxing of the ears." While it could be argued that Gandhi is merely employing figurative language and that a "boxing of the ears" could equally apply to punches as to slaps or cuffs, the fact is that the latter expression normally applies to slaps or cuffs to the head. One does not mix metaphors when one is offended. If violence of the kind described in the 1909 account had occurred, Gandhi would not be describing it so lightly as a "boxing of the ears" as he does in the later autobiography account given below:

> The man came down upon me and began heavily to box my ears. He seized me by the arm and tried to drag me down. I clung to the brass rails of the coachbox and was determined to keep my hold at the risk of breaking my wristbones.

As we can see, the word "heavily" does precede the words "to box my ears." Therefore, there is some correspondence between the 1925 and 1909 accounts insofar as "brutal" and "heavily" are synonymous in that they both describe extreme forms of violence. However, the fact remains that a "boxing of the ears" does not normally refer to a close-fisted blow or punch, but rather to a slap or cuff to the head. Surely a man subjected to so extreme a form of racial brutality and violence as to have received at least two "brutal blows," one to the head and the other nearly knocking him down, would not be describing them in a subsequent account given sixteen years later [1909 to 1925] as a mere "boxing of the ears."

In addition, the 1924 account makes no mention of the blow referred to in the 1909 account that nearly knocked Gandhi down. Instead of two brutal blows, one of which nearly knocked him off his feet, we have instead a series of blows described as a "boxing of the ears," which end with him being seized by the arm in an attempt to drag him down from his perch. While some might argue that the 1909 account is nearer to the event historically, sheer proximity to which inspires stronger language, we would argue that, for the event to remain at the forefront of Gandhi's mind so many years after, his outrage would not have dissipated at all, but would rather have grown in proportion to his fame and the resulting self-esteem this would have afforded. Memories of life's early indignities would have only increased in proportion to his rising status, since the disparity between his later fortunes and early indignities would have made the earlier life experiences that much harder to bear. Indeed, far from seeing a decline in emotional outrage, it is only logical that his anger over such offenses would have increased with time.

The disparity between these two accounts raises serious questions about the issue of credibility, especially when one contrasts these with the account given in Reverend Mott's interview in 1938. Either Gandhi is getting dotty in his old age or he has forgotten altogether the inventions he formulated earlier in his career. In the 1938 account, he clearly states that he was beaten by the coachman for moving from his seat and not as he has previously alleged, because he refused to move. It is no longer possible for Gandhi to get away with his equivocations. His statement in the 1938 account clearly demonstrates that his testimony is contradictory and no more reliable as evidence than a witness giving contradictory testimony in court, for in Rev. Mott's interview he states: "I was severely assaulted by the coachman for my moving from the seat he had given me."

Contrast this with the account dictated to J. J. Doke in 1909: "The coach was about to leave Paardeberg with Mr. Gandhi seated on the box when the guard, a big Dutchman, wishing to smoke, laid claim to this place, telling the Indian passenger to sit down at his feet." Without question Gandhi is being asked to move in the 1909 account and his refusal to do so results in a sound beating. Yet, the 1938 account makes it no less clear that he was assaulted for moving from the seat the coachman had assigned him. In addition, the 1909 account informs us that it is the "guard" not the coachman who is responsible for the beating, while the 1938 account informs us that it is the coachman and not the guard. On the basis of this testimony alone, Gandhi's case should be thrown out of the academic court. Either his entire testimony is false and predicated on fabrications or he is so dotty as to be a completely unreliable witness to incidents occurring in his own life. It is not legitimate to accept the testimony of someone simply because their name and reputations precede them. Were that the case, the historicity of Jesus and the testimony of the New Testament would not be subject to debate.

Amazingly, in Gandhi's case, many of his followers, even from within the Christian Church, have granted him a place even more elevated than Jesus Christ (see plate 4). Indeed, numerous commentators and scholars of the Bible have pointed out its many contradictions and when placed on the witness stand, the Gospel writers' testimony seems no more able to stand up under cross-examination than Gandhi's. What this demonstrates is that, as someone who is no greater a sacred cow than Jesus, his autobiographical and biographical accounts should be subjected to scrutiny, since his eyewitness testimony does not pass even the most basic scholarly test of consistency and accuracy. What is even more disgraceful is the fact that, as a scholar and a man trained in the law, one would expect Gandhi to be above such oversights. The fact that he has failed to render accounts that are the least bit credible due to their gross contradictions, inconsistencies, and anomalies raises serious questions about their authenticity and historicity. Are they in fact true accounts or the fabrications of an opportunist and con artist seeking political advantage from the politics of victimization?

Day 2:

The methodology of skeptical inquiry employed in this work of scholarship, consisting of legal argument and cross-examination, is fitting since Gandhi himself was a practicing lawyer trained in the law. It is only legitimate therefore, that Gandhi should be subjected to the same scholarly and jurisprudential rigors he was trained in as a lawyer. What is clear from the beginning is that none of the autobiographical or biographical accounts given of the racial train incident add up to a consistent train of logic, causality or chronology. Does it make sense that a scholar and lawyer trained in logical argument and consistency would be guilty of so many oversights in his account? The truth is that it makes no sense whatsoever. The only possible explanation for such gross oversights is that Gandhi fancied himself to be such an untouchable, such a sacred cow, that no one would dare question him or his motives or anything he had ever said or done without bringing an avalanche of criticism and censure down upon his head. No doubt this would have been true in Gandhi's day, but with so much water now under the bridge, it seems that we are significantly well placed downstream to launch an assault on that bridge and assail it with all the criticism we have at our disposal. Will the bridge collapse under Gandhi's feet? We believe that it will and that Gandhi will land in it, so to speak, up to his proverbial neck. It is not out of vindictiveness or malice or any kind of desire to see a hero toppled from his pedestal that we launch this skeptical inquiry, but simply out of a will to safeguard humanity from the deception and lies disseminated in the public arena, which the general public has a tendency to naively and rather gullibly believe, lies perpetrated by a global elite for their own purposes.

Let us now put Mr. Gandhi on the witness stand again and ask him the pressing questions related to the 1909, 1925, and 1938 accounts to see how he fairs under cross-examination. The examiner will now approach the witness stand.

> Mr. Gandhi, did you not solemnly swear that the "brutal blows" you were subjected to on board the coach were of substantial enough force to be designated "brutal"? The man who took your statement, Reverend Doke, employed the very words "brutal blow" when referring to the assault. You even insist that the second blow was sufficient to nearly knock you off your feet. Yet, in none of your eye-witness testimony do you make reference to your injuries. It occurs to the court that if blows of such violent a nature were to have occurred in fact and not in fiction, they would have been sufficiently violent as to result in injury. While the other litigants might object that we are invoking pre-supposition in assuming that injuries would have resulted from such violence, let me repeat Mr. Gandhi's own testimony as it was dictated to Rev. J. J. Doke, so that the academic court will be left in no doubt on the issue: "The result was a brutal blow in the face. The victim held on to the rail, when another blow nearly knocked him down." It should be clear to the academic court that the violence of

the blows involved would have most certainly resulted in the victim sustaining injury, yet there is no mention whatsoever of any injuries, nor of the subsequent medical treatment such injuries would have required.

Are you telling us, Mr. Gandhi, that you did not sustain any injuries or that the injuries were not serious enough to have warranted any medical attention? Does it seem likely Mr. Gandhi that the blows would have been as "brutal" as your testimony conveys if they resulted in no significant physical abrasions or harm? Does it seem likely that the blows would have been "brutal" at all as they are described as being in your witness testimony if they were insufficient in force to result in injuries that would have required medical treatment? If indeed you insist that they were as "brutal" as you allege, and did in fact cause bodily injury, why is there no mention of this in your testimony? And why is there no mention of any medical treatment if the blows were as "brutal" as you claim them to have been? Could it be, Mr. Gandhi, and it is only a question, Your Honor, that the entire account is fabricated? Does this not account for the gross anomaly between experiencing "brutal" violence with no resulting injuries? Could it be, Mr. Gandhi, that in your haste to invent a significantly moving story, you neglected to connect your story causally to its resulting effects and therefore neglected to include certain dctails in your story that would not be absent from a bona fide account?

And how, Mr. Gandhi, can you account for the gross disparity between the 1909 and the 1925 accounts of this incident? In your 1909 statement taken down by J.J. Doke, you refer to a "brutal blow" administered to the face, which could be none other than a close-fisted punch based on the language employed. Based on your statement, Rev. Doke then informs us that you received a second blow of sufficient force to nearly knock you off your feet. Yet in the 1925 account, you use entirely different language to describe what, in the language of the 1909 account, can only be the most extreme form of violence. The "brutal blow" to the face described in the 1909 account followed by a second blow that nearly knocked you from your feet transforms into a series of blows referred to as a "boxing of the ears."

Surely you can see the gross disparity here, Mr. Gandhi. How can "brutal blows" be reconciled with a "boxing of the ears"? Surely you can see that the violence being described is of two entirely different orders. A "brutal blow" to the face could be none other than a close-fisted punch, while a "boxing of the ears" would refer to cuffs or slaps to the head. We put it to you, Mr. Gandhi, that it is most fitting to place you on the witness stand and subject you to cross-examination precisely because, as one trained in the law, you would surely know what kind of testimony stands up in court. It is only fitting then that you should fall subject to the same rigors as any witness would, but you particularly as one trained in the law.

What perplexes us as litigants is that someone with your jurisprudential training could give such appallingly careless testimony, so full of anomalies and inconsistencies as scarcely to be believed. We can only conclude that you must have felt your unassailable reputation granted you such immunity that your testimony would have been beyond question. You must have felt that your reputation preceded you in a manner that left you entirely above censure or even skeptical inquiry. How wrong you were, Mr. Gandhi, and how far you miscalculated, for with the benefit of hindsight and the objectivity time and distance afford, you have been dwarfed and no longer stand in such stark relief to those who view you standing on your pedestal. Indeed, distance has granted us an objectivity that allows us to see you in a clearer light, not as a larger-than-life figure towering head and shoulders above the rest, but as a figure that has been dwarfed by time and distance, so that you have now sunk in our estimation sufficiently that you have joined the ranks of men and not the rank and file of gods and demigods.

As one trained in the law, Mr. Gandhi, you would surely know that the testimony given in the 1909 and 1938 accounts of the racial train and coach incidents do not stand up in court. In fact, no plaintiff would ever get away with this kind of witness testimony in court, testimony so riddled with contradiction the case would be immediately dismissed. Did you not state in your 1909 statement, Mr. Gandhi, that you were beaten by the coachman for your refusal to give up your seat? Yet in the 1938 account, do you not state unequivocally that you were subjected to a beating for having moved from your seat? And how do you account, Mr. Gandhi, for the fact that the assailant of 1909 swaps identities with the assailant of 1938? In 1909, it was the guard who set upon you, but in 1938, the villain in question is the coachman.

Would you care to account for these discrepancies in the two accounts, Mr. Gandhi? Can you not see, sir, that you have lost all credibility? It is not sufficient for you to say that you made a mistake or that you have become careless with details due to the passage of years. You see, Mr. Gandhi, for your account to be considered plausible, there would have to be some consistency in the overall story as rendered in the various testimonials of the incident you have given throughout your career. Yet the truth is that the various accounts are so anomalous and inconsistent as to beggar belief, which raises the suspicion that they are not based on any central canon of truth to which they refer, but to a grand lie and deception so shadowy and lacking in substance that the disparate accounts seem no more substantive than the fabrications upon which they are based.

To take our case further, let us examine what Gandhi has to say in the 1925 account. By the end of our skeptical inquiry, it should be clear that Gandhi has no case, and that his case is so full of holes that it can no more stay afloat than a leaky boat. As a plaintiff, he simply has no case. His statements just do not stand up to the rigors of skeptical inquiry. Based on his contradictory evidence and testimony, the case he has brought before the academic court must be dismissed. For instance in Gandhi's 1925 account, he states that he was able to reach Johannesburg without further incident. However, upon arrival in Johannesburg, a man had come to receive him at the station, but it appears that both Gandhi and his driver were unable to recognize one another and so Gandhi missed his ride. Instead of waiting, he decided to proceed to a hotel as he recounts: "Taking a cab I asked to be driven to the Grand National Hotel. I saw the manager and asked for a room. He eyed me for a moment, and politely saying, *I am very sorry, we are full up*, bade me good-bye." Gandhi informs us that, after being refused at the hotel, he then took a cab to Muhammed Kasam Kamruddin's shop. Here, Mr. Abdul Gani Sheth was waiting for him.

Abdul Gani received Gandhi's story with considerable mirth, when he was told of his hotel experience, inquiring, "How ever did you expect to be admitted to a hotel?" Gandhi, employing sound philosophical reasoning, then purportedly replied, "Why not?" His future friend Abdul Gani then allegedly replied, "You will come to know after you have stayed here for a few days," adding, "Only we can live in a land like this, because, for making money, we do not mind pocketing insults, and here we are." Unfortunately, the conversation does not ring true. What is clear from the conversation Gandhi is describing is that he is being portrayed as someone of significantly higher caste than his Indian peers or even superiors. The fact that he has obtained a law degree from England and has all the manners of an English gentleman appears to set him apart, but is this the reality or merely the impression he would like to give? His future friend purportedly flatters him further by saying, "This country is not for men like you."

What is shocking is that throughout the exchange, Gandhi raises not the slightest eyebrow, shows not the slightest surprise, and makes not the least protest. Indeed, he seems to take it for granted that he is something more estimable and significant than his Indian colleagues. One wonders if the passage is true or if Gandhi is actually trying to portray himself as a cut above. To repeat the words of Abdul Gani, he observes, "Only we can live in a land like this, because, for making money, we do not mind pocketing insults...." The fact that Gandhi makes no apology for these remarks means that he takes them for granted. He is portraying Abdul Gani and his other colleagues as opportunists lacking in the higher moral faculties of the philosopher and idealist. Gandhi hardly seems loath to accept such praise. In fact, he seems quite willing to "pocket" it to use his own terminology.

What is clear from the conversation is that he does regard himself as superior to his fellow Indians both in terms of caste and education, and is anxious to accord himself the same status over them that whites insist on holding over people of color. By portraying himself as a gentleman whose caste and education warrant respect, Gandhi is giving himself a promotion. He is already placing himself at the head of a movement, as the one divinely endowed with the gift of more articulate speech, more profound reasoning, with a purer, more untrammeled vision than other Indians. In other words, Gandhi sees himself as the elect, the chosen one, the messianic deliver and emancipator of his people, the avatar who has come to set his people free. It seems that Gandhi is his own best public relations officer, promoting himself to the status of leader, spokesperson and representative of his people long before the appointment is ever made. Whether the conversation he is recounting ever actually took place is irrelevant. What is clear is that, invented or not, the conversation reveals that he takes the flattery and praise of his future friend for granted. Showing none of the deference or humility that an inferior should show to his superior in the face of such flattery, Gandhi instead appears to take the words to heart and accept them *prima facie*.

The fact that Gandhi accords himself special status and insists on being treated with greater deference than his Indian colleagues is apparent in the following exchange with Abdul Gani. The conversation begins with the following advice from Abdul Gani:

Look now, you have to go to Pretoria tomorrow, you will have to travel third class. Conditions in the Transvaal are worse than in Natal. First and second class tickets are never issued to Indians. You cannot have made persistent efforts in this direction. We have sent representations, but I confess our own men too do not want as a rule to travel first or second.

This advice did not sit well with Gandhi. His pride and his general conviction that he occupied a higher status than his fellow Indians compelled him to examine the railway regulations more closely. His own training in jurisprudence had taught him that there is normally a legal loophole in the language of such documents to allow the intellectually nimble to circumvent their strictures. Gandhi appears to have planned to vault over this impediment to his freedom and civil rights by taking advantage of a legal loophole, for he states, "I sent for the railway regulations and read them. There was a loophole. The language of the old Transvaal enactments is not very exact or precise; that of the railway regulations was even less so."

What is significant here is not the fact that he should go to such pains to fight human rights abuses, but the fact that he is so obsessed with the issue of status that he insists on elevating himself above his peers by according himself greater privilege. Gandhi's own words tell us that he regards himself as a VIP who should not suffer the indignity of traveling beneath his station. In fact, he is even willing to add additional expense to the journey in order to accord himself proper dignity by traveling in luxury, as he explains to Abdul Gani: "I wish to go first class, and if I cannot, I shall prefer to take a cab to Pretoria, a matter of only thirty-seven miles."

The fact that even after being brutalized, he insists on traveling first class and even granting himself the luxury of a cab ride regardless of expense tells us how hung up on status he actually is. How anomalous this is with the image of the saint that walked in a loincloth while seeking the support of a staff. The contradictory imagery of the saint and his earlier incarnation as the aspiring English gentleman or "Wag" (white Asian gentleman) - an appalling term but one no less fitting in this context - does not end there, for his obsession with higher status motivates him to even write a letter to the Station Master in advance to request that a first class ticket to Pretoria be reserved for him at the station, for he writes:

> ...We sent a note to the Station Master. I mentioned in my note that I was a barrister and that I always travelled first, I also stated in the letter that I needed to reach Pretoria as early as possible, that as there was no time to await his reply I would receive it in person at the station, and that I should expect to get a first class ticket. There was of course a purpose behind asking for the reply in person. I thought that if the Station Master gave a written reply, he would certainly say "no," especially because he would have his own notion of a "coolie" barrister. I would therefore appear before him in faultless English dress, talk to him and possibly persuade him to issue a first class ticket. So I went to the station in the frock-coat and necktie, placed a sovereign for my fare on the counter and asked for a first class ticket.

What is revealing about the passage is how much in contrast it is with Gandhi's later incarnation as the holy saint inspired by teachings of non-violence. Not only are his actions aggressive, but show an obsession with class and status. Indeed, there is even a degree of vanity in his description of the foppish dandy "in faultless English dress" appearing at the station in "frockcoat and necktie." Is this the picture of a human rights leader or an opportunist pathologically obsessed with status, who will exploit any situation or advantage to seek ascendancy in his quest for fame and notoriety? Indeed, as with many leaders of civil rights movements, Gandhi seems more intent on according himself the status he feels he deserves than in campaigning for the rights of the oppressed class he purportedly represents. What is transparently clear is that in none of these accounts of the racial train and coach incidents do you see him showing any genuine attempt to champion the rights of his fellow Indians or indeed those of "colored" people in general. Instead, you see a man obsessed with and obsessing over his own status to the exclusion of all else, a man so anxious to obtain higher status for himself that he can think of nothing else, spending his days and nights hatching his next scheme.

The next exchange between Gandhi and the Station Master reveal far more about Gandhi's true character and intentions. "You sent me the note?" asks the Station Master. To which Gandhi offers the reply, "That is so. I shall be much obliged if you will give me a ticket. I must reach Pretoria today." The Station Master then responds, smiling according to Gandhi, and ostensibly with some pity:

> I am not a Transvaaler. I am a Hollander. I appreciate your feelings, and you have my sympathy. I do want to give you a ticket on one condition, however, that, if the guard should ask you to shift to the third class, you will not involve me in the affair, by which I mean that you should not proceed against the railway company. I wish you a safe journey. I can see that you are a gentleman.

The account is highly deceitful and manipulative. The fact that the Station Master is portrayed as a Dutchman and not as a Transvaaler is enormously significant from a political point of view. What Gandhi is in fact suggesting is that the superior treatment accorded him by this European is no accident, nor is the reference to his being a Hollander and not an Afrikaner. Gandhi is implying that the Europeans are of a more elevated moral education, sensibility and breeding than the colonialists. This, as we shall see, is politically expedient for Gandhi, since by flattering the vanity of the Europeans by portraying them as more civilized, he can come to expect or even demand such civility from them.

It is doubtful that the exchange took place with the so-called Hollander. However, even if it did, one can easily see that Gandhi is exploiting the incident to advantage, currying moral favor with the Europeans by manipulatively insinuating that they are somehow morally superior to the colonialists, whom he portrays as riffraff. This will allow Gandhi to later appeal to a British sense of fair play. By reminding the British and other Europeans that they are moralistically more upstanding and more progressive in terms of human rights, he can demand concessions and better treatment for his people at the hands of the British, while expecting them to live up to the good reputation he has granted them in this and other passages within his writing.

In the next passage from the 1925 account, Abdul Gani prepares Gandhi for the dangers ahead with a further admonition: "I shall be thankful if you reach Pretoria all right. I am afraid the guard will not leave you in peace in the first class, and even if he does, the passengers will not." This alleged warning in advance of the next leg of Gandhi's journey is as manipulative as it is portentous. To call it foreshadowing would be an understatement. We expect another incident. He is preparing us for it. It comes as no surprise then when Gandhi meets with another alleged incident in the first class section of the train bound for Pretoria. The entire fabricated story is so well planned one almost imagines it to be the work of a master fiction writer than a man professing to be giving us his autobiography, which he rightfully but no less ironically titles, *The Story of My Experiments With the Truth*. It is often said in English, "Speak of the devil and he shall appear." Small wonder then that he should appear in the very next passage describing Gandhi's confrontation with the ticket collector he has so nicely prepared us for by speaking of the devil:

> I took my seat in a first class compartment and the train started. At Germiston the guard came to examine the tickets. He was angry to find me there, and signaled to me with his finger to go to the third class. I showed him my first class ticket. *"That doesn't matter,"* said he, *"remove to the third class."* [emphasis added]

According to Gandhi, there was only one other passenger in the compartment at the time, who just happened to be English. Not only that, but the English gentleman intervenes on Gandhi's behalf and speaks up in his defense. The fact that a European, more specifically and importantly an Englishman, is represented as being morally superior to the Transvaalers is politically expedient for Gandhi. He can later appeal to British vanity by referring to this incident to remind the British ruling class in India that bad manners are not only inappropriate but un-English. Implicit in the passage is the fact that Gandhi is trying to portray the English gentleman in the most positive possible light as an angel Gabriel coming to defeat the principle of evil represented by the Transvaaler ticket agent:

> There was only one English passenger in the compartment. He took the guard to task. *"What do you mean by troubling the gentleman?"* he said. *"Don't you see he has a first class ticket? I do not mind in the least his travelling with me."* Addressing me, he said, *"You should make yourself comfortable where you are."* [emphasis added]

Gandhi can now appeal to the British sense of decency and fair play at a later juncture by having this notorious incident on hand to refer to. Should anyone in the British establishment fail to observe such protocol and fair play, they will be reminded of the Hollander and Englishman who interceded on Gandhi's behalf in yet another racial train incident that occurred many years before in South Africa. The fact that a European, particularly an Englishman, would be moved to exhibit such conduct in the most racially backward and morally unprogressive backwater in the world would be a harsh reminder to the British Raj that their regime is many years on and boasts greater civility, thus demanding conduct in accord with progress. The fact that Gandhi makes one more swipe at the Transvaaler following the Englishman's rebuke only brings the contrast between English gentility and Transvaaler barbarism into starker relief. According to Gandhi, the Transvaaler purportedly said to the Englishman, "If you want to travel with a coolie, what do I care?" The fact that any English incivility would be comparable to that of the Transvaaler is an excellent political expedient for keeping the British ruling caste in India honest. Should they show any kind of intolerance, racism, chauvinism, or lack of fair play, Gandhi need only refer to the example of the English gentleman in the train as a paragon of proper virtue.

Further anomalies occur in Gandhi's account of what transpired in his journey to and arrival in Pretoria. First, Gandhi informs us in his own words in his 1924 *Satyagraha* account that he suffered further assaults on his journey to Pretoria: "I suffered further insults and received more beatings on my way to Pretoria." Notice that Gandhi uses the word "beatings," which requires a degree of brutality that would have certainly resulted in injuries or at the least severe discomfort. Were the testimony true, one would assume that Gandhi would have arrived in Pretoria so pummeled and in such discomfort that it would at least bear a mention. Yet not the least mention of physical discomfort or injury is made in the more protracted 1925 account.

Instead, Gandhi refers only to his state of mental anxiety upon finding no one there to greet him at the station: "I was perplexed, and wondered where to go, as I feared that no hotel would accept me." In addition, not one word of the more lengthy 1925 account is devoted to details on the alleged "insults" and "beatings" that were supposed to have occurred en route to Pretoria. One would assume that if Gandhi had been subject to more humiliations, he would have wished to give a full account of them, since he had been so meticulous in his account of previous insults and injuries. Indeed, his statement, "I suffered further insults and received more beatings on my way to Pretoria" sounds too trite and matter of fact. The statement lacks credulity and rings hollow. Based on the triteness of the statement and the fact that it is supported by no eyewitness testimony whatsoever, it can safely be dismissed as testimony. Testimony requires a testimonial and no facts or details are given to support the allegation that the plaintiff suffered further assaults and human rights violations in the course of his journey to Pretoria.

As for Gandhi's account of what occurred upon arrival in Pretoria, this testimony is riddled with additional inconsistencies and anomalies. It is a pathetic self-portrait he paints of himself arriving at Pretoria Station and one calculated to elicit our sympathies. Presumably shell shocked by his experiences and in a state of semi-bewilderment, he arrives at Pretoria Station only to find that there

is no one there to greet him. Once again we run into disparities between testimonials given at two different periods in his career. In
the 1924 account, Gandhi informs us that the firm of Dada Abdulla
went to considerable pains to ensure that Gandhi was well looked
after in Pretoria. Having resolved to proceed to Pretoria, Gandhi's
acquaintances allegedly made efforts to look after him based on his
request for assistance as he states:

> Next morning I wired to the firm of Dada Abdulla and to
> the General manager of the Railway. Replies were received
> from both. Dada Abdulla and his partner Sheth Abdulla
> Haji Adam Jhaveri who was then in Natal took strong
> measures. They wired to their Indian agents in various
> places to look after me. They likewise saw the General
> manager.

The above passage leaves us in no doubt that Gandhi's colleagues went to considerable effort to ensure that Gandhi was well
looked after, as he clearly states that Dada Abdula and his partner
Sheth Abdulla Haji Adam Jhaveri took, as he claims, "strong
measures" on his behalf. Amazingly, the two men to whom he refers are actually the same individual.[5] Why would Gandhi fiction-
alize his own *Satyagraha in South Africa* and invent two men for
the same personage? Is this more of Gandhi's "experiments with
the truth"? Again, we must recapitulate our earlier argument that
one does not experiment with the truth. One either intends to give
the facts or to render fictions. In the case of truth, there is no room
for experimentation. Indeed, *The Story of My Experiments With the
Truth* is an unfortunate title for Gandhi to have chosen for his
autobiographical work, as it makes his motives rather transparent
and exposes his autobiography for what it is - an experiment with
truth - which no more approaches the truth as such than the fictionalized autobiographical writings of Dickens, and may be even less
authentic.

The question is, if Dada Abdulla had gone to considerable
lengths to ensure that Gandhi was well looked after on the subsequent legs of his journey, why was there no one there to greet him

when he arrived at Pretoria Station? Gandhi even informs us that he expected someone to be dispatched by Dada Abdulla's firm to escort him from the station:

> I had expected someone on behalf of Dada Abdulla's attorney to meet me at Pretoria station. I knew that no Indian would be there to receive me, since I had particularly promised not to put up at an Indian house. But the attorney had sent no one. I understood later that, as I had arrived on Sunday, he could not have sent anyone without inconvenience.

The inconsistency between the accounts becomes clear when we take into account the fact the Dada Abdulla had taken what Gandhi called "strong measures" to ensure his safety and comfort in the course of his journey, but seems to have taken no pains on behalf of the newcomer upon his arrival in another strange place, namely Pretoria, the final destination of his momentous journey. It is simply ridiculous to explain away this anomaly with the explanation that it was Sunday, a day of rest when it is difficult to do business. Knowing Indian culture and the rituals of hospitality it strictly adheres to, the idea of abandoning an Indian stranger to the fates upon his arrival in a strange place, when he had specifically asked to be looked after is patently ridiculous. Anyone familiar with Indian culture would know that, Sunday or not, inconvenient or not, someone would have been dispatched to Pretoria Station to meet Gandhi, particularly as such courtesies were requested in advance. In addition, knowing the difficulties attending a colored passenger in his journeys in Natal, the gravity of the situation would have required Dada Abdulla to send an escort for the sake of protecting his good name in addition to showing proper hospitality to a fellow countryman.

A stranger in a strange land, he is confused and wonders what he should do next: "I was perplexed, and wondered where to go, as I feared that no hotel would accept me." Gandhi then describes his state of mind in Pretoria Station, where we see him skulking in the shadows waiting for the other passengers to disperse before approaching the ticket collector to inquire after a hotel. The episode is clearly calculated to elicit our sympathies at his vulnerability. The pathetic figure he now cuts is in stark contrast with the proud barrister who insisted on traveling first class. Now he skulks around the station like a coward seemingly afraid to ask anyone the time. For this to be a coherent portrait of his character and real-life experiences, there would have to be some consistency in his behavior and conduct. Yet, the man we know as Gandhi goes through so many transformations of character and conduct over the course of this record as to beggar belief. Who is he really? Would the real Gandhi please stand up? We cannot help feeling that all of the Gandhis we see in these few pages of autobiography are fictions and no more consistent with the real-life Gandhi than a character in a novel. Yet, we are asked to believe that the pathetic skulking figure at the railway station afraid to beg the favor of a question is the real Gandhi:

> The lights were burning dimly. The travelers were few. I let all the other passengers go and thought that, as soon as the ticket collector was fairly free, I would hand him my ticket and ask him if he would direct me to some small hotel or any other place where I might go; otherwise I would spend the night at the station. I must confess I shrank from asking him even this, for I was afraid of being insulted.

Gandhi is so cynically experimenting with the truth in this and other passages that it is doubtful we can believe even so much as a word. How are we to believe that the same man who was cocky enough to travel to Pretoria by train in first class, inviting verbal or even physical abuse in the process, would now be afraid to approach a lone ticket collector to merely inquire after a hotel? When finally he does manage to approach the ticket collector to make inquiry, he informs us that, while polite, the man could apparently be of no assistance to him. It is at this juncture that Gandhi is allegedly approached by an "American Negro," who kindly offers him some assistance. The problem with this account is that it is entirely lacking in any linguistic integrity, since there is not the slightest trace of an African-American dialect. In fact, the African-American speaks the Queen's English rather as one would expect a British subject or a British South African colonial subject to speak it. How, pray tell, could he therefore identify the man as an "American Negro?" We will ask the reader to examine the words of the African-American for himself to judge the authenticity of his speech in terms of the African-American dialect in question:

> *"I see,"* said he, *"that you are an utter stranger here, without any friends. If you will come with me, I will take you to a small hotel, of which the proprietor is an American who is very well known to me. I think he will accept you."* [emphasis added]

As an experiment with truth, this is an abject failure. If a black man attempted to talk in this dialect in any American city, he would either be laughed at or thought crazy. African-Americans simply do not talk like this. The expression "utter stranger here" is British to the extreme. The expression "without any friends" is another expression of Anglo origin rather out of place in an African-American cultural context. "If you will come with me" is all too formal an expression for any American and would be regarded as pretentious. The construction "of which" is a refinement of the English educated class and would no more make it across the Atlantic than the repressive class system it hearkens to. The expression "who is very well known to me" would be very well known in the British Isles, but utterly unheard of in the Americas. As for the expression, "I think he will accept you," such a choice of words would be utterly alien to an American of any color both for ideological reasons as well as simple linguistic unfamiliarity. These are British expressions through and through. There is nothing in any of his speech to hint at his origins. He is no more African-American than Afrikaner from a linguistic point of view. The dialect has absolutely no resemblance to the words Gandhi has put in his mouth.

The question that naturally arises is how could Gandhi identify this man as African-American, when he shows not the slightest sign of understanding what the African-American dialect sounds like? And if there is no authenticity to the account, why has Gandhi chosen an African-American as the character in his mini drama? Could it be that Gandhi is attempting to create the impression that only a black man in the Transvaal would have the humanity to reach out to a person of color? Is the passage not precisely designed to make it appear that this person of color was his only friend in the world at that moment? We maintain that this passage, along with the rest of the flawed account, is so blatant a fabrication as to warrant an investigation into Gandhi's true identity and past. He seems in every conceivable way to be a conman extraordinaire.

Gandhi then recounts how the African-American gentleman allegedly led him to a hotel, where the proprietor, Mr. Johnston, agreed to put Gandhi up if he agreed to have dinner served in his room instead of eating with the other guests. Mr. Johnston purportedly apologetically explained to Mr. Gandhi that the other guests were European and might not appreciate sharing the dining room with a person of his persuasion. Mr. Johnston's words if they can be believed are indeed offensive:

"I assure you," said he, "that I have no colour prejudice. But I have only European custom, and, if I allowed you to eat in the dinning room, my guests might be offended and even go away."

Gandhi meanwhile, having retired to his room, expecting to be served dinner there, is revisited by Mr. Johnston who informs him that the other guests have considered the matter and wish for him to join them. The civility these so-called European guests exhibit mirrors the conduct of the other Europeans we see depicted elsewhere in the account, as you can see from the proprietor's explanation:

I was ashamed of having asked you to have dinner here. So I spoke to the other guests about you, and asked them if they would mind your having your dinner in the dinning-room. They said that they had no objection, and that they did not mind your staying here as long as you liked.

The fact that Europeans are once again depicted as the bastion of civility and good manners in South Africa is more political expedience on Gandhi's part. This is more flattery designed to elicit the support of liberals and moderates within the imperial camp. By continually depicting the Europeans as the epitome of refinement and good manners, Gandhi is attempting to show that any kind of ill-mannered or vulgar conduct is simply un-European and not to be tolerated.[6] In terms of the master/slave dialectic he is employing, this is masterful diplomacy. In essence, Gandhi has created a slave morality value system in these few pages specifically designed in the Nietzschian (From *The Genealogy of Morals*) sense to make the master feel guilty for his privilege, while making the slave feel empowered by the master's awakened sense of moral conscience. Did any of these incidents actually happen? Certainly not in the way they are portrayed. At the very least, they are embellished accounts at gross variance with actual events. What is more likely, however, is that they are complete fabrications with no more resemblance to actual events than a doctored photograph bears to the original.

SUMMATION

In order to substantiate our claim that Gandhi's experiments with the truth are an abject failure, let us summarize our findings in our summation before the academic court. First of all, Mr. Gandhi was quite evasive when asked to solemnly swear that he would tell the truth, the whole truth and nothing but the truth before the whole world court. In his own words, he describes his 1925 autobiography as *The Story of My Experiments With Truth*. This is a perplexing and disturbing title. What does he mean by "truth"? Does he mean that he is experimenting with "truth" per se as a philosopher might experiment with an authentic way of living and being or does he mean that he is experimenting with the "truth," as in toying or playing with various versions of the "truth"? Perhaps both meanings are implied, such that those who are initiated into his political game plan know exactly what he means by his enigmatic choice of words. What is clear is that, experimental or not, in terms of "truth" or "authenticity," Mr. Gandhi's testimony fails to convince. As an experiment with the "truth," it is a complete failure and the result is that the evidence fails to support the premise, the premise being that the plaintiff suffered serious human rights violations on his train and coach journeys in Natal and the Transvaal.

Additionally, Mr. Gandhi's testimony is riddled with inconsistencies and anomalies throughout. For instance, throughout his career, Gandhi gives contradictory accounts of what occurred in the different legs of his journey by train and coach across South Africa. Even the identity of the assailants involved in the alleged racial train and coach incidents changes. What makes it particularly difficult for the plaintiff's charges to stick is the fact that he picks so many different suspects out of the lineup. For instance, accounts differ on what occurred at Maritzburg. Gandhi identifies two different suspects as his assailants in this case. In the 1909 account, his assailant is a police constable, but in the 1938 statement given to Reverend Mott, Gandhi maintains that the assailant who threw him off the train was a railway guard. This might be forgivable were it not for the fact that the same case of mistaken identity occurred in his account of what took place on board the coach in his journey across the Transvaal. In the 1909 version, he alleges that it was the guard who attacked him for refusing to give up his seat, while in the 1938 account, he claims it was the coachman who set upon him for moving from the seat to which he had been assigned. Not only does he pick a different suspect from the lineup, but the motive for the crime has changed as well. In fact, it is not just the identity of the suspects that change over time, but the number of assailants involved as well. For instance in the 1925 account, Gandhi informs us that one of the passengers went to complain about finding Gandhi in the first class section and came back in as Gandhi writes with, "one or two officials." As testimony this is exceedingly faulty. For an event of this kind to have taken place, Mr. Gandhi would be in no doubt about what occurred at that moment. It would not be a question of a passenger returning with an unclear number of railway officials. Gandhi would know and would state the exact number if he truly knew. Due to the traumatic nature of the event, he would have known the exact number of assailants involved. The fact that he is unclear about the exact number raises suspicions about the authenticity of the account. Moreover, if we believe the 1924 account, Gandhi was not only racially humiliated but also assaulted at the Maritzburg railway station.

Additionally, the 1924 and 1925 accounts given of the racial train incidents occur well on in Mr. Gandhi's career. No accounts contemporaneous to the events in question are given. The earliest reference to these alleged events occurs sixteen years after the incidents in question and not even in Mr. Gandhi's own autobiographical accounts, but rather in an interview with J. J. Doke. Further, the 1925 account is so much more meticulous and detailed in its account of events than the account of one year previously that we are left asking why greater circumspection was not invoked at an earlier juncture. Indeed, it seems likely that Mr. Gandhi felt compelled to lend a greater sense of authenticity and ring of truth to the account by embellishing the tale and adding an additional layer of characterization and plot. Could it be that doubts were raised about Mr. Gandhi's account of events, requiring that he add more detail to immunize himself against skeptical inquiry and charges of inventing tall tales? Sadly for Mr. Gandhi, it is precisely this attempt to add more characterization and story line to the plot that alerted us to certain discrepancies in the first place.

As mentioned previously, accounts even differ on the nature of the attacks that allegedly occurred on board the coach. In his 1909 statement to Rev. J.J. Doke, Mr. Gandhi alleges that the assailant administered a "brutal blow" to his face followed by another that nearly knocked him from his feet. In the later 1925 account, Mr. Gandhi exchanges these "brutal blows" for a "boxing of the ears." It has to be one kind of blow or the other; it cannot be both. A "brutal blow" is of an entirely different order from a "boxing of the ears." They are as irreconcilable as play-fighting to gang warfare. A "brutal blow" to the face can be interpreted as none other than a close-fisted punch, while a "boxing of the ears" is understood as nothing more than a cuff or slap to the head.

If Gandhi is providing testimony for the same incident, it is inadmissible in the academic court because of its sheer inconsistency. The blows described in the two accounts of the same incident are of a different status and kind. Gandhi is essentially describing two mutually exclusive forms of violence for the same alleged incident. How can this be? Is it because the entire story has been fabricated? He even maintains in the 1924 account that he sustained further injuries en route to Pretoria: "I suffered further insults and received more beatings on my way to Pretoria." With all these "beatings" and "brutal blows" one would have thought Mr. Gandhi would be staggering off the train and limping down the platform at Pretoria. Yet not even a single mention of his physical injuries is given in the lengthy account offered in his autobiography. Nor is there any mention of medical treatment or the administering of a wet cloth, plaster or bandage. The beatings described are inconsistent with the injuries sustained. If we are to believe the account, Gandhi appears to have been emotionally scared only. There is no evidence that he sustained any physical injuries whatsoever. This being the case, we can only assume that the "brutal blows" and "beatings" to which he refers either did not occur or were exaggerated for purposes of eliciting greater sympathy. However, as historians, it is our considered opinion that the accounts given are so inconsistent causally, chronologically and historically as to be completely unworthy as testimony and must be deemed inadmissible in any academic court where true standards of skeptical inquiry are maintained.

The racist incidents that Mahatma Gandhi recounts in his autobiographical writings would be disturbing if they were true. Unfortunately, none of them have the sonorous ring of truth that true stories should have. They seem rather to be manufactured truths crafted to match the truth he would like to present to the world. "Manufactured truths" are carefully orchestrated lies geared to fit a pre-structured ideology and policy agenda. A political opportunist would be well served by such distortions and a lawyer trained in the law would be ideally suited to manufacturing such mistruths toward a preconceived political goal. Exploiting the politics of victimization as a catalyst and springboard to a higher agenda and a larger political goal is precisely what a political opportunist would do.

The first thing to say about Gandhi's "manufactured truth" is that there is such a litany of contradictions in his own accounts as to beggar belief. How could someone who had been so deeply insulted as he claims to have been have such a foggy recollection of the events being represented that the accounts are neither consistent chronologically nor factually? Does it seem likely that someone who had been so deeply outraged by an event that he was motivated to speak and write about it decades later would fail to recall the incidents that occurred at that time with co-relevant consistency? What is even more telling is the fact that none of the accounts are told contemporaneously with the time at which the outrage occurred. One would think that a man of Gandhi's stature, feeling the wound of racial discrimination, would feel motivated to write about the incident at the time it occurred, yet he seems not to have felt the compulsion to write about the racial train and coach incidents until years later. It should be obvious to anyone researching the incident that anyone suffering the sting of racial injustice would feel motivated to write about it immediately. The fact that Gandhi should fail to recount the incident until a full sixteen years later suggests that he was either suffering from psychological denial or that he had not yet invented the story that would prove so dramatic in his attempts to elicit the support of a sympathetic audience, which would serve as a locus for his political movement.

We know that Dada Abdulla[7] was a successful seasoned businessman and possessed a high degree of awareness on the relevant political issues directly affecting Indians. Knowing that, why would he buy a first class ticket for Gandhi? If we believe what Gandhi is telling us, then Dada Abdulla would have had to know that traveling in the first class compartment was "illegal" in practice for Indians, so why would he jeopardize the safety of his newly hired attorney? Why would the railway authorities issue first class tickets to this Indian knowing full well the racial and legal consequences? Ironically, Gandhi stayed in South Africa for a tumultuous twenty-one years. He traveled extensively by way of trains. How is it that he never faced another racial incident of the same kind?[8] Why did they occur only when he landed in Natal and the Transvaal in June 1893 for the first time?

Interestingly, Henry S. L. Polak, Gandhi's closest white disciple in South Africa made a note that "the 'coolie lawyer' (the foolish epithet by which he was commonly known) was a well-known passenger, as he went about the country on professional or public business and he generally had the compartment (a first-class one, in those days) to himself."[9] Polak had known Gandhi from 1904 to 1914 while in South Africa. If we can believe Gandhi's autobiography, he had taken a vow of poverty in 1906 and from 1906 to 1914 he was embroiled in the *Satyagraha* [nonviolent resistance] movement against the government. Even under such circumstances, according to Polak, our Gandhi had been traveling routinely in the first class compartments, and come to think of it, apparently never faced any such racial humiliation.

Part Three

Would Gandhi hold his own were he placed on the witness stand in answering the questions posed thus far? At least once he made a statement on September 25, 1939 accounting for the general disparities. According to him:

At the time of writing I never think of what I have said before. My aim is not to be consistent with my previous statements on a given question, but to be consistent with truth, as it may present itself to me at a given moment. The result has been that I have grown from truth to truth; I have saved my memory an undue strain; and what is more, whenever I have been obliged to compare my writing even fifty years ago with the latest, I have discovered no inconsistency between the two. But friends who observe inconsistency will do well to take the meaning that my latest writings may yield unless of course they prefer the old. But before making the choice, they should try to see if there is not an underlying and abiding consistency between the two seeming inconsistencies.[10]

This statement rather than responding to the dilemma has only complicated the matter still further. Upon further pinning him down, Gandhi may say the following:

1. My statements are rooted in my spiritual development and only I know the positive effects that these racial events had upon me. And

2. Who are you to question me? I am a world-class states-man. You have insulted me by placing me on the witness stand. Nobody before you has questioned me the way you are questioning me. My reputation is at stake and I will not allow you to scrutinize me lest it affects my good name and my following throughout the world. And

3. Understand that the four statements attributed to me on the racial train incidents were said and written long after the actual events. Therefore, the discrepancies that you have brought to light can be easily explained. Given the long time intervals involved between accounts, it would be strange if there were not some discrepancies in the accounts owing to memory lapse. Underlying these alleged contra-dictions and discrepancies, there is a constant commonality between the four accounts: I encountered racial discrimina-tion. Period. That is the abiding consistency throughout these four accounts. You see my case is not much different from that of Jesus Christ whose four gospels attest to the remaining consistency of the truth of the resurrection de-spite what modern scholars have pointed out regarding the alleged inconsistencies and contradictions. And

4. You are correct, as you pointed out, that the first report in the literature occurred in 1909 in a book titled *M. K. Gandhi: An Indian Patriot in South Africa*. Please keep in mind that this account was brought out sixteen years after the occurrence of the racial incident(s). Just because I have

brought the incident to the world's attention sixteen years after the fact doesn't mean that the incidents never took place. The fact is that the incidents happened and my political history going back on these sixteen years (before 1909) attests to these facts. Look at the history of those sixteen years (from 1893 to 1909) and you will see underlying consistent truths scattered throughout in spite of the alleged discrepancies you have pointed out.

Dear Mr. Gandhi, let us be candid with you. We have no intention of maligning your character and reputation just for the sake of doing so. At every given opportunity we would like to give you the benefit of the doubt. In that spirit, we will definitely conduct research on the records you have kept between 1893 and the time of your first biography by Reverend Doke in 1909. Also Mr. Gandhi, we have done something else that has never been done before, which is to construct a timeline of your journey from Durban to Pretoria based upon your testimony. Since you mentioned disembarking at Pretoria on Sunday evening and staying the night there, we are using that as our starting point, we have retraced your steps from that point and this is what we have discovered. You boarded the train at Durban on a Wednesday. Since your journey was interrupted, you spent that Wednesday night at Pietermaritzburg. You spent the entire day on Thursday in Maritzburg. Whether you remained at the railway station or went into the city with or without the company of Indians, we simply cannot determine. Anyway, at 9 p.m. on Thursday, you re-boarded the train with Charlestown as your destination. You spent Thursday night on the train while traveling. On Friday, just before noon, you disembarked at Charlestown, and due to the length of your visit, you were forced to switch your mode of travel to the stagecoach. In spite of the beatings that you encountered at Pardekoph, you reached Standerton and that's where you spent the Friday night. On Saturday, you continued your journey by stagecoach and reached Johannesburg in the evening. Clearly, it is evident that you spent the night in Johannesburg.

Given the above timeline with respect to the days of the week, we have one shortfall: We have no way of knowing the exact dates of your travel and in your testimony you never mentioned the dates. Your diehard followers celebrate June 7, 1893 as the day commemorating what transpired on that occasion at Maritzburg train station. It seems that they have done their homework because June 7, 1893 turns out to have been a Wednesday. At another place, we are given June 3, 1893 as the date given for what took place at Maritzburg, which happens to be a Saturday (see Appendix II).

As evidenced by the aforementioned, the timetable brings into relief several problems with Gandhi's autobiographical accounts of the racial train incident that took place at Pietermaritzburg, which would otherwise have remained in the shadows and would have most assuredly been overlooked. First, Gandhi is quite explicit about the arrived time: "The train reached Maritzburg, the capital of Natal, at about 9:00 p.m." The train timetable for the historical time period in question indicates that the arrival time was actually 8:42. Let's give Mr. Gandhi the benefit of the doubt and imagine that the train did indeed arrive at around about 9:00. It was winter, so this would fix the train's arrival time after dark as he contends in his 1925 autobiographical account. He then proceeds to tell us that it is the dead of winter and bitterly cold at that time of year: "It was winter, and winter in the higher regions of South Africa is severely cold. Maritzburg being at a high altitude, the cold was extremely bitter." He then informs us that he is thrown off the train at Maritzburg, where he must brave the winter cold in a waiting room, where he is forced to spend the night. He later informs us that he does not in fact spend the night alone in the waiting room, which is strange, but is joined sometime after entering the vacant waiting room by another passenger: "A passenger came in at about mid-night and possibly wanted to talk to me. But I was in no mood to talk."

This is where the timetable raises problems. Let's check our watches. The train arrives at around 9:00 p.m. Gandhi is thrown off the train at around 9:00 p.m. He spends approximately three hours shivering in the dark in a waiting room, when he is suddenly joined by a fellow passenger at around midnight. What is contradictory here is the fact that it is late at night, midnight to be precise, and cold, bitterly cold so we are told, and yet, of all unlikely events, Gandhi is met by a fellow passenger, who like him is prepared to spend the night in the bitterest cold of the dead of winter for the next train, which will not arrive till the next morning. Why would a passenger, any passenger, wish to spend the night in a waiting room on a train station platform in the fierce cold of winter? Gandhi never addresses this or accounts for it. Gandhi makes no mention of a passenger disembarking from another train.

However, even if he had, why would the passenger not seek shelter for the night in a proper guesthouse or hotel? What would possess the man to spend the night in the appalling cold of the South African highlands? The explanation that the passenger had just arrived and was waiting for the next available train makes even less sense, since he had obviously deserted a warm place of shelter to spend the night in the most absurdly inhospitable conditions imaginable. What would possess a person to have so early a start that they set out for the railway station instead of repairing to a warm hotel or guesthouse for the night? Would they prefer the unspeakable boredom and discomfort of a railway station waiting room to the comforts of tea, coffee, a newspaper, warm slippers and other amenities? The fact that Gandhi should be spending the night in a waiting room with anyone on one of the coldest nights of the Natal provincial winter makes no sense and no more rings true than an improperly tuned instrument.

And why, additionally, would Gandhi not seek some kind of shelter? Gandhi even states that the man who entered the waiting room around midnight appeared to want to talk to him. Why would Gandhi deny himself the luxury of a companion with which to while away the dark, cold hours in conversation? Why, additionally, if the man appeared friendly as Gandhi alleges, would Gandhi not turn to the man to inquire after lodgings or a place of shelter for the night? True, most people in the province would have regarded him as an unwelcome stranger and would have been reluctant to provide him with lodgings, but why would Gandhi not seek out the chance of hospitality from a fellow passenger who appeared friendly enough, and even seemed willing to strike up a conversation with the lonely Indian gentleman. To repeat Gandhi's own words in this context, "A passenger came in at about midnight and possibly wanted to talk to me. But I was in no mood to talk." Why on earth not? Does it seem sensible or even rational to turn down an opportunity of this kind? Why would he not take advantage of a situation in which he is presented with a friendly stranger? While the race of the individual in question is not mentioned, the fact that the issue is overlooked suggests that it is not a person of color, but a friendly white man. Why would Gandhi not then take advantage of an encounter with a friendly white man in order to seek some advantage for himself? Could this stranger not in fact provide some welcome advice or even hospitality in a situation of obvious undesirability?

The other problem with the 1925 autobiographical account is that it is contradicted by the account Gandhi gave in the interview with Reverend Mott. In the 1938 interview, Gandhi stated, "I entered the dark waiting-room. There was a white man in the room. I was afraid of him." Contrast this with the account he gave in 1925: "There was no light in the room. A passenger came in about midnight and possibly wanted to talk to me. But I was in no mood to talk." What is self-evident from reading these two accounts of what allegedly transpired that night in the waiting room is that the accounts don't match. In fact, they are diametrically opposed. In the 1938 account, the stranger is already in the waiting room when Gandhi enters and is clearly identified as a white man. Gandhi also claims that he is afraid of the man because he is white. Yet, in the 1925 account, the waiting room is empty when Gandhi first arrives and it is not until three hours later that a man appears, who Gandhi identifies as a passenger, but gives no indication of his race. This man, Gandhi tells us, appears sociable enough and even willing to talk. Yet, it is Gandhi and not some formidable white man, who is described as unsociable on this occasion.

The fact that the timetable should conflict with probability is no surprise when we consider the fact that the entire episode appears to have been fabricated. That any passenger besides Gandhi should be in the waiting room at so late an hour on so cold a night seems extremely improbable. Its sheer unlikelihood only makes the account more dubious, when one considers the fact that there are so many disparities between the 1925 and 1938 accounts. What this suggests is that the entire incident has been staged by a master dramatist who wishes to have the strongest possible effect upon his audience. Not only is the fictional passenger's presence on the stage more dramatic in the later 1938 account, but seems designed to be so. Gandhi now has the momentum of history behind him. He can now exploit the politics of victimization more readily. He can now exaggerate the role of the white man in the scene in the waiting room. He can make his presence seem all the more threatening, as a symbol of everything that stands in the way of racial tolerance and progress. This is not even to criticize Gandhi's methods as dishonest, deceitful, and opportunistic or anything of the kind. It may even have been necessary for Gandhi to tailor his story for the mass media market by sensationalizing it. It may also have been a political expedient for a just cause. The fact remains, however, that subjecting the account to methods of modern skeptical inquiry exposes certain inconsistencies and contradictions in the accounts that have been entirely overlooked by previous researchers.

Gandhi goes on to recount in the 1925 account how he sent a long telegram to the General Manager of the Railway and also to Abdulla Sheth, who immediately met the General Manager. He then tells us that Abdullah Sheth wired the Indian merchants in Maritzburg as well as friends in other places and told them to look after their esteemed colleague. Gandhi tells us that he spent the day with them. He then departed for the Maritzburg railway station that evening. "The evening train arrived. There was a reserved berth for me," he recounts. This suggests that there is only one train passing through en route to Charlestown each day. The timetable indicates that the arrival time for the Durban to Charlestown train is 8:42, with a 9:00 departure time. If trains run so infrequently on this route that one has to wait a full 24 hours for the next train, why would anyone choose to spend the night in the waiting room in the Maritzburg railway station? Gandhi's account simply does not ring true. If he spent the night in the waiting room, it is most likely that he was the sole occupant. The stranger he alleges passed the night with him, a man who is given two different stage cues in the 1925 and 1938 accounts, making his entrance at two different times, is more likely to be a phantom of his imagination. Whatever the case may be, Gandhi's testimony is clearly unreliable.

Other inconsistencies emerge in the autobiography when we subject it to close comparative analysis with the railway and coach timetable then in operation. In the 1925 account, Gandhi tells us that, after some reflection on his circumstances, he resolved at the train station at Maritzburg to carry on with his train journey, "So I decided to take the next available train to Pretoria." There is no direct train from Maritzburg to Pretoria. The train only goes as far as Charlestown and from there you must take a coach to reach Standerton. Gandhi later corrects this slip by telling us that the train from Maritzburg went to Charlestown: "The train took me to Charlestown." What is odd, however, is the arrival time Gandhi gives for the train to Charlestown: "The train reached Charlestown in the morning." According to the timetable, the arrival time for the train to Charlestown was 11:50, which is in fact noon or mid-day. Why would Gandhi not give the arrival time as indicated on the timetable as midday if he were familiar with the route? This may seem like a minor point, but the following evidence suggests that Gandhi may not have been as familiar with the route as he purports to be. In the 1925 account, he claims he proceeded from Charlestown by coach and that the next arrival point was Parde-koph, where another racial incident allegedly took place. To make the point clear, it is necessary to quote the passage in full:

> At about three o'clock the coach reached Pardekoph. Now the leader desired to sit where I was seated, as he wanted to smoke and possibly to have some fresh air. So he took a piece of dirty sack-cloth from the driver, spread it on the footboard and, addressing me, said, "Sami, you sit on this, I want to sit near the driver."

The timetable actually indicates that 4:00 p.m. is the arrival time for the coach at Pardekoph, but we'll give Gandhi the benefit of the doubt on that issue. What is of far greater concern is the tes-timony he gives in the 1909 account by Doke. Here Gandhi main-tains that the next arrival point by coach was Paardeberg and not

Pardekoph, and that it was here that the next racial incident took place:

> The coach was about to leave Paardeberg with Mr. Gandhi seated on the box when the guard, a big Dutchman, wishing to smoke, laid claim to this place, telling the Indian passenger to sit down at his feet.

What this demonstrates is that Gandhi is not as familiar with the route as he would have us believe. This is not to suggest that he never traveled by train or coach. He certainly would have had to travel by train in South Africa. On the contrary, the point to be made here is that he confuses the towns Paardeberg and Pardekoph.[11] This is significant. The timetable indicates that the next town on the train route is Paardekop, which Gandhi misspells as "Pardekoph." Two things are problematic here. The first issue of whether Gandhi misspells the place name Paardekop as "Pardekoph" is a minor one. The second issue is more serious. He also mistakes the place name in the earlier account of 1909 as Paardeberg. What this demonstrates is that Gandhi is not as familiar with the train line as he alleges. Had the incident in question actually taken place in Paardekop as he claims, he would have certainly remembered the name in 1909 and would surely not have misspelled the name of the town in the 1925 account, the place and the incident being so indelibly etched upon his memory. Also, for witness testimony to hold up in court, the witness must be able to identify a consistent place or locale where the assault took place, and not display this kind of confusion over the setting of the incident.

Further inconsistencies arise concerning accounts on the last leg of the journey. In Doke's account based on an interview with Gandhi in 1909, the assault that took place on the coach from Paardekop to Standerton was the last such incident. We are informed that, from Standerton, nothing further transpired, because "...at Standerton the coach was changed, and the rest of the journey was accomplished without incident." However, according to Gandhi's own 1925 account, it is not true that the rest of the journey was accomplished without incident. When the train stopped at Germiston, Gandhi experienced another incident of racial harassment. Granted this situation did not turn violent, but the 1925 account depicts it as serious enough to conflict with the 1909 version of events, in which we are told "the rest of the journey was accomplished without incident." According to the 1925 account, Gandhi was about to encounter another racial episode when a fellow white passenger rescued him from another humiliation before he reached his final destination in Pretoria. The story of what transpired at Germiston is given in Gandhi's 1925 version of events, where he boarded the train in first class and was ordered by the guard to remove to third class:

> I took my seat in a first class compartment and the train started. At Germiston the guard came to examine the tickets. He was angry to find me there, and signalled to me with his finger to go to the third class. I showed him my first class ticket. "That doesn't matter," said he, "remove to the third class."

It is hard to imagine how Doke could have responsibly dismissed this part of the journey as passing without incident or how Gandhi could have possibly given Doke that impression, since what happened at Germiston is clearly, while not violent, an incident nonetheless. According to the 1925 account, the racial confrontation with the guard is likely to have escalated to a more aggressive confrontation were it not for the intervention of a fellow white passenger as Gandhi recounts:

> There was only one English passenger in the compartment. He took the guard to task. "What do you mean by troubling the gentleman?" he said. "Don't you see he has a first class ticket? I don't mind in the least his traveling with me."

Taken to task by the white passenger for his racial harassment of Gandhi, the guard backs down, but not before making another

Singh & Watson

insulting racial remark on the way out: "If you want to travel with a coolie, what do I care?"

We return to our cross-examination:

Well, Mr. Gandhi, while you are still on the witness stand, we would like to bring to everyone's attention including yours some more mysterious questions surrounding your testimony in the 1925 autobiography and we do not expect you to have a ready answer for any of them:

1. You said that at Maritzburg station "another official" told you, "Come along, you must go to the van compartment." We are wondering why you weren't told to go to the second or third class compartments? In your autobiography, contrasting the conditions of railways in India, you stated:

"In Europe I traveled third - and only once first, just to see what it was like - but there I noticed no such difference between the first and the third classes. In South Africa third class passengers are mostly Negroes, yet the third class comforts are better there than here. In parts of South Africa third class compartments are provided with sleeping accommodation, and cushioned seats. The accommodation is also regulated, so as to prevent overcrowding, whereas here I have found the regulation limit usually exceeded."[12]

Mr. Gandhi, if the black natives of South Africa traveled in the third class compartment in South Africa, then who traveled in the van compartment? Are you telling us that the whites in southern Africa treated you worse than they treated the South African natives by directing you to go to the van compartment?

2. Moreover, we have another problem and that deals with your altercations involving injustices and slights occurring in India shortly before you left for South Africa (see Appendix III). Our purpose in alluding to this rather petty and

inconsequential affair is to make the point that you were not in the habit of pocketing insults of any kind. Any altercation, however slight, appears to have galvanized you into action whenever such an avenue seemed open to you. In this case, you were left with no apparent option but to back down. The official with whom you were at odds was simply too powerful and influential for you to take on. However, it is clear that your pride was so strong that you were ill inclined to forgive any kind of insult to your caste. The question arises, then, as to why you did not take similar action in South Africa. As a commissioned lawyer, you surely held higher status under South African law than a ticket inspector or coachman. Arguably, you would have found it more difficult to proceed against the police constable who threw you off the train at Pietermaritzburg train station. But still, it does appear odd and inconsistent, from the perspective of your earlier actions in India that you did not proceed against the railway authorities in South Africa.

3. By alluding to your purchase of a bedding ticket at Maritzburg, you seem to be suggesting something. Are you telling us that if you had the bedding ticket, perhaps, you might have escaped the racial train incident? On Thursday, late in the evening at about 9 p.m., you re-boarded the train going to Charlestown and this time you paid some extra money to buy the bedding ticket. Even though you make no mention of it, the obvious conclusion to be drawn from this is that you were seated in a first class compartment. That scenario raises more problems. You see Mr. Gandhi since the railway personnel work in shifts, this makes it very likely that the railway employees who threw you out of the train on Wednesday night at Maritzburg would most likely be back on duty on Thursday evening. Knowing their negative racial attitude toward you, we are baffled as to how they would allow you to return to the first class compartment with the added luxury of a bedding ticket! Mr. Gan-

dhi, you will have to forgive us, the facts just do not match your story.

4. After reaching Standerton and relating the story of your misfortunes to the local Indians, where did you stay the night? You make no mention of the person or persons that put you up for the night, nor of the residence or domicile in which you stayed upon that occasion. Also, we are baffled that late at night you wrote a letter to the agent of the coach company, who miraculously replied to you in writing that same night. As you indicate that you sent a "wire" to the Station Master the following day, it is very probable that your "letter" as you call it, would have to be a telegram. According to your own testimony given in the 1925 account, you composed a letter that very night to alert the agent of the Coach Company about the whole affair. In your own words you claim to have written him a letter: "So I wrote him a letter, narrating everything that had happened, and drawing attention to the threat his men had held out." We know this correspondence is alleged to have occurred in the middle of the night, for you state: "I also asked for an assurance that he would accommodate me with the other passengers inside the coach when we started the next morning." The question is, Mr. Gandhi, was it a letter or a wire? You will, we hope, forgive us for saying so, but "a letter, narrating everything that happened" does sound more like a letter to us. Telegraph wire messages are usually brief messages and for economy, usually consist of short phrases, not long letters detailing everything that happened. The question is how were you able to dispatch this long letter detailing everything that happened and then hear back so quickly, before the break of day in fact? Of course we may be mistaken about it being a letter. It could be a wire.

But then how could a wire contain so detailed an account of events that it "narrated everything that had happened"?

Still, even if it was a wire, it seems bewildering that the Agent of the Coach Company would be on hand in the middle of the night to receive your telegram and reply to it posthaste.

5. In Johannesburg, you met and conversed openly with Abdul Gani. Where did you stay the night? Is it possible that both at Standerton and Johannesburg, you spent the night at the homes of unnamed fellow Indians? Did they fail to offer you proper hospitality? Were they so un-Indian?

6. We are wonderstruck that you could encounter anything so baffling. During your stops at Maritzburg, Standerton, Johannesburg, and Pretoria, the number of Indians that came to see you decreased correspondingly as your journey progressed and when you reached your final destination of Pretoria, there was no Indian waiting to greet you at the station. Are you telling us the truth? Even more surprising is that you knew that no Indian would be there to receive you at Pretoria and you "vowed that you would not agree to being put up at the Indian's house." Why would you make such a vow? Did Indians at Standerton and/or Johannesburg insult you? Surely you stayed at Indian residences, did you not?

7. As you stated, you reached Pretoria on Sunday at about eight o'clock in the evening after catching a train from Johannesburg, a journey of only 37 miles. Mr. Gandhi, we are having difficulty understanding you on this point. You see, at Johannesburg, an evening before (that is on Saturday) you were in a hurry to reach Pretoria. As it turns out, the train journey from Johannesburg to Pretoria could not have been more than two hours if you reached Pretoria at 8 p.m. That means you boarded the train no later than 6 p.m. at Johannesburg on Sunday evening. The question we would like to ask therefore is: Where were you and what were you

doing all day on Sunday in Johannesburg? Since you were in a hurry to reach Pretoria why would you stay in Johannesburg all day until 6 p.m.?

8. Mr. Gandhi, we have the train schedules from Durban to Charlestown. You know very well that the train stopped at many locations along the way. Given the nature of your racial encounters, your employer must have made arrangements to have Indians meet you at the train stations of Ladysmith, Newcastle, and Charlestown. And yet you are silent on that score. Why would Indians meet you at Maritzburg and at none of the other locations in Natal colony?

9. You said that when the stagecoach reached Johannesburg, there was one Indian who had come there to welcome you. However, failing to recognize each other, you were left stranded. We are again having problems here accepting your story in light of the following facts: You were the only Indian traveling in the coach in the company of a number of white people. And since you hardly look like a Caucasian, how could anyone miss you in broad daylight?

You see Mr. Gandhi we have done our homework and now we are going to take your words seriously and examine the historical records from the time you landed in South Africa until the time you left in 1914.

NOTES

---

[1] Burnett Britton. *Gandhi Arrives in South Africa.* Canton, Maine: Greenleaf Books, 1999.

[2] Gandhi assigns the date April 2, 1924 to the preface of *Satyagraha in South Africa.* Therefore, we have used the year - 1924 - as a focus for analysis purposes only.

[3] Gandhi assigns the date of November 26, 1925 to the introduction section of *An Autobiography or The Story of My Experiments With Truth.* Therefore, we have focused on the year - 1925 - focus for analysis purposes only.

---

[4] Friedrich Nietzsche. *The Genealogy of Morals*, ed. and trans. Oscar Levy, London: Foulis Ltd, 1913.

[5] Fatima Meer, ed. *The South African Gandhi: An Abstract of the Speeches and Writings of M. K. Gandhi 1893-1914*. Durban, South Africa: Madiba Publishers, 1996. On page 103, Dada Abdulla's full name is given as Abdulla Haji Adam Jhavary. On page 83, his brother's full name is given as Abdul Carrim Haji Adam Jhavary. On pages 1193-94, one can read brief descriptions of these two brothers.

[6] Gandhi assures us that the gentleman he meets at Pretoria Station, who provides intelligence on local hotels is an African American, whom he identifies as an "American Negro" as we have noted. This same man offers to direct Gandhi to a hotel run by a man whom he claims is a fellow American. The American who runs the hotel, and who receives Gandhi with due ceremony, informs him that he only has European custom. Does it seem likely that, in this caste-obsessed society of South Africa, an American would be running a hotel frequented by Europeans, who would doubtless seek a more befitting room with a view than one in a hotel run by a "Yankee"? Considering that the African American claims to be on familiar terms with the American hotel proprietor named Mr. Johnston, he is confident that he will put Mr. Gandhi up for the night. Given that status is everything in this racial based society, does it seem likely that a white American proprietor of a hotel in the Transvaal would be willing to risk his business by having people of color staying at a hotel frequented by Europeans. Keep in mind that Mr. Johnston equivocates on the issue of his clientele by stating, "I assure you...that I have no color prejudice. But I have only European custom, and, if I allowed you to eat in the dinning room, my guests might be offended and even go away." How can he have no color prejudice and at the same time have only European custom at the hotel? This makes no sense whatsoever. Clearly, Mr. Johnston does have color prejudice even if it is only from business motivations. So concerned is he about the color issue that he is afraid to take Mr. Gandhi down to the dining room for fear of the consequence it might have for his business. Given that he is concerned enough to avoid making a scene in the dining room, he would presumably be equally concerned about having people of color sauntering in and out of the hotel.

This being said it is no more likely that Mr. Johntson would be any more willing to have an African American in his hotel than a colored man of Indian persuasion. It is also worth noting that America is no less color blind in the time period in question than South Africa. Is it likely that a white American would be any more hospitable toward the custom of an African American than any white colonial subject Transvaaler? The social and historical record of the time would suggest not. This being the case the entire account is likely to be another example of Gandhi's fanciful imagination.

[7] Abdulla Sheth and Dada Abdulla are different names for the same individual.

[8] In September 1913, while in the midst of the Satyagraha campaign, Gandhi and his associates faced a minor racial incident while traveling on the train at Ladysmith in Natal. This incident is discussed in the next chapter.

[9] Quoted in *Incidents of Gandhiji's Life*, page 239, edited by Chandrashanker Shukla. Vora & Co. Pub., Bombay, 1949. How is it that Gandhi was able to gain such privilege? Interestingly, in the concluding chapter of this book, we have the testimony of F.E.T. Krause on that score, who informs us that Gandhi had received a special pass (railway included) from the Attorney General of the Transvaal Republic, Krause's brother in fact, which exempted him from showing papers and other requirements of people of color. Also, according to Krause's testimony, Gandhi was treated like a dignitary whenever they were together. Was Gandhi's status as a mere barrister sufficient to warrant such privilege that he was able to rub shoulders with the white establishment of South Africa? We think it highly unlikely that such a chauvinistic community would have allowed him into their ranks without a very special reason. We believe there was a special reason for such preferential treatment. We believe Gandhi had affiliations and connections, which the scholarly community has never before examined or even been aware of, largely due to incompetence and poor sleuthing ability. We will examine these affiliations, possibly from which Gandhi gained privilege and power in chapter 8.

[10] D. G. Tendulkar. *Mahatma: Life of Mohandas Karamchand Gandhi*, Vol. 5., New Delhi: The Publications Division, Government of India, 1952, p. 168.

[11] In modern times, *Illustrated Atlas of South, Central, East Africa* has named the town as Perdekop.

[12] Mohandas K. Gandhi. *An Autobiography or The Story of My Experiments With Truth*. Boston: Beacon Press, 1957, page 239.

Six

Historical Inquiry

~

In the midst of humiliation and so-called defeat and a tempestuous
life, I am able to retain my peace, because of an underlying faith in
God, translated as Truth. We can describe God as millions of
things, but I have for myself adopted the formula - Truth is God.
~ Mahatma Gandhi
The Mind of Mahatma Gandhi

Historical inquiry into the alleged incidents, a little more than a hundred years after, is not an easy task. No one ever looked into these incidents at the time when Gandhi was alive. Even today, had it not been for the project of the Collected Works of Mahatma Gandhi (CWMG) undertaken by the government of post-British India, the task of undertaking an historical inquiry would have been next to impossible. The CWMG project has already been published in a total of six editions, the last revised edition in 2000. The one hundred volumes of the CWMG, especially the first fourteen volumes (all chronologically arranged) cast a startling light on Gandhi's history in South Africa. This is a highly prized product delivered by a tax-funded group. Gandhi himself would have been appalled and might have resorted to another hunger strike to stop it, had he lived. In addition to letters and petitions, the CWMG incorporates the contents of Gandhi's *Indian Opinion*, a weekly newspaper of his own creation, whose first issue appeared on June 4, 1903. *Indian Opinion* had sections in four languages - English, Gujarati, Hindi, and Tamil. Shortly after the first issue, the Hindi and Tamil sections were dropped. Only the English and Gujarati sections remained. The following analysis into the alleged train incidents is based upon the sixth edition of CWMG combined with Gandhi's other writings.

One is hard pressed to find anything concerning the train incidents in the month of June 1893 in the pages of CWMG. That in itself does not prove that the incidents did not take place. However, when analyzed within the context of what Gandhi experienced before (in May 1893), the alleged racial train incidents and other encounters that occurred after, in the month of June 1893, seem unlikely. Luckily for us, Gandhi himself has left us a stream of contemporary records that we were able to analyze.

What is clear from the literature is that Gandhi arrived in Durban in May. After a day or so, his employer took him to the court where an incident allegedly took place as described in the 1909 biography and in the Autobiography.

From the pages of the CWMG, we learn the following as the above incident was reported in *The Natal Mercury* on May 26, 1893:

> An Indian entered the Court House yesterday afternoon and took a seat at the horseshoe. He was well-dressed and it was understood that he was an English barrister, on his way to Pretoria, where he is reported to be engaged in an Indian case. He entered the Court without removing his head-covering or salaaming, and the Magistrate looked at him with disapproval. The new arrival was courteously asked his business, and he replied that he was an English barrister. He did not attempt to present his credentials, and, on returning to the horseshoe was quietly told that the proper course for him to pursue, before taking up his position at the Bar, was to gain admission to the Supreme Court.[1]

What we learn from this article is that Gandhi entered the court on May 25. It is likely that he landed in Durban on 23 May, though one can never be one hundred percent certain. What does come as a surprise is the fact that Gandhi read the above report in the *Natal Mercury* and immediately on the same day responded in a letter to the editor of the *Natal Advertiser*, which the newspaper published on May 29, 1893!

SIR, I was startled to read paragraph in your today's issue referring to myself, under the heading, "An Unwelcome Visitor." I am very sorry if His Worship the Magistrate looked at me with disapproval. It is true that on entering the court I neither removed my head-dress nor salaamed, but in so doing I had not the slightest idea that I was offending His Worship, or meaning any disrespect to the Court. Just as it is a mark of respect amongst the Europeans to take off their hats, in like manner it is in Indians to retain one's head-dress. To appear uncovered before a gentleman is not to respect him. In England, on attending drawing-room meetings and evening parties, Indians always keep the head-dress, and the English ladies and gentlemen generally seem to appreciate the regard which we show thereby. In High Courts in India those Indian advocates who have not discarded their native head-dress invariably keep it on.

As to bowing, or salaaming as you would call it, I again followed the rule observed in the Bombay High Court. If an advocate enters the Court after the judge has taken his seat on the bench he does not bow, but all the advocates rise up when the judge enters the Court, and keep standing until the judge has taken his seat. Accordingly, yesterday when His Worship entered the Court I rose up, and took my seat only after his Worship had done so.

The paragraph seems to convey also that though I was told privately not to keep my seat at the horseshoe, I neverthe-less "returned to the horseshoe." The truth is that I was taken by the chief clerk to the interpreters' room, and was asked not to take my seat at the horseshoe the next time I came unless I produced my credentials. To make assurance doubly sure I asked the chief clerk if I could retain my seat for the day, and he very kindly said "yes." I was therefore really surprised to be told again in open court that in order to be entitled to the seat I had to produce credentials, etc.

Lastly, I beg His Worship's pardon if he was offended at what he considered to be my rudeness, which was the result of ignorance and quite unintentional.

I hope, in fairness, you will extend me the favour finding the above explanation a space in your paper, as the paragraph, if unexplained, would be likely to do me harm.[2]

From the evidence of all the contemporary accounts available, in May 1893, Gandhi did experience a minor incident in the court. Apparently, the Magistrate looked upon Gandhi with disapproval. That in no way implies that Gandhi had experienced a racial incident at that time. There is hardly a doubt left that the issue really hinged upon the protocol of presenting credentials, and in Gandhi's case, it was no different from those protocols expected from any new lawyer in a preliminary hearing in a court of law. It seems the court clerk handled Gandhi courteously. However, in the 1909 biography as well as the *Autobiography* accounts, Gandhi has changed the story by injecting a previously unmentioned issue of ethnic discrimination. In this account, the Magistrate ordered him to remove his turban and rather than accept an insult, Gandhi walked out of the court. Here they are:

From the 1909 biographical account:

Here in Natal, it was all changed. When, on the following day following his advent, according to Eastern habits of respect, he wore his barrister's turban in Court, sitting beside his client's solicitor at the horse-shoe, and was rudely ordered to remove his hat, he left the building smarting under a sense of insult.[3]

While in his *Autobiography*, Gandhi wrote:

On the second or third day of my arrival, he [Abdulla Sheth] took me to see the Durban court. There he introduced me to several people and seated me next to his attorney. The Magistrate kept staring at me and finally asked me to take off my turban. This I refused to do and left the court.[4]

Gandhi's actions of May 1893 call for more circumspect analysis. We know of no other similar example. Here is a 23-year-old failed lawyer from India who had landed in Durban only three days earlier and is writing a letter to the editor in reply to a reported minor incident. Another strange mystery concerns the fact that Gandhi wrote to the *Natal Advertiser* rather than the *Natal Mercury*. Why? We have not been able to solve this mystery. In any case, we can reasonably conclude that in May 1893, Gandhi is active and certainly would not one to shy away from expressing his opinions in public even over a minor incident.

As for June 1893, we have detailed in Chapter Four the litany of racial incidents that Gandhi encountered while traveling to Pretoria. Strangely, there is nothing written on the subject contemporaneous with the events in question in the CWMG. Again, we can draw only one conclusion: Gandhi wrote no letters to the editor of the *Natal Advertiser*. If he had experienced the racial incidents on the train, then judging from his previous actions of May 1893, he would have definitely written some letters to the editor. Could it be that the train incidents never took place?

Now Gandhi is in Pretoria, capital city of the Transvaal, and an adjoining province to Natal. In the month of September 1893, Gandhi reads a report in the "Transvaal Advertiser" and immediately dispatches a "correction letter" dated September 16, to the *Natal Advertiser*, a newspaper located about 400 miles away.

SIR, My attention has been drawn to the reproduction of Mr. Pillay's letter to The Transvaal Advertiser in your paper with comments thereon. I am that unfortunate Indian barrister-at-law who had arrived in Durban, and who is now in Pretoria; but I am not Mr. Pillay, nor am I a Bachelor of Arts.[5]

The Natal Advertiser published Gandhi's letter on September 18, 1893. At the bottom of page 58, the editors of the CWMG inserted a footnote: "Pillay's complaint was that he was violently pushed off the footpath." There is some confusion here. Considering there were more individuals named Pillay, which Pillay is Gandhi referring to? Apparently, Mr. Pillay, an Indian located in Natal or the Transvaal, faced a racial incident, in which he was pushed off the footpath. It is clear from the CWMG that Pillay wrote a letter of unknown date to the *Transvaal Advertiser* complaining about the incident. In the preceding letter, Gandhi inserted himself in the story. Whether Gandhi himself faced a racial incident in Natal (or elsewhere) similar to that of Mr. Pillay is not clear. In his 1925 autobiography, Gandhi narrates the racial incident of being kicked and pushed off the footpath while walking in Pretoria, Transvaal.[6] Strange as it may sound, on September 19, Gandhi dispatched a long letter to the *Natal Advertiser* briefly mentioning the controversy generated by Pillay and a few other issues relating to Indians experiencing difficulties. The *Natal Advertiser* published the letter on September 23, 1893.[7] Lo and behold, he dispatched another long letter on September 29, which was published on October 3 in the *Natal Advertiser*.[8] In these long letters there is no mention of the racial train incidents, nor can one discern anything relating to the footpath incident. Here is a man who loves to write and complain. And yet he does not mention a single word about the racial train incidents. Another curious matter is that he writes a prolific volume of letters to the editor of the *Natal Advertiser* while living in the Transvaal. T. K. Mahadevan, in his *The Year of the Phoenix* has produced at least two of Gandhi's letters that were written before Gandhi penned his related letter about Mr. Pillay. For some unknown reason, the editors of the CWMG failed to incorporate those letters into the volume.[9]

Gandhi routinely traveled by train in South Africa. His notation in his diary, dated June 29, 1894 clearly remarked that he was traveling in Natal in the first class compartment along with Sir Harry

Singh & Watson

Escombe and Hitchens, two very senior white leaders.[10] Amazingly, before Gandhi left South Africa and went back to India on June 5, 1896, there is not a single shred of evidence that he had commiserated with anyone over the degrading and humiliating racial train incidents at that time.

Gandhi stayed in India for the next six months and here was an open opportunity for him to express his sorrow to his countrymen concerning that awful place called South Africa. Expectedly, Gandhi fully exploited the opportunity to let the Indians know of all the terrible things to which Indians were subject in South Africa. In not a single place are these racial incidents that he is alleged to have experienced even once mentioned. In India, Gandhi traveled extensively, going to Bombay, Calcutta, Madras, Gujarat (his home place), Poona, and so forth, and at each place he gave speeches detailing the deteriorating racial situation in South Africa. He went even further. He authored a booklet of about 33 pages titled, "The Grievances of the British Indians in South Africa: An Appeal to the Indian Public."[11] Gandhi exploited one opportunity after another to let his readers and listeners know about all the things that were wrong with South Africa and yet he failed to mention anywhere what allegedly transpired in June 1893. Could it be that the incidents never happened? In one place in a letter to the editor of the *Times of India*, dated October 17, 1896, Gandhi addressed the issue of railway and tram-car officials in Natal who mistreated Indians terribly: "I have been witness myself to not a few such cases. What is it if it is not being treated as a beast, to be removed three times during a single night journey from one compartment to another, to suit European passengers?"[12] Here, Gandhi has clearly stated that he has witnessed "not a few such cases" of Indians suffering mistreatment by railway officials while traveling on the South African railways. In no way do his words allude to any such incidents happening to him. He seems to be aware of at least one case, in which an Indian traveler moved three times from one compartment to another in a single night's journey.

This example is in no way similar to the incidents he is supposed to have experienced in June 1893. If there is one place where Gandhi could have easily narrated his pathetic racial encounters on the train, it was in this letter to the editor of the Times of India.[13] We can thank Pyarelal, Gandhi's famous biographer, for bringing to our attention an incident that occurred in the last week of November 1893: "A Muslim leader Tyab Mohamed, a resident of Durban, was thrice ejected with insults and threats from one second class carriage to another during a train journey from Pietermaritzburg to Durban."[14] In all likelihood, Gandhi is alluding to the case of Tyab Mohamed. Here is a great example of an incident that occurred while in India, in which Gandhi remembered a slight experienced by a fellow Indian in the month of November 1893 - only a few months after the alleged train incidents that he himself encountered. The point here is: Had there been any truth to the racial incidents of June 1893, Gandhi would have certainly taken this opportunity to make mention of them.

In January 1897, Gandhi returned to South Africa and because of his strong anti-South African rhetoric in India, he was assaulted by a Durban mob only to be rescued by the timely efforts of Mr. R. C. Alexander, the superintendent of police and his wife. So if we go by the history given to us, by January 1897, Gandhi had already faced two separate assaults: one in June 1893 and one in January 1897. Yet, immediately after the assault of 1897, he and his friends wrote numerous letters and petitions to the colonial authorities.[15] Not once is the assault of June 1893 even referred to. Could this be because it never happened?

Gandhi maintained complete silence on the train incidents while staying in South Africa, until October 1901, when he left again for India. This time he stayed in India for a little more than a year until December 1902. As before, he traveled in India going to various cities giving lectures and writing petitions. Here again he could exploit an opportunity to relate to his world audience the story of what had transpired in June 1893, but astonishingly not so much as a single word is uttered about the racial train and coach incidents.

Once having returned to South Africa and settling in the Transvaal, he established the *Indian Opinion* in Natal, a weekly newspaper in June 1903. In 1906, he participated in a war against blacks and two months after he launched the Satyagraha movement or his version of nonviolent passive resistance against the repressive race laws. This campaign continued till the tail end of his stay, at which time he left South Africa for India via England. One can't help but notice that not a single word escapes his mouth about the train incidents as recorded in the CWMG. In September 1913, at the tail end of his Satyagraha campaign, Gandhi encountered a minor incident while traveling on the train and he wrote a letter of complaint about it to the General Manager of the South African Railways on September 12, 1913:

SIR, With two other Indians I was traveling by the Kaffir Mail that left Durban on Thursday to the Transvaal. We were all traveling third-class. We occupied one of the corridor third-class compartments which are usually attached to the Natal trains. My companions and I were put in the compartment we occupied by one of the conductors. At Ladysmith, however, the new conductor came and told me that we would have to shift from the compartment we were occupying to another. On enquiring for the reason I was told that the compartment we were occupying was meant for Europeans only. I drew the conductor's attention to a compartment which was so labeled, also to the fact that our compartment was not labeled at all, and that I had traveled in such compartments several times on the Natal line. I informed him also that the conductor said that I was to obey instructions or to get permission from the Station Master to remain where I was. Thereupon, I saw the Station Master, but I must say that, in rather a rude manner, he told me that I was to do as the conductor asked me, and that I ought to know that the conductors could ask passengers to shift as many times as they chose without giving any reason whatsoever. I did not argue the matter with the Station Master but simply went and occupied the compartment I was in and awaited developments there. Meantime, unknown to me, a friend who happened to be on the platform, and who knew me, disclosed my identity to the conductor who subsequently spoke to me and told me that, in asking me as he had done to remove, he was only carrying out instructions, but that he would not do.... I was told by the Indians who were on the platform at the time, and who were watching the proceedings, that such difficulties happened to Indian passengers often. I do not know what truth there is in what the conductor told me. I can only hope that he misread the instructions of the administration, because, in my humble opinion, it would be preposterous if even third-class Indian passengers may not travel without being disturbed, and without being told that the nicest compartments were always reserved for Europeans.

I hope that you will be good enough to investigate this matter and do whatever you consider is necessary. I feel that high officials, such as Station Masters, ought to be told to realize their responsibility and behave courteously towards passengers even though they may not belong to the European race. I hardly think that it was necessary for me to disclose my identity before I could claim courteous treatment from the Station Master.[16]

When it comes to historical inquiry, we find that the section of the CWMG pertaining to the South African period provides us with no information on what happened on June 1893. However, as we have elaborated on previously, Reverend Doke referred to the train incidents in the biography of Gandhi that he authored. Here is some background: In 1908, in the midst of the Satyagraha campaign, a fellow Indian, a Pathan (in company of his friend) by the name of Mir Alam, thinking that Gandhi was playing a double game, assaulted Gandhi on February 10, 1908, and in the process badly hurt him. Under such circumstances, Gandhi's bruises were nursed at the home of Joseph J. Doke, a local Baptist. Their acquaintance soon grew into a friendship of exceeding intimacy. Doke wrote the biography with the aim of acquainting the people in England with Mr. Gandhi. It is quite apparent that in 1908, when Gandhi was "dictating" his biography to Rev. Doke, it was virtually the first time Gandhi had mentioned what had transpired on the trains in June 1893. Since the book, *M. K. Gandhi: An Indian Patriot in South Africa* was published in London, it is safe to assume that those who read the book in England became aware of the racial incidents in question. However, there are a number of problems associated with this book and the role both Doke and Gandhi had in it. These problems are discussed in the next two chapters.

Once Gandhi left South Africa for London en route to India, he had an opportunity to meet Oxford University classicist professor, Gilbert Murray, in 1914. Gandhi narrated his history to him, which Murray published in article form in 1918. Regarding the period in question, we read:

> He came as a barrister in 1893; he was forbidden to plead. He proved his right to plead; he won his case against the Asiatic Exclusion Act on grounds of constitutional law, and returned to India. The relief which the Indians had expected was not realized. Gandhi came again in 1895.[17]

Here in London in 1914, Gandhi failed to mention the racial train and coach incidents of June 1893. Why?

In Gandhi's extensive literature (called Gandhiana), there is only one place where an eyewitness account of the incident that allegedly transpired at Pietermaritzburg train station appears in print. In this case, the eyewitness is none other than the Railway Guard himself:

> I was a guard on the train on which the young lawyer, M. K. Gandhi, traveled from Durban, South Africa, in 1893, on the first stage of his first journey to Johannesburg. He had bought a first-class ticket, but I threw him off the train because he was an Indian and had dared to travel with white people.

> That was only one of many such episodes. He was insulted, thrashed, savagely attacked again and again. Of necessity so, for we have to keep the colored races down in their places as servants. The mere fact that one of them gets him-

self educated does not mean that all the regulations can be broken in his favor. It is all the more necessary to keep that kind of Indian from getting uppish, for if you give them an inch they will take a mile.

Remember, we in South Africa are a small white minority in a whole continent full of blacks. Race lines must be drawn clearly and race barriers enforced, or we are submerged. That is why we South African whites insist on a system of passes and poll taxes and segregated areas for Indians. We also bar colored people from taking skilled jobs in industry. The race regulations on the railroads are only the outward sign of a fundamental prop of our whole outlook on life, that we whites are to be the ruling race. That is why I threw Gandhi out of that train.

But I must say he took it well. There was no sniveling and no ill will. He stood up for his rights fearlessly and said he had paid his fare and had the right to travel in the carriage. When it did no good, he took his punishment like a man. It was the same every time he was insulted and beaten. He fearlessly protested against what he thought was unjust, and suffered patiently the results of his protest. I can see how such a man could put a new spirit into the Indians.[18]

Here we have some problems. The railway guard has not provided his name. He doesn't refer to the season or time of year in 1893 in which the alleged incident of throwing Gandhi off the train occurred. He hasn't provided us with the date on which the alleged testimony given above was issued. Amazingly, this letter was published in a book in 1947 - nearly fifty-four years after the incident. How did John S. Hoyland, the author of *They Saw Gandhi* get a hold of this railway guard or his undated letter? As it happens, the Fellowship Publications published the book and in the entire narrative one gets the distinct impression that *They Saw Gandhi* is a work of pure fabrication and fiction, an imaginary work of Reverend Hoyland, a Christian missionary in India. This information about the fictionalized account is recorded by the Fellowship Publications on the jacket of the book. Where did Hoyland get the details as mentioned in the above letter? In all probability, Hoyland accompanied Reverend Mott to meet Gandhi in 1938, and based upon what Gandhi told Mott, Hoyland took the liberty of fabricating the corroborating evidence provided by his fictional railway guard so that the Gandhi story could be cross-referenced.

NOTES

[1] CWMG, Vol. 1, p. 56

[2] Ibid., pp. 56-57.

[3] Joseph J. Doke. *M. K. Gandhi: An Indian Patriot in South Africa.* London: Indian Chronicle, 1909, p. 44.

[4] Mohandas K. Gandhi. *An Autobiography or The Story of My Experiments With Truth.* Boston: Beacon Press, p. 106.

[5] CWMG, Vol. 1, p. 58.

[6] Mohandas K. Gandhi. *An Autobiography or The Story of My Experiments With Truth.* Boston: Beacon Press, p. 130.

[7] CWMG, Vol. 1, pp. 58-60.

[8] Ibid., pp. 62-64.

[9] T. K. Mahadevan. *The Year of the Phoenix: Gandhi's Pivotal Year, 1893-1894.* Chicago: World Without War Publications, 1982, pp. 36-41.

[10] CWMG, Vol. 1, p. 123.

[11] Ibid., pp. 359-93.

[12] Ibid., p. 420.

[13] Ibid., pp. 420-23.

[14] Pyarelal. *Mahatma Gandhi: The Early Phase*, Volume 1. Ahmedabad: Navajivan Publishing House, 1965, p. 306.

[15] CWMG, Vol. 2, pp. 1-150.

[16] CWMG, Vol. 13, pp. 329-330. Also read pp. 331-32.

[17] Gilbert Murray. "The Soul As It Is, And How To Deal With It." Hibbert Journal, January 1918, p. 200.

[18] John S. Hoyland. *They Saw Gandhi*. New York: Fellowship Publications, 1947. The quote is taken from the 2nd edition published by National Education Association of the United States, 1953, page 15 under the heading "We Saw What He Did About Race Oppression: The Railway Guard."

Seven

Gandhi's First Biography

~

I have in my life never been guilty of saying things I did not mean-my nature is to go straight to the heart and if often I fail in doing so for the time being, I know that Truth will ultimately make itself heard and felt, as it has often done in my experience.

~ Mahatma Gandhi
The Mind of Mahatma Gandhi

G iven all that we have presented and analyzed concerning Gandhi's encounters on the trains and coaches, we have no choice but to pay close attention to *M. K. Gandhi: An Indian Patriot in South Africa*, Gandhi's first biography and also the first source of information that described the racial incidents in question. There are a series of questions surrounding this biography that are puzzling and convinced us to take a closer look.

Keeping the political context in view, we know that the ongoing Satyagraha struggle made it possible for Rev. Doke to meet Gandhi no less than four times, including an opportunity to nurse him back to health following the Indian Mob attack led by Mir Alam, before sitting down with Gandhi to discuss the idea of writing a book on him. Doke himself committed a few lines to paper regarding his conversation with Gandhi that first prompted him to write the biography:

"My friend," I began, "I want to ask you a strange question - how far are you prepared to make a martyr of yourself for the good of the cause?" he looked a little surprised but said quietly, "I think you should know that by this time." "No," I said, "candidly I do not." "Well," said he, his face kindling, "it is a matter with me of complete surrender. I am nothing. I am willing to die at any time, or to do anything for the cause." "Take care," I rejoined, "perhaps I shall ask something too great." "You cannot do that," he replied calmly. Then I saw my opportunity, and drew the toils about him. "Listen," I said. "It appears to me that what we are doing now is merely tinkering at the Asiatic settlement - our fight with this Government is only part of a much greater fight, to be fought out on a greater battlefield. The question of the status of British Indians throughout the whole Empire will have to be solved, and in the settlement of that vast problem, you should have much to say. The question is - how can we best prepare for that future?" he nodded in his own quick, incisive way. I proceeded. "You know very well that, with us Europeans, character and personality are of the first importance. It is so here, and it must be so at home. You yourself are the chief asset of the Indian cause. It is a great thing to know and trust the leader of such a movement." He was about to speak, but I stopped him. "Let me continue," I said. "Your position as leader makes your personality of great importance to the cause. It has occurred to me that if I could write a short book - bright, graphic, and reliable - making your personality real to the people of England, it might do something to help the cause in the great struggle that is to come." The emphatic nods became appreciably weaker, but they did not altogether cease, so I went on: "You will see, however, that my power to do this depends altogether upon yourself. You must tell me about your childhood and youth, allow me to picture your personality, and depict your character, and if I know anything of you, to submit to this will be the severest kind of martyrdom that you can suffer." "Ah," he said, as my purpose dawned upon him, "you have caught me completely." "But," said I, "would this help your people?" He thought a moment, and then replied, "Yes, in England." "Well, can you go so far?" "For the cause, I can," he said. And then, "What do you want me to do? You don't want me to write anything, do you?" "No," I replied, "not a word; just let me question you about that Indian city where you were born, that beautiful home of yours far away in the East, the very thoughts of your heart, your struggles and sacrifices and victories. What you cannot tell me, others will help me to discover." So, silently, with a grip of the hand, we confirmed the bond, and this is how this story was born.[1]

Before analyzing this passage, we ask the reader to employ the methods of skeptical inquiry and explore the passage for himself first. The opportunistic nature of the enterprise is there in plain language for him to read. Let's begin by examining one of Doke's key statements on the subject of the biography, "But," said I, "would this help your people?" To which Gandhi replied, "Yes, in England." There is no room for equivocation here. It is clear from Doke's question and Gandhi's reply that the enterprise is being conceived in the form of a P.R. campaign for Satyagraha at best and at worst a cynical and calculated propaganda campaign. One thing is certain: The book they both have in mind is not an authentic biography, but a blatant attempt at self-promotion. Then, Doke asks Gandhi how far he is willing to go with the enterprise, "Well, can you go so far?" To which Gandhi replies, "For the cause, I can." This last exchange is central to our whole argument for opportunism because it provides evidence of an ethical dilemma they are able to justify on the basis of a means-ends relationship. Doke, the man of the cloth, is indisputably asking Gandhi if he is prepared to go all the way with the scheme they have devised. Gandhi's reply indicates that for the sake of the cause he is willing to do anything, turn himself into a martyr, saint, avatar if need be, whatever is necessary to further the cause. For Gandhi, the ends justify the means. This in itself does not make him Machiavellian, but it does raise questions. If he were willing to embellish the story of his life to further the political cause, what wouldn't he do on behalf of the cause or anything else he believed in? How authentic was the man really? If he could win converts in England by turning himself into a martyr-hero, he could certainly absolve himself of the sin of hyperbole.

The next question Gandhi puts to Doke eliminates all doubts about Gandhi being the consummate opportunist. Gandhi asks, "What do you want me to do? You don't want me to write anything, do you?" This is pure opportunism. It is also highly irregular and improper. Only an opportunist would ask if he could contribute to the writing of a biography being written about him. This undermines the ethical and professional integrity of the biography and calls the legitimacy of the entire enterprise into question. Gandhi's question makes explicit the fact that he is a consummate opportunist. His words prove that he conceives of the biography in terms of P.R. only. In fact, we would go so far as to call it a propaganda exercise and nothing else.

How many sessions the pair had in order to complete the manuscript is not known. We can reasonably assume that both exhausted considerable hours in this endeavor. They had finished the manuscript by the end of October 1908. One thing can be verified beyond doubt from the above conversations: That the purported biography was originally meant for an English audience. Then on June 21, 1909, Gandhi (in company with Hajee Habib, his associate) left Johannesburg for Cape Town en route to England and carried with him Doke's manuscript. In England, he was to plead and represent the Indian case to the highest colonial authorities. He reached London on July 10 and stayed in London until November 13, 1909. All in all, in the course of these roughly five months, Gandhi was successful in getting the biography published. From the literature we were able to put together the sequence of events that took place in Gandhi's effort to get his book published. This sequence is as follows.

Gandhi landed in London on July 10 and started to look for a publisher. Most likely he had someone in mind.

He found Mr. N. M. Cooper, publisher of *London Chronicle* with the address: 154 High Road, Ilford, Essex. How he actually found him is not clear. Most likely the avenue of approach occurred as the result of a parallel case, involving one Madanlal Dhingra, a local Indian resident who had assassinated Sir Curzon Wyllie, political Aide-de-Camp to the Secretary of State for India, on July 1. As a follow up to the case reported in the press, another unnamed Englishman, a printer by profession, was arrested for apparently printing the cause of the Indian nationalists who had justified this assassination. Clearly, this Caucasian printer was a regular printer hired for Mr. Cooper's business adventures. We believe quite possibly that Gandhi had read the story in the local press of this printer's agony over being unjustifiably imprisoned and that this paved the way for Gandhi to contact Mr. Cooper. We believe that Gandhi made this contact sometime in the latter half of July. It is also quite possible that someone in the local Indian community referred Gandhi to Cooper.

Based upon his negotiations with Mr. Cooper, Doke's manuscript was put through the process of proofreading and possibly editing. Whether Cooper handled the editing process or someone else was employed, we will never know. Then on August 9, Gandhi dispatched a letter to Lord Ampthill:

> I have now received the somewhat delayed proof of the Rev. Mr. Doke's book, which I am very anxious to see published as early as possible. I might mention in passing that I have received a number of subscriptions from subscribers in advance.

> I know you are very busy and I have hesitated to burden you further with the perusal of this proof and with the writing of the introduction, which you were good enough to promise, if the proof should meet with your approval. Nevertheless you will, I hope, find time - as I sure you have the desire - to give this matter your very kind attention.

> I am forwarding the proof under separate cover.[2]

Clearly, Gandhi had requested Lord Ampthill write an introductory chapter for Doke's biography. On August 26, Lord Ampthill finished the introduction and passed it along to Gandhi who eventually found a publisher for it.

In a letter to Henry S.L. Polak (who is by this time in India), dated September 16, Gandhi expresses signs of growing frustration:

> Mr. Doke's book is still unpublished; it is likely to be in the first week of October. For reasons I need not go into this week. I am thinking of buying out the whole of the edition, more for the sake of Mr. Doke than anything else. He will be very much cut up if there is a fiasco, and there might be. The publisher has not put his heart into it, and as many copies will have to be distributed free of charge, I thought I should pocket my own personal feelings and deal with the thing myself. I fancy that Dr. Mehta will guarantee any deficit. I have already corresponded with him in the matter. You may, therefore, be on the lookout for any bookseller who would care to take up the book. The best thing will be, perhaps, for Kaliandas or Chhaganlal's cousin, or both of them, to take the book personally to many people. In any case, there should be no credit given to any booksellers on whom you cannot rely implicitly....[3]

Mr. Polak responded with some good news on the subject: "Natesan will take 250 copies for distribution here among booksellers for sale. When Chhaganlal comes here, he will make enquiries in Bombay. You may be sure that no credit will be given to unreliable booksellers."[4]

In another letter to Polak, dated October 6, Gandhi updated the progress by writing, "Mr. Doke's book will probably be in my hands next week. Mr. Cooper promised a few copies even on Saturday."[5]

In a follow up letter to Polak, dated October 14, Gandhi's frustrations are obvious, "I am sorry Mr. Doke's book is not yet ready. I have just got two advance copies, but I suppose it is not necessary for me to send one out to you. As soon as the copies are ready, I shall ask Mr. Cooper to send 250 to Mr. Natesan."[6]

Singh & Watson

A week later, on October 21, sensing some progress, Gandhi dispatched a letter to Cooper with the following request:

Will you kindly send Mr. Doke's book as follows: 24 copies to Dr. Mehta, 14 Mogul Street, Rangoon, India; 250 copies to Messrs Natesan & Co., Booksellers, Madras, India.

250 copies to the Manager, International Printing Press, Durban, Natal, South Africa. (Postal address, Box 182, Durban, Natal).[7]

The next day, October 22, in a letter to Polak, Gandhi expressed his frustrations in the following words:

Mr. Doke's book cannot still be delivered. Poor Cooper is at his wit's end. His printer being in gaol, the printer's wife has not been able to keep her promise. Next week, I think, delivery will take place without fail.[8]

Finally, on October 29, the apparent good news is announced: The book has been published and Gandhi dispatched a long letter giving precise instructions to Polak:

At last Mr. Doke's books are ready. I enclose herewith a list of complimentary copies to the newspapers in India. If there are any newspapers left out which, in your opinion, should get complimentary copies, please take them from the parcel that will be received by Natesan, not, I fear, by the mail that takes this letter but by the following mail. I have had great difficulty in getting the copies. Ritch and I have come to the conclusion that, apart from the newspapers, no public men should receive complimentary copies. None have therefore been sent, but if you think that any should be sent on your side, you should consult Dr. Mehta and then distribute. Dr. Mehta has bought 25 copies for such distribution. You may either get some of these or, in order that the same person may not get two copies, after having learnt from him the names of those who may receive his copies, you will be able to get them from Natesan. I take it you have come to some arrangement with Natesan so that we may receive cash without delay. 85 complimentary copies have been distributed here. Of these 81 are to newspapermen. Will you please arrange for cuttings containing the reviews to be sent to Mr. Doke.[9]

There is something curious about the preceding letter to Polak that cannot be passed over. Gandhi specifically instructs Polak that newspapermen are the only public men who are to receive complimentary copies, writing: "...Apart from the newspapers, no public men should receive complimentary copies." There are two ways of reading this. Neither, as it happens, is particularly flattering to Gandhi. First, one can assume that Gandhi does not want the biography falling into the wrong hands. Second, and more probably, he wishes to exploit the situation to his advantage by distributing the highly prized complimentary copies only to members of the press most probably to publicize both himself and his cause. There is an opportunism here motivated by personal or political ambition, which is certainly not the Gandhi we all know and love and is so at odds with the original portrait painted of him by biographers and filmmakers as to make this Gandhi unrecognizable. This is not the Gandhi we have learned about in school, but a consummate propagandist and opportunist engaged in a public relations campaign as cynical as those launched in a corporate boardroom today. The opportunistic nature of the enterprise cannot be made clearer than through Gandhi's own succinct words on the subject: "85 copies have been distributed here. Of these 81 are to newspapers." He also instructs Polak to await news from Dr. Mehta and to act on the basis of his list of names in distributing copies. It is very clear that this effort is being promoted in a business-like manner as a P.R. if not propaganda campaign. Now we would ask our readership to match this Gandhi with the one promoted by popular culture for nearly a century! We will now ask our readers a question: Does the image of the Gandhi presented by mass media and academia match the one more careful reading and analysis brings to light?

In another follow up letter to Polak, Gandhi apprised him of another development:

> Mr. Doke's book has been received in the Edinburgh Evening News in about 20 lines. The Times has just acknowledged it, giving a 4-line notice. I do not think it has been received anywhere else yet.[10]

Only three days before his departure from London, on November 10, Gandhi mailed one complimentary copy of the Doke biography to Leo Tolstoy in Russia:

> I beg to send you herewith a copy of a book written by a friend - an Englishman, who is at present in South Africa, in connection with my life, in so far as it has a bearing on the struggle with which I am so connected, and to which my life is dedicated.... It has not been possible for me to advertise the struggle as much as I should like. You command, possibly, the widest public today. If you are satisfied as to the facts you will find set forth in Mr. Doke's book, and if you consider that the conclusions I have arrived at are justified by the facts, may I ask you to use your influence in any manner you think fit to popularize the movement?[11]

Before Gandhi left South Africa, he had arranged for Mr. Polak to go to India. In the interval, while both Gandhi and Polak were away from South Africa, Rev. Doke assumed the duties of editor-in-chief for the *Indian Opinion*. From the passages cited above, we can draw some reasonable conclusions. It seems that Mr. Cooper, the publisher, harbored a few qualms about Doke's manuscript and he reluctantly published the book, perhaps under some unidentifiably compelling factors. It is also apparent that Gandhi himself went through frantic efforts to get the book published in London. Why would he put himself in such a situation considering that there was an easy alternative? He could have easily published the book through his printing press from where *Indian Opinion* was being published in South Africa. And he could have brought the books with him to London for distribution. What advantage did it serve for Gandhi and his Satyagraha movement to publish the book in England? There are many more questions. What intrigues us is the speed with which the book was published. It appears that in roughly three months, Gandhi was able to meet the publisher, present Doke's manuscript, sign a contract, and get it published. Not since St. Paul have we seen this kind of evangelical zeal to get the word out. What sort of contract did Gandhi sign? How much money did Gandhi pay the publisher for publication? We don't know. You would think that it would have been more appropriate for Rev. Doke, he being the author, to have gone to all these lengths to get the book published. Why is Gandhi, the subject of the book, exhausting so much time and money on promoting a book that is being published so far from South Africa and the Satyagraha movement?

It is also clear that Gandhi bought all the books that were published - about 700 in all.[12] This most likely means the *Indian Chronicle* was not a traditional commercial publisher. Rather, it would have resembled today's version of subsidy publishing. It is clear that Gandhi is hoping to win some publicity from the book. He details his promotional efforts in London, India, and Russia. On October 29, Gandhi has earmarked 85 copies, out of which 81 copies are to be distributed to newspapermen in England. We can be sure that Gandhi presented at least one copy to Lord Ampthill. The reason Gandhi is directing the book's distribution to the journalists is simple: to elicit a favorable review in the local newspapers. In India, he sent 250 copies to Mr. Natesan. In accordance with the instructions to Polak, Gandhi is again, as in London, targeting newspapermen with complimentary copies of the book with the aim of soliciting good reviews. Amazingly, he chose Leo Tolstoy as his point man to do the same job in Russia.

Something is very odd here. Gandhi is promoting his book in England, India, Russia and Burma. The geographic location where Gandhi's book is most likely to have the biggest impact is South

Africa. Yet ironically, Gandhi is taking no pains to promote the book in South Africa. Why? Already he had dispatched 250 copies to the "International Printing Press" in Durban, which means he essentially mailed it to himself. Following his return to South Africa, the literature is silent on what he did with those copies. Moreover, not once does he announce the book's release to the readers of the *Indian Opinion*. Not once did he inform the non-Indian communities of South Africa of the existence of this book. Why would Gandhi and Doke exercise such silence in their own locale and sphere of major influence? Judging from the literature, we believe Mr. Cooper had refused to take on the extra burden of sending book parcels to overseas locations as Gandhi had instructed him to do earlier. We believe Gandhi himself mailed these parcels. Tallying up the 700 books, we have broken down the distribution as follows: (1) 250 copies to India, (2) 250 copies to South Africa, (3) 25 copies to Burma, (4) 1 copy to Russia, and (5) 85 copies distributed in England. This gives us a total of 611 copies. The rest of the roughly 89 copies are unaccounted for - most probably distributed as extra complimentary copies in India, some more in London, and a few he probably hand carried on his way back to South Africa. Whether Dr. Mehta received 24 or 25 copies is irrelevant. If one happens to believe that Cooper mailed the books himself, then a case can be made for Mehta being the ultimate recipient of 49 copies. We believe he purchased only 25 copies for distribution in Burma.

Dr. Mehta was in Europe during the time in question and Gandhi had met and corresponded with him quite regularly before Dr. Mehta left for Burma. It also appears that Gandhi lied to Lord Ampthill in a letter dated August 9 when he told him, "I have received a number of subscriptions from subscribers in advance." Another irony is that Gandhi came to London to extract the best political advantage from the book. However, the book was not published until October 29, only twelve days before Gandhi left for South Africa. This situation must have left an unfavorable impression upon him and whatever political advantage he could derive from the book had to be minimal. However, because this book was selectively promoted in India, B.P. Wadia (1881-1958), who at that time closely worked under the tutelage of Annie Wood Besant, wrote a book review of this biography by Doke. The Theosophist magazine published it in July 1910:

> From time to time we come across a biography which creates in us a genuine admiration for the hero of the book.
>
> When it is a living hero in the thick of his battle, manifesting a strength of character met with but rarely, our sympathy and love go out to him and we look for ways and means of giving him a helping hand. Such a man we have found in the hero of the book. We have heard and read much about this clever, hard-working, self-sacrificing [individual, which] from a sympathetic pen enhances the value of Mr. Gandhi in our eyes. The biographer, Mr. Doke, is a Christian, a Baptist Minister at Johannesburg and a friend of his hero, who has been watching him and his work for some years. The whole story from beginning to end is thrilling with life, and to enjoy it one must read it. Its graver mission is the arousing of genuine sympathy for Mr. Gandhi's noble cause, and it is a matter, as Lord Ampthill points out in his Introduction, "which touches the honor of our race and affects the unity of the Empire as a whole." Mr. Gandhi is so much at one with his cause that it is difficult to speak of him apart from his work; and yet in reading the book it is the personality with all its romance and pathos that attracts us more than the cause. Mr. Gandhi seems to us to be a true Theosophist in principles and spirit, though he is reported to have said: "No, I am not a Theosophist. There is much in Theosophy that attracts me, but I have never been able to subscribe to the creed of Theosophists." But Theosophists have no creed. It is not of grave consequence, however, that Mr. Gandhi is not a member of our Society; he lives the life of a Theosophist, preaches our ideas and ideals in his own language and acts as we should wish to act. What more do we need?[13]

Plate 1

Gandhi's Journey from Durban to Pretoria in 1893.

Plate 2

Pietermaritzburg Railway Station, photo taken in about 1884. Source: *The Birth and Development of the Natal Railways.*

Plate 3

Gandhi & his staff in Johannesburg. H.S.L. Polak, M.K. Gandhi, Sonja Schlesin seated in the front row. Source: *Mahatma Gandhi* (1949).

Plate 4

A messianic Gandhi compared to Krishna, Jesus, Buddha, Tolstoy, Lenin, and Prof. McSweenie. This "photo" was circulated in the early 1920s.

Plate 5

Gandhi as a Sergeant Major during the 1906 Zulu War.

Plate 6

Gandhi and his stretcher-bearer corps during the 1906 Zulu War.

Plate 7

A statue of Gandhi which stands in Pietermaritzburg, South Africa.

Plate 8

Former President of South Africa, Thabo Mbeki, pays his respects at Raj Ghat, Gandhi's state memorial in India. Source: Press Information Bureau, Government of India.

The Orwellian "doublespeak" repeatedly found in this review does not fall on deaf ears. Gandhi's denial that he is a Theosophist is a trifle dubious when we consider his close association with Annie Wood Besant of the Theosophical Society. Why write the review unless Gandhi somehow espoused or supported views in accord with those of the Theosophical Society, which B.P. Wadia does in fact purport in his review?

As has been argued earlier, Gandhi never promoted this book in South Africa from the 1910-1914 periods onward. He mentioned the title of the book incorrectly only once in 1913, an issue that will be discussed in the next chapter. In 1910, Rev. Doke went on a trip to the United States, and before going he received well deserving accolades no less than four times, as seen in CWMG, Vol. 10, documents 246, 249, 250, and 262. Not once did Gandhi in his public speeches mention the book by name or title or even thank him for writing the biography. Why? After spending so much of his own money, why wouldn't he promote the book in South Africa? Surely, by promoting the book in South Africa, Gandhi would have easily recuperated the publication costs. Was there something in the book that he didn't want anyone in South Africa to read? Is it possible that he knew that major contents of the book, including the train and coach incidents, were false and that there were people living in South Africa, who had known Gandhi from his earliest days and knew the truth concerning his habitation in South Africa all too well? Had Doke's book come into the hands of these knowing individuals, it is quite likely someone would have blown the whistle on Gandhi's campaign of lies. We believe this was the prime reason why Doke's book was not promoted in South Africa. We believe we have valid reasons to question the very historicity of these train and coach incidents. Our claim is given greater credence by the following two cases, one concerning Polak and the other Mehta.

First, as was said earlier, Polak (1882-1959) was in India during this period promoting the cause of Indians in South Africa. He followed through on the advice given to him by Gandhi regarding Doke's book. Strangely, as the literature shows, Polak did something more while in India: He wrote two small books. One is titled

The Indians of South Africa and the other *M. K. Gandhi*, both published by Natesan in 1909 and 1910 respectively.[14] Perplexingly, *M. K. Gandhi* is not to be found anywhere in the literature, perhaps because it was eliminated intentionally. Instead, we have a book naming Polak as the author, *M. K. Gandhi: A Sketch of His Life and Work*. Amazingly, the racial train and coach incidents are entirely missing from this biography.[15] Upon Polak's return to South Africa, Gandhi in a jubilant mood introduced Polak to his *Indian Opinion* readers. He specifically wrote a news report titled, "Polak's Book" where he introduced *The Indians of South Africa*. Nowhere did Gandhi mention anything about Polak's writings about him[16]. Why would Gandhi go to such lengths to make sure that nobody in South Africa knew about his earliest biographies? We also learn from Sushila Nayar (Gandhi's close associate and physician in India) that Polak's friendship with Gandhi fell apart in the 1940s, and that he turned against Gandhi.[17]

Second, Dr. P. J. Mehta (1858-1932) was extremely close to Gandhi over the years and was another recipient of Doke's biography. He wrote a "biography" which was also published by Natesan. Surprisingly, the racial train and coach incidents are entirely absent from this biography.[18] Both Polak and Mehta must have read Doke's biography and yet somehow totally ignored the record of the racial train incidents in their biographies. Why? Is it possible that they knew their man well enough to know that the purported racial incidents were altogether false?

Mr. G. A. Natesan (1873-1949), the publisher of G. A. Natesan & Co. as well as Ganesh & Co. mounted a propaganda blitz promoting Gandhi, first in India and then abroad. In a timely fashion in 1919, he published the Indian edition of Doke's biography. Later on, he too fell out of favor with Gandhi and a bitter exchange of letters between the pair ensued. Lord Ampthill (1869-1936), who had written an introduction to Doke's book, received not so much as a word of thanks from Gandhi, not even a word of gratitude after he passed away.

NOTES

[1] J. J. Doke. *M. K. Gandhi: An Indian Patriot in South Africa.* London: Indian Chronicle, 1909. Check chapter 4 titled "A Compact." The quote is taken from reprint.

[2] CWMG, Vol. 10, p. 15.

[3] CWMG, Vol. 10, p. 96.

[4] Ibid.

[5] CWMG, Vol. 10, p. 151.

[6] CWMG, Vol. 10, p. 167.

[7] Ibid., p. 183.

[8] Ibid., p. 184.

[9] Ibid., pp. 194-195.

[10] Ibid., p. 207.

[11] Ibid., pp. 223-224.

[12] Sushila Nayar mentioned the count of 700 in her book, *Mahatma Gandhi: Satyagraha At Work* (Vol. 4), page 473.

[13] Annie Wood Besant. "Theosophist Magazine July 1910-September 1910." Whitefish, Montana: Kessinger Publishing; 2003; pages 1355-56. It is not clear whether Gandhi himself knew of this book review. If he knew of it and decided not to inform the South Africans, that action of his is understandable in the overall context of his secret and evasive strategies.

[14] Henry S. L. Polak, H. N. Brailsford, and Lord Pethick-Lawrence. *Mahatma Gandhi.* London: Odhams Press Ltd, 1949. Polak mentioned the title of "M. K. Gandhi" as a footnote on page 76. Otherwise we would have never known of this book's occurrence.

[15] Henry S. L. Polak. *M. K. Gandhi: A Sketch of His Life and Work.* Madras: G.A. Natesan & Co. 1910. Subsequent editions after 1922 were published under the title, *Mahatma Gandhi: The Man and His Mission.*

[16] CWMG, Vol. 10, pp. 371-372.

[17] Pyarelal and Sushila Nayar. In *Gandhiji's Mirror.* Delhi: Oxford University Press, 1991, page 299. Professor Thomas Weber of La Trobe University in Aus-

tralia, in his book *Gandhi As Disciple and Mentor* (Cambridge University Press, 2004), acknowledges the falling out between Gandhi and Polak but never penetrated beneath the surface to ascertain what lay beyond the lines written by Pyarelal and Sushila Nayar.

[18] P. J. Mehta. *M. K. Gandhi and the South African Indian Problem.* Madras: G. A. Natesan & Company. [1912?]

Eight

Probing the Doke-Gandhi Connection

~

There is no religion higher than Truth and Righteousness.
~ Mahatma Gandhi
Ethical Religion (1930)

A few words on the background of Reverend Doke would be helpful here before unfolding our story. Based upon what is reported in the popular Gandhian literature, he was born at Chudleigh, South Devon in England on November 5, 1861, about eight years before Gandhi. With little early education to his credit, he became a pastor at the age of seventeen, and three years later, moved to Cape Town in South Africa. With some more foreign travels as a missionary, he returned to South Africa in 1903 and in 1907 a pastoral opening brought him to Johannesburg.[1] [2] [3] The ongoing Satyagraha campaigns brought the two personalities closer together, their relationship deepening as a result of Gandhi's convalescence in the Doke family home.

The best person to bring on side in any political cause is a man of God or holy man. Nothing grants greater credibility to a cause than a man of God who swears by the Almighty to be a vessel of the truth and a proponent of righteousness. In the case of the Christian community, the mere sight of a collar, cross, ministerial garb and other accoutrements of the Christian leader inspire a certain reverence among his flock and a feeling of awe mixed with respect. The Satyagraha movement would definitely have benefited from such an influential religious figure and certainly would have wished to recruit one of such stature to the cause. Reverend J. J.

Doke, missionary and zealous converter of the multitudes, would have jumped at the chance to serve a popular movement of the masses such as Satyagraha. He would have equally wished to convert a figure like Mahatma Gandhi to his religion in order to initiate mass conversions under the leadership of a human rights proponent he would single-handedly turn into a saint in his own Gandhi biography. Gandhi never did convert to Christianity as Reverend Doke, the consummate religious opportunist, had hoped, but he did function, as Doke had wished, as a Christian paradigm of Doke's own invention, a modern day saint who would give Christianity the hormone injection it required. In essence, Doke was a kind of Pygmalion who had fashioned a saint in his own image. Gandhi was an invention who would convince the Christian world that the miracle of Christ really had been possible. If the miracles of healing the lame and feeding the multitudes could be recapitulated in the form of a modern day miracle, people's faith in Christ would be restored and the churches would be filled once more. Gandhi couldn't walk on water, heal the lame and blind, or turn water into wine, but what the Satyagraha movement would prove, through the public relations campaign orchestrated by Doke, is that he was capable of performing a modern day miracle: Defeating an imperialist power through passive resistance. The Satyagraha movement would have with equal fervor wished to bring a man of God into its fold who would give its cause the legitimacy it sought, a man of the cloth whose reputation would precede him and with sufficient power to convince the masses that, his word being as good as gold, the movement for which he stood really was legitimate.

Doke's letter to *The Transvaal Leader* on the "Immigrants Restriction Act" and "peace preservation permits" shows how politically savvy he actually was. The language he employs in his letter to the editor is calculating and manipulative. It is intended to elicit shame in the white rulers of South Africa by highlighting how reasonable the Asiatics and their demands really are. A certain degree of irony can be detected, sufficient to inflict the appropriate sting. What in essence Doke implies in the letter is that the Asiatics are not protesting laws that violate their basic human rights, but only the practice of leaving the decision in the hands of officials subject to racial bias and questionable ethics. The letter implies that the Asiatics wish their cases to be referred to legitimate courts and that they be granted the right of appeal. The irony of course is that, if the Asiatics were actually to be given such entitlements, it would be tantamount to granting them the very human rights they see themselves as being denied. The strategy employed in Doke's letter is admirably sophisticated, but not entirely genuine in import by being so:

> The Asiatics claim simply the interpretation and protection of the Supreme Court. They do not resent the "Immigration Restriction Act." They only claim that it be not interpreted by any official, however exalted he may be, but by the recognized Court, and by that judgement they will stand. They do not resent the rejection of Asiatics by Mr. Chamney, and their deportation, but they claim that no official shall be made supreme. They ask for the right of appeal in such cases to the well-balanced judgement of a properly constituted tribunal.[4]

What the letter shows is that, while a man of the cloth, Doke is a political animal. His use of language is highly manipulative and far from genuine. Granted, the cause is just, but the language employed is conceived in the spirit of "the ends justify the means." He is not being entirely genuine. This in itself is no fault. The point we are making is that he is politically savvy and a master propagandist. He is also given to employing language in a manipulative and even coercive fashion. We present this as evidence that he is capable of being manipulative or even lying to get what he wants. From a means-ends standpoint this can be justified if the cause is just. This we do not dispute. We simply wish to show that there is no reason for believing that this man of the cloth is above lying. There is a tendency for scholars and the reading public to be persuaded that the good reverend's biography of Gandhi is entirely genuine and aboveboard because it is written by a man of the cloth, but we intend to show that it is not written to be a genuine account at all, but rather as "an experiment with the truth" to use Gandhi's own language. Experimenting with the truth in essence is to experiment with a lie, since to employ disparate versions of the truth in order to witness their effect is tantamount to telling lies in order to assess their true impact. Dr. Goebbels's maxim: "The bigger the lie the more people will believe it" is apropos in the case of Gandhi and Doke, the master manipulators.

There is another question to examine in relation to Doke's biography of Gandhi. Is it professional for a biographer to establish a friendship with his subject? Additionally, is it appropriate from the standpoint of professional ethics to associate oneself with the political movement of the biographical subject? Is it acceptable for a professional biographer to be part of the same political struggle as the biographical subject? Is there a conflict of interest in writing a biography on a subject with whom you are both a friend and a professional colleague? There are such instances of course, but is it ethical from a professional standpoint? This is the question we would like our readers to ask themselves.

Doke's biography *M. K. Gandhi: An Indian Patriot in South Africa* is dated 1909, yet it can be established from the evidence of several letters written in the year 1908 that an intimate friendship and political alliance had been forged between Gandhi and Doke well in advance of the biography's publication. The following letter by Gandhi to Rev. Doke dated October 8, 1908 is a fine example:

Dear Mr. Doke,

I received your note at Phoenix. The expected has happened. I think it is well. I have arrived just in time. There were serious differences between two sections here. They are by no means over yet. You will say I have accepted the hospitality before the "settings" were finished. I think it was better that I should do that than that the invitation should be rejected for the sake of the "settings." After all I have done nothing. For six days I may carry on correspondence. If you think I should answer any questions, you may write. I must now stop as I have been called away to give digit impressions. Please excuse me to Olive for not writing.[5]

What this letter reveals is that Gandhi has become a friend of the Doke family and is on intimate terms with husband and wife. It is also clear from the letter that Gandhi appeals to Doke for advice and counsel and that they are political colleagues. The fact that Gandhi invites Doke to write to him should he have any questions implies that the reverend has become so intimate an associate that Gandhi's personal welfare has become a matter of greatest concern to his champion and defender. There is nothing cynical about the friendship and political alliance. What we question is whether such a relationship represents a conflict of interests from the standpoint of a professional biographer. There is no way that the friendship and political alliance forged between the two men could fail to color the tone of the biography.

A letter from the same year reveals how close the relationship between the two men had become. Gandhi writes to Doke from the Court House. The tone and nature of Gandhi's letter implies that he is attempting to relieve his friend of any anxieties he might be entertaining on his account. The tone of the letter is most consoling:

Dear Mr. Doke,

I am writing this from the Court House. I had hoped to be able to send you something before I was fixed up. But I have been too busy otherwise. I thank you very much for your good wishes. My sole trust is in God. I am therefore quite cheerful.[6]

There is another letter from Doke that shows the great depth of Doke's friendship and love for Gandhi. The letter is dated September 30, 1908 well before the publication date of the biography. There is no doubt that the friendship has moved well beyond acquaintance and mutual self-interest. A bond has been forged be-

tween the two men that is lifelong, so deeply felt on Doke's part
that he would willingly lay down his life for Gandhi:

> Your beautiful present of the *Song Celestial,* I appreciate
> very much. In every respect it is one of the choicest treas-
> ures which I have - dainty in appearance - fascinating in its
> contents - and of great value and a memento of a friendship
> which I shall always regard with gratitude. Yes, even if the
> darling wish of your heart is fulfilled and I get into prison
> for it.[7]

Then we have Rev. J. J. Doke's letter to the editor of the *Rand
Daily Mail*, in which he protests the arrest of Gandhi. What is clear
from the letter is that he has received regular updates from Gandhi
on the treatment he has received at the hands of the authorities.
This means that no one member of *Satyagraha* is more concerned
with the personal well being of Mahatma Gandhi than Rev. Doke.
He has taken it upon himself to be his champion and defender. His
good name and standing in the community as a reverend of untar-
nished respectability would make his letter to the editor both credible and morally persuasive. It is likely that both Gandhi and Doke
would have recognized the political expediency of using the merits
of a man of the cloth to influence public sentiment. There is no
doubt from the tenor of the letter that it is intended to make the
citizens rise up in moral outrage:

> Yesterday it was necessary that he should appear in some
> case in the Magistrate's Court. I understand he was brought
> there from the cells, dressed in civilian clothes, but hand-
> cuffed! Of course, there may be amongst us those who will
> be glad to hear that indignities are being heaped on this
> great Indian leader; but I venture to hope that the great ma-
> jority of our colonies will feel ashamed and angry that a
> man of the character and position of Mr. Gandhi should be
> needlessly insulted in this way.[8]

Singh & Watson

What emerges from the letter is the fact that Doke has risen to the stature of serving as Gandhi's champion. No matter how politically and socially compromised he might be in the corrupt white establishment of South Africa, he is prepared to put his life and reputation on the line in defense of Gandhi. No higher level of commitment could be shown by one human being to another in defense of their mutual cause than that shown by Doke to Gandhi and *Satyagraha*.

How did they meet? How did they come to know each other? And under what compunction were they brought together? While we have addressed these questions based on what has been reported, we nevertheless need to ask: Was there a fraternity to which they both belonged that preceded *Satyagraha* and the European Committee of which they were both active members? What force drew Doke from New Zealand to South Africa, providing him with the opportunity to seize the hand of his confederate? There is an answer to this and the evidence for it rests with a speech Gandhi gave at a Masonic Hall, of all places, in Johannesburg. The description of the gathering given below reveals a great deal about the organizations to which Gandhi and Doke were mutually affiliated:

> The Masonic Hall, Jepper Street, Johannesburg, was the scene of a brilliant mixed gathering of Europeans, Chinese and Indians on the night of the 18th instant in honour of the British Indian community. Mr. Hosken was in the chair. Mr. Doke was on his right and Mrs. Doke on his left. Mr. Cachalia occupied a seat to the right of Mr. Doke.
>
> Mr. Quinn and his Chinese friends were also present.[9]

The first thing to observe about the preceding description of the banquet is that it was held in a Masonic Lodge and that Mr. Hosken, the leader of the European Committee to which both Gandhi and Doke belong, is the Grand Master of the Masonic Lodge on Jepper Street in Johannesburg where the banquet is being held. We know this because of what is stated in the above passage, that,

"Mr. Hosken was in the chair." This means that he is in the chair where the Worshipful Master or Grand Master of the Masonic Lodge presides. This means that he is a 33rd Degree Freemason and the supreme head of this particular Temple. The fact that Gandhi and Doke are present and that Gandhi is giving a speech in honor of Rev. Doke in a Masonic Lodge hosted by the Grand Master of the Lodge and leader of the European Committee, Mr. Hosken, is strong evidence supporting Gandhi's and Doke's Freemason affiliations. The fact that Mr. Hosken is both the Grand Master of the Temple and the leader of the European Committee of which all three are members suggests that the links between the three men go beyond the European Committee to another overriding organization, the very organization in whose Temple the current banquet is being hosted, namely Freemasonry. We would go even further and suggest that the European Committee is a sub-committee set up by Freemasonry for vested political reasons and toward a defined political goal. The description of the content of Gandhi's speech given below establishes the Masonic affiliations of all three men beyond doubt:

> Speaking of Mr. Doke's Asiatic work, it is not possible to refrain from speaking in praise of the work of the European Committee of which the chairman (Mr. Hosken) was the president. Mr. Gandhi frankly confessed that passive resistance might have broken down without the magnificent support rendered by the European Committee.[10]

What the preceding passage reveals is what it doesn't reveal, namely, the text of Gandhi's speech. We only have a description of the speech made at the so-called banquet. While some might object that, just because all three men are attending a meeting held in a Masonic Lodge, in no way proves that they are Masons, the fact that this is an official meeting and Gandhi's speech is unavailable because the meeting is official and secret proves that all three men are at the least affiliated with Masonry.[11] Again, some might argue that just because the meeting is held in a Masonic Temple does not mean that everyone present is a Mason, including possibly some of the Chinese delegates present, the fact that this is an official Masonic meeting is proven by the fact that the text of Gandhi's speech is not available. We only have the minutes pertaining to the alleged content of Gandhi's speech. This means that Gandhi's speech and its contents are secret. Let's not forget that Freemasonry in its modern form is based on the 33 Degree organizational model. Freemasonry maintains that it is "not a secret society, but a society with secrets." This is a matter of semantics and wordplay. Whether secret or not, the organization lacks transparency. We have provided evidence, which if not proving the case beyond a reasonable doubt, certainly points to the likelihood of Gandhi and Doke being Freemasons. In the instance described above, they appear to be attending an official Lodge meeting, in which fellow Lodge members are hosting a farewell dinner for one of their own members, Rev. J. J. Doke.

Gandhi's obituaries to the late Rev. J. J. Doke in 1913 reveal a great deal about the reverend's motives for writing the biography. Gandhi's own words imply that the primary aim of the biography was not to glorify the Indian leader, but to promote the cause of *Satyagraha*, and Indian home rule. Gandhi's first obituary to the late Rev. Doke reveals the book's true *raison d'etre*:

> He wrote an *Indian patriot in South Africa* - a popular history of the story of Indian passive resistance. Lord Ampthill wrote a very flattering introduction to it. To Mr. Doke it was purely a labour of love. He believed in the Indian cause and the book was one of the many ways in which he helped it.[12]

The express purpose for Doke writing the Gandhi biography, as Gandhi himself admits was to promote the cause of passive resistance first and foremost. Why would Gandhi misquote the title of the book? Moreover, *M. K. Gandhi: An Indian Patriot in South Africa*, is really a biographical sketch of Gandhi and the issue of Indian passive resistance is secondary to the greater issue of Gandhi himself. Gandhi states unequivocally that, rather than being a simple biography, Doke's book was written as "a popular history of the story of Indian passive resistance" to use Gandhi's own words. Gandhi, the leader of the movement, was just a means to an end, a rallying cry, a voice capable of mustering forth a throng of supporters toward a common cause. By turning Gandhi into a martyred saint, fictionalizing his early life to depict him as a messianic figure, who had miraculously risen from defeat after being beaten down by his oppressors, would give the cause the locus and impetus required to get it off the ground, to give it wing, make it fly, if not soar. What is also evident from Gandhi's first memoir and obituary to the late reverend is that he is on such intimate terms with Doke that he knows his personal and family history nearly as well as his own, i.e.:

> The late Rev. Doke had very little schooling, owing to delicate health. At the age of 16 he lost his mother. At the age of 17, on the resignation of his father from the pastorate, he became pastor. At the age of 20 he came to South Africa, where he was in Cape Town for a short time....[13]

What is revealing about the preceding memorial account is the fact that the writer of the first major biography on Gandhi was on such friendly terms with the subject of the biography as to have been a confidante, best friend, and virtual family member. In addition to being a friend of intimate acquaintance, colleague and brother-in-arms, he was a strong supporter of the same political struggle. This intimacy of association violates the professional ethics of the biographer, who is supposed to maintain a certain objectivity and professional distance from his subject. For a biographer, or any historian of personages, to be too close to the subject he is memorializing is bound to distort and color the portrait.

To add to this memoir, we have the second of Gandhi's obituaries to the late reverend also written for the *Indian Opinion*. Gandhi's second obituary in honor of Doke demonstrates beyond doubt that Doke was a proponent of Gandhi's cause of passive resistance and had been so practically upon arrival in South Africa:

When Mr. Doke came to the cause, he threw himself into it heart and soul and never relaxed his efforts on our behalf. It was usual with Mr. Doke to gain complete mastery over the subject he handled. He, therefore, became one of best informed men on the subject in South Africa. He loved passive resisters as they were his own congregation. The poorest Indian had free access to this pious Englishman. His pen and his eloquence were continually used by him during the troublous times through which the community has passed. He missed no opportunity of visiting passive resistance prisoners in gaol. And at a critical period in the history of the community and this journal, he magnanimously and at no small inconvenience to himself, took charge of the editorial department, and those who came in contact with him during that period know how cautious, how painstaking, how gentle and how forbearing he was.[14]

What the passage makes explicit is that, not only is Doke an active proponent of Gandhi's cause of passive resistance, but is deeply committed to it as an adherent. From the standpoint of a professional biographer, his Gandhi biography would be regarded as little more than a propaganda and public relations exercise rather than a genuine biography. As Gandhi says of the reverend, "He loved passive resisters as they were his own congregation." His mission then was to champion the cause of his congregation. One wonders whether his sermons were geared toward liberating their immortal souls or their minds and bodies from the material bondage to which they were subject. Gandhi adds of the good reverend that, "His pen and his eloquence were continually used by him during the troublous times through which the community passed." There is no equivocation here. Gandhi states explicitly that the pen and the eloquence of the good reverend "were continually used by him," that is continually, unremittingly used by "him" for the furtherance of the cause of passive resistance. Gandhi leaves us in no doubt that he has used the reverend as a propaganda agent in promotion of the cause, "continually" implying from the beginning and without interruption. Gandhi then informs us that his colleague took charge of the editorial department, which suggests that Doke was in complete charge of the P.R. machine behind the *Satyagraha* movement as the Editor-in-Chief of the *Indian Opinion*, controlling what got printed and by whom. The fact that he functioned as Editor-in-Chief of the *Indian Opinion* only makes the conflict of interests in writing the Gandhi biography that much more self-evident. How can an advocate of the cause and an editor of the propaganda vehicle of the movement, the *Indian Opinion*, be expected to write an objective and unbiased biography of the leader of the movement?

Should any doubts remain about the level of commitment demonstrated by Reverend Doke to the cause, Gandhi tells us unreservedly in his final tribute to Rev. Doke, written for the very newspaper the reverend himself headed, that Doke had been committed to the Indian cause practically from the day he arrived:

In 1907, when preparations for the Satyagraha campaign were in full swing, Mr. Doke had recently come to the Transvaal from New Zealand. He began taking a keen interest in the Indian problem from the very day he arrived, and continued to help till he died. With the exception of one or two, no other Englishman, and hardly any Indian, had such clear grasp of our problem as Mr. Doke.[15]

Doke's loyalty to the cause was as unrelenting as his faithfulness to its leader. As Gandhi himself states, *Satyagraha* became his *raison d'etre* from the day he arrived until the time of his death. There is no doubt then that the 1909 biography of Gandhi is colored by an emotional investment on the part of the biographer to the subject and the cause to which both subject and biographer are committed. The biography by Doke is neither scholarly nor professional, but is colored by the biographer's own biases and commitment to the cause. It does not maintain any of the professional detachment, distance, dispassionate objectivity that a bona fide biography is required to maintain. Should there be any question then about the authenticity of Doke's account of the racial train incidents in South Africa, let us remind ourselves of the purpose of the biography. The purpose of the biography as Doke explicitly stated to Gandhi was to promote Gandhi as the martyr figure and hero of the Indian passive resistance movement.

There is another suspicious circumstance concerning Doke's biography of Gandhi. The foreword is written by Lord Ampthill. In the foreword, Lord Ampthill takes care to distance himself from the author. He even goes so far as to deny even knowing him, saying, "The writer of this book is not known to me personally, but there is a bond of sympathy between him and me in the sentiments which we share in regard to the cause of which he is so courageous and devoted an advocate."[16]

Why does this passage from Lord Amptill's foreword pique our curiosity? Why does it raise our doubts? We invite the reader to employ our methodology and scrutinize the passage for himself before reviewing our analysis. A perceptive reader will have his own suspicions aroused after rereading the preceding passage carefully. The first suspicious element is that Lord Ampthill begins the foreword with a denial of any firsthand acquaintance with the author, "The writer of this book is not known to me personally...." Why deny knowing someone, especially at the outset, unless you desire to distance yourself from having any association with the person in question. While some might argue that this is probably because Lord Ampthill did not want to be politically compromised by association with *Satyagraha* or the movement for home rule, his own words show this not to be the case, for he adds, "...but there is a bond of sympathy between him and me in the sentiments which we share in regard to the cause...." It is self-evident that Lord Ampthill feels no need to distance himself from the cause. So why distance himself from the personage of Rev. Doke? It is rather odd that he should seek to do so, since the reverend is obviously respected, of good standing in the community, and wears a collar. Is Lord Ampthill being genuine in his claim not to know the reverend "personally" as he puts it? This is hardly likely, since his own words in reference to Doke's character give him away - "...the cause of which he is so courageous and devoted an advocate." How is Lord Ampthill able to vouch so strongly for the character and commitment of a man he has never met? Why deny knowing someone unless you wish to disassociate yourself from the individual in question? Were Lord Ampthill to have an association with Doke, Gandhi and others, there might be a very good reason to deny his having any association with the good reverend. Were he a fellow Freemason or a member of the European Committee or in some way more intimately tied to the political struggle to which both Gandhi and Doke are committed, there might be a very good reason for denying any association with the good reverend. Based on a cable sent by Gandhi to Lord Ampthill on December 24, 1913, there is evidence that such an intimate political association would have and actually did exist.

The cable from Gandhi reads, "Hosken issued public appeal supporting our letter."[17] Hosken, our reader will recall, was presiding as the Worshipful Master at the farewell dinner for Rev. Doke held at the Masonic Lodge meeting in Johannesburg. Hosken was also the head of the European Committee. The fact that Gandhi mentions Hosken[18] in the cable without any honorific title before his name suggests that he is a well-known member of the old boys' network and an intimate associate of them both. This suggests either that Lord Ampthill was an active member of the same Masonic Lodge or intimately associated with its members, as well as some of those associated with the European Committee. Gandhi's connection to Freemasonry must be investigated and carefully evaluated knowing fully that his literature is scant on these matters (see Appendix IV).

NOTES

[1] James D. Hunt. *Gandhi and the Nonconformists: Encounters in South Africa.* New Delhi: Promilla & Co. Publishers, 1986, pp. 98-123.

[2] Sushila Nayar. *Mahatma Gandhi: Satyagraha at Work* (Vol. 4). Ahmedabad, India: Navajivan Publishing House, 1989, pp. 468-74.

[3] CWMG, Vol. 13, pp. 258-62.

[4] CWMG, Vol. 8, p. 495.

[5] CWMG, Vol. 9, pp. 193-194.

---

[6] Ibid., pp. 204-205.

[7] Ibid., p. 482.

[8] Ibid., p. 489.

[9] CWMG, Vol. 13, p. 420.

[10] Ibid.

[11] On October 22, 2005, G. B. Singh (one of the authors of this book) held a dialogue over dinner with Kanu Gandhi, one of the grandsons of Mahatma Gandhi. During the course of the conversation, Kanu Gandhi admitted that his grandfather had rather close associations with Freemasonry in South Africa. Kanu Gandhi also emphasized the unique position he occupied within the Gandhi clan as the only living relative of Mahatma with an intimate knowledge of his grandfather's activities and ideals considering that Mahatma Gandhi's four sons and other grandchildren were not close to the Mahatma, a privilege known only to Kanu Gandhi himself.

[12] CWMG, Vol. 13, p. 258.

[13] Ibid. p. 260.

[14] Ibid., p. 262.

[15] Ibid., pp 263-64.

[16] CWMG, Vol. 10, p. 485. Also read the introduction in *M. K. Gandhi: An Indian Patriot in South Africa.*

[17] Cable to Lord Ampthill, Durban, Dec. 24, 1913, Colonial Office Records: 551/52, Vol. 13, p. 439.

[18] Mr. William Hosken (1851-1925) is reported to have been an "ardent Wesleyan." He immigrated to the Transvaal in 1874 where he once held a job as the manager of a gold mine.

Nine

Sergeant Major Gandhi
and the War on Blacks

~

I make no distinction, from the point of view of ahimsa, *between combatants and non-combatants. He who volunteers to serve a band of dacoits* [robbers], *by working as their carrier, or their watchman while they are about their business, or their nurse when they are wounded, is as much guilty of dacoity* [robbery] *as the dacoits themselves. In the same way those who confine themselves to attending to the wounded in battle cannot be absolved from the guilt of war.*

~ Mahatma Gandhi
An Autobiography

W hen Rev. Mott interviewed Gandhi in 1938, he asked him: "What have been the most creative experiences in your life? As you look back on your past, what, do you think, led you to believe in God when everything seemed to point to the contrary, when life, so to say, sprang from the ground, although it all looked impossible?" Gandhi answered, "Such experiences are multitude."[1]

Preceding chapters focused exclusively on rigorous examination of one famous yet fabricated experience that Gandhi and the historians claim as a deciding factor in his life. However, in light of his response to Rev. Mott, one might wonder whether there is some other pivotal experience in Gandhi's life worthy of investigation. Perhaps the best place to look is in the events surrounding Gandhi's famous *Brahmacharya* vow of celibacy and poverty.

Gandhi Under Cross-Examination

Gandhi was supposedly inspired to take that vow after leading a British stretcher-bearer corps during the Zulu War of 1906. The history books depict Gandhi's role in the war as that of a Florence Nightingale, ministering selflessly to injured Zulus. This was a life-changing experience similar to the racial humiliations in Pietermaritzburg. After witnessing the atrocities committed by the white British against the black Zulus during the war, Gandhi was led to take his *Brahmacharya* vow of celibacy and poverty. This is not so different from a modern-day soldier who, physically and mentally scarred and suffering from post-traumatic stress disorder, dedicates his life to being a peace activist or humanitarian.

We want to ensure a fair and enlightening study of Gandhi, particularly the events of his genesis. The *Brahmacharya* vow is considered just as momentous as the train incident, so to get the most benefit from our study of Gandhi it is imperative that we investigate both events. This gives us more than one set of actions on which to evaluate Gandhi and discover his character, goals and motivations while in South Africa. We have no desire to topple the Mahatma from his saintly pedestal without due process, and we hope to grant him a fair hearing within these pages.

The Zulu War, more commonly known today as the Bambatha Uprising, is considered the beginning of the black struggle against apartheid. The war began in February 1906 when Zulus near modern-day KwaZulu-Natal killed two British officials who were collecting a new poll tax. In the resulting chaos, Zulu chief Bambatha kaMancinza emerged as the leader of the rebellion. The British responded by declaring war and deploying a military force to suppress the black Zulus. As the British flogged, shot, and hung thousands of blacks, Gandhi led a relentless campaign to raise and equip an Indian stretcher-bearer corps.

When the British accepted his offer, Gandhi was again plunged into the thick of battle, merely a decade after his post office segregation victory in Durban. So he hung up his lawyer's suit, which he had claimed to use to fight racism, and put on British colonial army fatigues bearing the rank of a Sergeant Major, which he claimed was to serve the downtrodden Zulus. Soon he was marching with the British Army while administering the soothing balm of Gilead to wounded black brows.

Unlike the Pietermaritzburg incident, where one is left to guess whether the incident really took place or not, Gandhi's service as a British Sgt. Major is beyond question. However, what he did during the war and how it influenced his life are issues open to scrutiny. Again we turn to the historians to see what the Gandhi propaganda machine has to say. Fatima Meer, a well-known Gandhi scholar from South Africa, describes Gandhi's activities and thoughts during the war as follows:

> He soon realized that he was on the wrong side, that this was no rebellion but stark repression, that justice was on the side of the Zulus who were treated with inhumanity for doing no more than resisting a poll tax similar to that imposed on the Indians. The Indian stretcher-bearers redeemed themselves by nursing the Zulu prisoners of war abandoned by the British. For Gandhi, the brutality against the Zulus roused his soul against violence as nothing had been done up to then; he sought answers and found them in his traditional scriptures. He returned from the war determined to give himself wholly to serving the people.[2]

This same account has permeated the annals of Gandhian history, whether through truth or sheer repetition we will yet decide. A passage from "Mahatma: Life of Mohandas Karamchand Gandhi" by D.G. Tendulkar more explicitly associates the Zulu War with the *Brahmacharya* vow:

> The Zulu 'rebellion' was an eye-opener to Gandhi. He saw the naked atrocities of the whites against the poor sons of the soil.... Marching through the hills and dales of Zululand, Gandhi often fell into deep thought. Two ideas which had been floating in his mind became fixed. First, an aspirant after a life exclusively devoted to service must lead a life of celibacy. Secondly, he must accept voluntary poverty."[3]

Gandhi Under Cross-Examination

Calvin Kytle is a civil rights activist and the former acting director of the U.S. Community Relations Service. In his book "Gandhi, Soldier of Nonviolence," Mr. Kytle describes Gandhi during the Zulu War:

> In May of 1906, Gandhi's routine was shattered by news of the Zulu Rebellion in Natal....
>
> For a good part of his six weeks' service, Gandhi was in motion, sometimes marching as much as forty miles a day. On these long, silent marches through the sparsely populated land Gandhi fell to thinking about the purpose of life, the senseless war that he was in, the meaning of renunciation, the nature of God, and his own future in South Africa...
>
> His experience brought home the horrors of war more vividly than anything he had seen during the Boer War. Violence, he decided irrevocably, was an insult to God's intent for man. He could ease his conscience only with the thought that if it had not been for him the Zulus would not have been cared for at all.
>
> In the midst of these pitiful, frightened, and dying black men - in the employment of men who seemed to value life only if it came packaged in a white skin - Gandhi came to equate life with time and to see the acceptance of death as a condition of freedom.... From this moment of resolution, Mohandas Gandhi became the most believing, the most living man of the twentieth century.[4]

Mr. Kytle obviously repeats most of the same points as other historians: Gandhi did his thinking during the long marches, cared for the Zulus when no one else would, and took a vow after the war. However, he puts his own unique spin on the tale by depicting Gandhi's postwar vow as an earth-shattering, transcendental experience. As he tells it, this vow alone was monumental enough to secure Gandhi's place in history for ten thousand years. Through the vow Gandhi became "the most living man of the twentieth century."

The last version of Gandhi's war experience we shall examine is one related by Louis Fischer, that famous political writer. He was quite poetic, saying of Gandhi: "The suppression of the tribesmen, with its insane cruelty of man to man, depressed him. The long treks to the hamlets of the suffering Negroes afforded ample opportunity for self-analysis; he must do more to make a better world."[5]

These select biographers, like most, draw their accounts of the Zulu War nearly verbatim from Gandhi's own autobiography, the aptly titled "An Autobiography, or The Story of My Experiments With Truth." Considering this is Gandhi's officially approved version, one would presume it is the most reliable place to learn about his activities during the war. This is what Gandhi himself said:

Even after I thought I had settled down in Johannesburg, there was to be no settled life for me. Just when I felt that I should be breathing in peace, an unexpected event happened. The papers brought the news of the outbreak of the Zulu 'rebellion' in Natal. I bore no grudge against the Zulus, they had harmed no Indian. I had doubts about the "rebellion" itself. But I then believed that the British Empire existed for the welfare of the world. A genuine sense of loyalty prevented me from even wishing ill to the Empire. The rightness or otherwise of the "rebellion" was therefore not likely to affect my decision. Natal had a Volunteer Defence Force, and it was open to it to recruit more men. I read that this force had already been mobilized to quell the "rebellion."

I considered myself a citizen of Natal, being intimately connected with it. So I wrote to the Governor, expressing my readiness, if necessary, to form an Indian Ambulance Corps. He replied immediately accepting the offer.

I had not expected such prompt acceptance. Fortunately I had made all the necessary arrangements even before writing the letter. If my offer was accepted, I had decided to break up the Johannesburg home. Polak was to have a smaller house, and my wife was to go and settle at Phoenix. I had her full consent to this decision. I do not remember her having ever stood in my way in matters like this. As soon, therefore, as I got the reply from the Governor, I gave the landlord the usual month's notice of vacating the house, sent some of the things to Phoenix and left some with Polak.

I went to Durban and appealed for men. A big contingent was not necessary. We were a party of twenty-four, of whom, besides me, four were Gujaratis. The rest were ex-indentured men from South India, excepting one who was a free Pathan.

In order to give me a status and to facilitate work, as also in accordance with the existing convention, the Chief Medical Officer appointed me to the temporary rank of Sergeant Major and three men selected by me to the rank of sergeants and one to that of corporal. We also received our uniforms from the Government. Our Corps was on active service for nearly six weeks. On reaching the scene of the "rebellion," I saw that there was nothing there to justify the name of "rebellion." There was no resistance that one could see. The reason why the disturbance had been magnified into a rebellion was that a Zulu chief had advised non-payment of a new tax imposed on his people, and had assailed a sergeant who had gone to collect the tax. At any rate my heart was with the Zulus, and I was delighted, on reaching headquarters, to hear that our main work was to be the nursing of the wounded Zulus. The Medical Officer in charge welcomed us. He said the white people were not willing nurses for the wounded Zulus, that their wounds were festering, and that he was at his wits' end. He hailed our arrival as a godsend for those innocent people, and he equipped us with bandages, disinfectants, etc., and took us to the improvised hospital. The Zulus were delighted to see us. The white soldiers used to peep through the railings that separated us from them and tried to dissuade us from attending to the wounds. And as we would not heed them, they became enraged and poured unspeakable abuse on the Zulus....

The wounded in our charge were not wounded in battle. A section of them had been taken prisoners as suspects. The General had sentenced them to be flogged. The flogging had caused severe sores. These, being unattended to, were festering. The others were Zulu friendlies. Although these had badges given them to distinguish them from the 'enemy,' they had been shot at by the soldiers by mistake.

Besides this work I had to compound and dispense prescriptions for the white soldiers. This was easy enough for me as I had received a year's training in Dr. Booth's little hospital. This work brought me in close contact with many Europeans.

We were attached to a swift-moving column. It had orders to march wherever danger was reported. It was for the most part mounted infantry. As soon as our camp was moved, we had to follow on foot with our stretchers on our shoulders. Twice or thrice we had to march forty miles a day. But wherever we went, I am thankful that we had God's good work to do, having to carry to the camp on our stretchers those Zulu friendlies who had been inadvertently wounded, and to attend upon them as nurses.[6]

Gandhi's *Satyagraha in South Africa*, published a year before his autobiography, provides the crucial details of his *Brahmacharya* vow:

While I was working with Corps, two ideas which had long been floating in my mind became firmly fixed. First, an aspirant after a life exclusively devoted to service must lead a life of celibacy. Secondly, he must accept poverty as a constant companion through life. He may not take up any occupation which would prevent him or make him shrink from undertaking the lowliest of duties or largest risks.[7]

As the world's most famous pacifist, Gandhi clearly needs to convince the reader that his service in the British Army bore a net positive outcome. Knowing that he must somehow justify his voluntary military duty, he offers the highly unusual explanation that his "main work" consisted of caring for wounded enemies. This upper-caste man walked among the savage Zulus, gracing them with his healing lantern of moral humanity. Not stopping there, he tells us that his participation in the Zulu War directly caused him to seek a "life exclusively devoted to service." In this way the *Brahmacharya* vow becomes more momentous than the transfiguration of Jesus Christ or the awakening of the Buddha.

There are four major points Gandhi wants to establish. First: "The wounded Zulus would have been left uncared for, unless we had attended to them." Second: "I bore no grudge against the Zulus, they had harmed no Indian" and "my heart was with the Zulus." Third: "Our main work was to be the nursing of the wounded Zulus." Fourth: "[During the war] two ideas which had long been floating in my mind became firmly fixed... a life of celibacy" and "voluntary poverty."

We have spent the majority of this book learning how Gandhi deceived the world with his Pietermaritzburg story. Did he decide to stop experimenting with the truth and actually tell it when he related his actions during the Zulu War? Does his medical care for the Zulus represent a change of heart from his racism detailed in Chapter Two? Did the war truly cause Gandhi to plumb the depths of his soul? These are the answers we're searching for in our quest to understand the true historical Gandhi.

Thus far all the information we've seen about the Zulu War of 1906 has come from his autobiography, which was not even begun until 1925. The Gandhi propaganda machine has done an extraordinary job of making this version of events a universally known story. However, our examination of the train incident clearly revealed that Gandhi is hardly at his most reliable when relating an incident decades after the fact. His autobiography sparks more questions than it answers. Did Gandhi really join the British Army to help nurse wounded enemies? Was his heart really with the black Zulus?

The best place to find answers to these questions is within Gandhi's contemporary writings. While none of the famous biographies deal exclusively with them, Gandhi wrote frequent articles about the war for his own newspaper, the *Indian Opinion*. Thanks to their inclusion in the "Collected Works," we fortunately do not have to second guess Gandhi or apply skeptical theory to his official version of the Zulu War. Rather, we can simply contrast that version with his accounts from the actual era.

Gandhi claims the war was an "unexpected event," yet his *Indian Opinion* articles tell a different story. Wars do not simply pop up out of the blue, and this one had been openly germinating for some time. In 1905, economic hardships in both the black and white communities resulted in a draconian poll tax on the Zulus, aggravating tensions all around. Although Gandhi says that the "papers brought the news" of the rebellion, he actually spent three months before the war, which began in February 1906, vigorously advocating for a volunteer corps to "share in the defence of the Colony." He initiated his campaign with the November 1905 issue of the *Indian Opinion*:

> The Government simply do not wish to give the Indians an opportunity of showing that they are as capable, as any other community, of taking their share in the defence of the Colony. At the time of the Boer War, it will be remembered, the Indians volunteered to do any work that might be entrusted to them, and it was with the greatest difficulty that they could get their services accepted even for ambu-

lance work. General Buller has certified as to what kind of work the Natal Indian Volunteer Ambulance Corps did. If the Government only realised what reserve force is being wasted, they would make use of it and give Indians the opportunity of a thorough training for actual warfare. There is, too, on the Statute-book, a law for the purpose, which has been allowed to fall into desuetude from sheer prejudice. We believe a very fine volunteer corps could be formed from Colonial-born Indians that would be second to none in Natal in smartness and efficiency, not only in peace but in actual service also.[8]

Gandhi's remark about the difficulty in being accepted "even for ambulance work" makes one wonder if Gandhi considered such medical work a distasteful consolation prize. Was unarmed nursing of the wounded not his first choice during the Boer War? It is clear that during the Zulu War he considers it an insult to his community for the British to not recruit and train them for "actual warfare." Although years later Gandhi told the world that his "heart was with the Zulus," at the time he offered three reasons for Indians to participate in the coming war. First, Indians are capable of defending the colony. Second, so the "reserve force" might not be wasted. Third, an old law allows for Indian volunteers. In Gandhi's eyes, it's an honor for the colonial-born Indians to be selected for military service.

Over the next few months, Gandhi pursued this goal of raising an Indian volunteer corps for the British Army. In the December 1905 issue of the *Indian Opinion*, he wrote:

Our note on the subject of Indian volunteering, we are glad to notice, has been warmly taken up by *The Natal Witness*, and some correspondence has appeared on the subject. We hope, now that the matter has been taken up by the Press, that it will not [be] allowed to die out without an expression of opinion from the Government as to its policy. Law No. 25 of 1875 was specially passed to increase "the maximum strength of the Volunteer Force in the Colony by adding

thereto a force of Indian Immigrants Volunteer Infantry."
Under the Law, the Governor is authorised "to accept, with
the consent of the employer, the services of any Indian
Immigrants who may be willing to be formed into a Volunteer Corps"... If the Government only wanted the Indian
immigrant to take his share in the defence of the Colony,
which he has before now shown himself to be quite willing
to do, there is legal machinery ready made for it.[9]

As we can see, Gandhi's campaign had begun to garner attention in the mainstream press of the day. Without explanation as to
why Indians should fight for the British against the blacks, Gandhi
begins arguing that an old law conveniently provides the framework for a volunteer corps. Oddly, he offers neither justification
for such voluntary service in the British Army nor any caveat that
resulting military assignments must be of a nonviolent, medical
nature. There is no mention of treating Zulus, but rather a discussion of "Volunteer Infantry."

Gandhi started to publish a number of editorials in the *Indian
Opinion* which essentially comprise a recruiting campaign. In
March 1906 he wrote "A Plea for Indian Volunteering." This arti-
cle, which constituted Gandhi's first step in organizing against the
Zulu rebellion, is reproduced here in its entirety:

The Natal Native trouble is dragging on a slow existence.
There can be no doubt that the imposition of the poll-tax is
itself the immediate cause, though probably the trouble has
been brewing for a long time. Whosesoever the mistake
may be, report has it that it is costing the Colony two thousand pounds per day. The white colonists are trying to cope
with it, and many citizen-soldiers have taken up arms. Today, perhaps, no further assistance is necessary, but this
trouble ought to suggest reflections to the Government, as
also to every thinking colonist. There is a population of
over one hundred thousand Indians in Natal. It has been
proved that they can do very efficient work in time of war.
The suspicion that they were worthless in emergencies has

been dispelled. In the face of these incontrovertible facts, is it prudent for the Government to allow a source of strength, which always lies at its disposal, to run to waste? Our contemporary, The Natal Witness, has recently written a very thoughtful editorial on the Indian question, and has shown that, some day or other, the question of Indian representation must be seriously taken up by the colonists. We agree with the view, though Indians do not aspire to any political power in the Colony. All they require is a guarantee of full civil rights under the general laws of the Colony. This should be the birthright of every British subject living in a British territory. Refusal to accept anybody as an immigrant is, in certain circumstances, justifiable, but imposition of disabilities upon well-behaved and physically sound immigrants can never be justified either on economic or political grounds. Whilst, therefore, the question of Indian representation is undoubtedly very important, we consider that the question of Indian volunteering is more important because it is more practicable. There is, it is nowadays fully recognised, work in the field which does not require the bearing of arms, but which is just as useful and quite as honourable as the shouldering of a rifle. If the Government, instead of neglecting Indians, were to employ them for volunteering work, they would add appreciably to the utility of the Militia, and would always be able in times of trouble to rely upon Indians giving a good account of themselves. The Government, we doubt not, recognise that it is impossible for them to drive Indians out of the country. Why not, then, make the best of the material at hand, and convert a hitherto neglected community into a permanent and most valuable asset of the State?[10]

Gandhi makes a very pragmatic case. The war has been "dragging," but an Indian volunteer corps would make quick work of the Zulus, and any shrewd government would use the Indians. Once the government agrees to take on a volunteer corps, they'll quickly discover the Indians are a "valuable asset" and employ them as a permanent force. The reader should also notice that contrary to his autobiographical claim that the war was an "unexpected event," Gandhi admits "the trouble has been brewing for a long time."

Within two weeks, his demand for a volunteer corps, even if unarmed, included a call for weapons training. In response to an editorial in another paper, Gandhi invoked a section of the Militia Act to support arming the Indians:

> Our contemporary rightly gives Indians and Coloured people the credit due to them. It also points out that Section 83 of the Militia Act states that no ordinary member of a Coloured contingent shall be armed with weapons of precision, unless such contingents are called out to operate against [persons] other than Europeans. Now it is evident that, in the unfortunate event of such a state of affairs arising as to necessitate the arming of an Indian contingent, the arms would be useless in the hands of inexperienced men. Why will not the authorities adopt the suggestion we made some time ago, and raise a volunteer corps from amongst Indians? We feel sure the Colonial-born Indians especially - Natal's own children equally with the whites - would give a good account of themselves. Why do not the Colonists insist on these, at all events, being given a chance to prove their mettle?[11]

Gandhi's efforts to this point had been dedicated to convincing the British of the need for an Indian volunteer corps. In April 1906, he initiated a recruiting campaign within the Indian population to convince members of his community to volunteer. This began with his article, "The Natal Rebellion," written in Gujarati for the *Indian Opinion*:

> Though twelve Kaffirs were put to death, the rebellion, instead of being quelled, has gathered strength. Bambata, the Kaffir Chief, was deposed and another installed in his place, because the behavior of the former was not satisfactory. Seizing the right opportunity, Bambata kidnapped the

new Chief and rose in revolt. And the disturbance continues in Grey Town. The region in which Bambata in operating as an outlaw is in difficult terrain full of bushes and trees where the Kaffirs can remain in hiding for long periods. To find them out and force a fight is a difficult job.

What is our duty during these calamitous times in the Colony? It is not for us to say whether the revolt of the Kaffirs is justified or not. We are in Natal by virtue of British power. Our very existence depends upon it. It is therefore our duty to render whatever help we can. There was a discussion in the Press as to what part the Indian community would play in the event of an actual war. We have already declared in the English columns of this journal that the Indian community is ready to play its part; and we believe what we did during the Boer War should also be done now. That is, if the Government so desires, we should raise an ambulance corps. We should also agree to become permanent volunteers, if the Government is prepared to give us the requisite training.

Such a step would be considered proper, even if we viewed it from the standpoint of our own interests. The case of the twelve Kaffirs shows us that whatever justice we may seek is to be had ultimately from the local Government. The first step in trying to get it is to do our own duty. The common people in this country keep themselves in readiness for war. We, too, should contribute our share.[12]

Gandhi begins his letter with a propaganda tactic, insisting, "It is not for us to say whether the revolt of the Kaffirs is justified or not." The article also outlines the Zulu situation for Gandhi's Gujarati readers as he importunes them to serve in the war. Notice that there is no mention of how Gandhi's "heart was with the Zulus." The only reasons he gives for joining the British Army are out of duty to the British Empire and to protect their own self-interests. With any luck, they might be rewarded with the "requisite training," meaning weapons training, for becoming "permanent volunteers."

Shortly thereafter, on the evening of April 24, 1906, several hundred Indians gathered at the Congress Hall in Durban to discuss the community's response to the Zulu rebellion. Differing opinions apparently floated around as to the cause of the rebellion, but Gandhi was adamant that "it was their duty not to be prejudiced by any such thoughts."[13] This is another of his propaganda tactics - don't analyze the problem, simply react with blind loyalty to the Empire. Gandhi wrote a press report on the meeting for the *Indian Opinion*:

> The meeting held under the auspices of the Natal Indian Congress the other day is to be congratulated on having passed a resolution offering the services of Indians in connection with the Native revolt... We trust that the Government will see their way to accept the offer, and give the Indian community the chance once more of proving its worth.

> But whether the offer is accepted or not, it shows most clearly the importance of the Government turning to good account the Indian willingness to take its share in the defence of the Colony by giving Indians a proper previous training. We have more than once pointed out the criminal folly of not utilizing the admirable material the Indian community offers for additional defensive purposes. If it is not possible to turn the present Indian population out of the Colony, it is surely elementary wisdom to give it an adequate military training.[14]

In May, Gandhi resorted to scaremongering to elicit greater Indian support for the British war effort. He presented his Gujarati readers with an emotional appeal:

> In sending an offer of help to the Natal Government we took the right step. Because of this, we can face others with some measure of confidence. But that is not enough. We should strive harder with a view to playing [a more direct]

part in times of war. Under the Militia Law, enlisting is compulsory for whites when war breaks out. If we can also prove our willingness and ability to fight, our disabilities may possibly disappear....

There is rumour of a revolt in Swaziland. The Natal Government has ordered huge quantities of ammunition. All this goes to show that the Natal rebellion will last many more days. And if it spreads further, it might affect the whole of South Africa. This time help from the Transvaal has already reached Natal. The Cape has promised aid, and an offer has been made by England also. If we keep aloof at such a time, it is bound to create a bad impression about us. It is necessary for every Indian to consider this matter very seriously.[15]

Gandhi hammers his readers with dire prophecies, beating the war drums to summon Indian volunteers. His smoke and mirrors attempted to magnify the situation in his readers' minds, warning them of a war-engulfed South Africa if they neglect to help fight the blacks. His war cries had one goal, which was to unify the region against the blacks.

His final recruiting appeal was published on May 12, 1906 as a response to commentary in a white paper called *The Natal Advertiser*. Titling the article "Indian Volunteering," Gandhi wrote:

One of them has satirically suggested that Indians, so that they may not run away, should be placed in the front-line, and that then the fight between them and the Natives will be a sight for the gods. We propose to take the correspondent seriously, and venture to suggest that, if such a course were adopted, it would be undoubtedly the very best that could happen to the Indians.... But the pity of it is that the Government, and the European Colonists who have dictated the policy to the Government, have not taken the elementary precaution of giving the necessary discipline and instruction to the Indians. It is, therefore, a matter of physical impossibility to expect Indians to do any work with the rifle; or, for that matter, to do any work in connection with war with much efficiency. The Indian Ambulance Corps, at the time of the late war, did excellent work, without the necessary instruction and discipline, only because the Indian leaders who joined the Corps had previously been instructed and prepared under Dr. Booth.

Another correspondent has suggested that Indians should not be armed, because if they were, they would sell their arms to the Natives. This is a suggestion which is made wickedly, and without any foundation in fact. Indians have never been armed; it is, therefore, sheer folly to say that, if they were, they would act in a particular direction. It has also been suggested that the offer has been made to gain cheap applause, and also to gain something not made apparent in the proceedings of the Congress meeting. The first statement is slanderous, and the best way to disprove the stricture is for these correspondents to make the Government accept the offer, and to see whether the response is adequate or not. The second statement is difficult to understand. If it is intended to convey the impression that Indians, by serving during war time, hope to obtain a redress of their wrongs, the statement is true, and no Indian should be ashamed of such a motive. What can be better and more praise worthy than that Indians, by standing shoulder to shoulder with their fellow-Colonists in the present trouble, should show that they are not unworthy of the ordinary rights of citizenship which they have been claiming all these years? But it is equally true also that the offer has been made unconditionally, as a matter of simple duty, and irrespective of whether there is any redress of the grievances granted or not. We, therefore, consider it to be the special aim of every Colonist to support the Indian community in the offer it has made, and thereby to show prudence and foresight, for it cannot be seriously argued that there is any wisdom or statesmanship in blindly refusing to make use of, for purposes of war, one hundred thousand Indians who are perfectly loyal, and who are capable of good training.[16]

In this passage, Gandhi divulges more than he perhaps realizes. His ulterior motive for boasting about the Ambulance Corps is to suggest that that the Indians could do far better if allowed "necessary discipline and instruction." Of course, by this Gandhi means they should receive weapons training so they can "work with the rifle." Only when the Indians are armed will they be capable of engaging in "actual warfare" against the blacks.

Furthermore, Gandhi is clearly again trying to arouse his readers to enlist. He pumps up the collective Indian ego, describing his community as "fellow-Colonists" who must stand by their white brothers to preserve colonial suppression of the blacks. A couple of weeks later, Gandhi elaborated on this notion, writing (as a member of the British Indian Association) that he "has always admitted the principle of white predominance and has, therefore, no desire to press, on behalf of the community it represents, for any political rights for the sake of them."[17]

Finally, thanks to Gandhi's brilliant campaign, the British agreed to Gandhi's demands. On June 9, 1906, he broke the good news to his Indian community, writing in the *Indian Opinion*:

The Government have at last accepted the offer of the Indian community, and put it upon its mettle. By way of experiment, they want a corps of twenty stretcher-bearers. The Natal Indian Congress has sent in a prompt reply. We think the Congress has done well in offering to defray the wages of the bearers, so long as the corps remains in the experimental stage.

The acceptance by the Government synchronizes with the amendment of the Fire-Arms Act, providing for the supply of arms to Indians, and the statement made by Mr. Maydon to the effect that the Government intended to give Indians an opportunity of taking their share in the defence of the Colony.

Indians have now a splendid opportunity for showing that they are capable of appreciating the duties of citizenship. At the same time, the fact of the corps being raised is nothing to be unduly proud of. Twenty Indians, or even two hundred, going to the front is a flea-bite. The Indian sacrifice will rightly be considered infinitesimal. But it is the principle involved which marks the importance of the event. The Government have, by accepting the offer, shown their goodwill. And if Indians come successfully through the ordeal, the possibilities for the future are very great. Should they be assigned a permanent part in the Militia, there will remain no ground for the European complaint that Europeans alone have to bear the brunt of Colonial defence, and Indians will cease to feel that, in not being allowed to participate in it, they are slighted.[18]

Gandhi is pleased with the amendment to the "Fire-Arms Act," which he seems to think will make it easier to eventually raise an armed Indian corps. As usual, however, he does not breathe one word about nursing the wounded Zulus. His eyes are set solely on the goal of fighting in "defence of the Colony" and eventually obtaining his prized weapons training. Could it be that he never even had an interest in caring for the blacks?

Most of June 1906 was spent forming the Corps. While Gandhi waited for this task to be completed, he began a new campaign within the pages of the *Indian Opinion*. Now he began preaching the necessity of material Indian support for the war effort. It wasn't enough that Indians were going to the battlefront. Those staying behind must supply the British soldiers with money and care packages.

He first broached the topic in "The Natal Rebellion," writing: "It is necessary that Indians help in the way they did when a fund was started at the time of the Boer War. It will be good to collect some money and send it to the Government or to some Fund that might have been started. We shall then be considered to have done our duty to that extent. We hope the leaders of the community will take up this matter."[19] Following this, he published "Soldier's Fund," writing:

> The Durban Women's Association has started a special fund for the soldiers who have gone to the front to fight the Kaffirs. All leading men have contributed to the Fund and some Indian names are seen among the contributors. It is our advice that more Indians, traders and others, should subscribe to the Fund....

> The soldiers' life is a hard one. The salary and allowances that the Government pay them are not always enough. Those, therefore, who do not go to the front should, in order to express their sympathy, raise a fund for the purpose of sending the soldiers fruits, tobacco, warm clothing and other things that they might need. It is our duty to subscribe to such a fund.[20]

Gandhi was so passionately dedicated to the war effort that not even raising a Stretcher-Bearer Corps satisfied him. Obviously, supplying British soldiers at the warfront with all the comforts of home is much different from nursing wounded Zulus. This no expenses spared approach is most baffling when contrasted with Gandhi's leadership of the South African Phoenix Settlement, an experimental commune he founded in 1904. Millie Polak, a close friend of Gandhi, wrote about the settlement at which she was a resident, saying: "Money was always too scarce to enable the well to be dug, and so the problem of giving to the thirsty Zulu wayfarer a cup of water had to be dealt with by each householder, and much heart-searching and real unhappiness was caused by the necessity of refusing the simple request."[21] Why was Gandhi, the great humanitarian, missing in action when it came to helping parched Zulus? Were members of the black race beyond the limits of his humanity? Have historians somehow overlooked a stark defect in Gandhi, who refused water to blacks yet helped fund the British military that fought the Zulus? Can such a man as this be a Mahatma?

While he was in the process of forming the Stretcher-Bearer Corps, Gandhi published two core letters which comprise his recruiting campaign for a future Volunteer Corps. As premier examples of propaganda, these two commentaries should be taught in all military colleges. The first article, "Indian Volunteers," was published on June 23, 1906. Gandhi wrote:

Between this proposal and the Stretcher-Bearer Corps that has already been raised, there is much difference. The Stretcher-Bearer Corps is to last only a few days. Its work will be only to carry the wounded, and it will be disbanded when such work is no longer necessary. These men are not allowed to bear arms. The move for a Volunteer Corps is quite different and much more important. That Corps will be a permanent body; its members will be issued weapons, and they will receive military training every year at stated times. For the present they will not have any fighting to do. Wars are not fought all the time. A war breaks out, roughly speaking, once in twenty years. It is now more than twenty years since the last Kaffir rebellion broke out. There is, therefore, absolutely no risk in joining the Volunteer Corps. It can be looked upon as a kind of annual picnic. The person joining it gets enough exercise and thus keeps his body in good trim and improves his health. One who enlists as a volunteer is much respected. People love him and praise him, calling him a civilian soldier.

If the Indians are given such a status, we believe it would be a very good thing. It is likely to bring in some political advantage. Whether or not any advantage is to be derived, there is no doubt that it is our duty to enlist. Hundreds of leading whites enlist themselves and take pride in doing so. Under the prevailing law, it is open to the Government to enlist compulsorily. We ought to obey the laws designed for the defence of the country we live in. Therefore, considering the matter from any point, it is clear that, if we are able to join the Volunteer Corps, the reproach against us would be lived down, once and for all.

For fifteen years now the whites have accused the Indians that, if it came to giving one's life in defence of Natal, they would desert their posts of duty and flee home. We cannot meet this charge with a written rejoinder. There is but one way of disproving it - the way of action. The time to act appears to have come now. But how is it to be done? Not by making volunteers out of the poor labourers freed from their indentures. It is the duty of the trading community to take part in the movement themselves. Many men can be trained up even if each shop offers only one man. Trade will not suffer. The condition of those who join will improve. They will gain in strength and energy and will be deemed to have done their duty as citizens.

It is sheer superstition to believe, as some appear to do, that there is greater risk to life in going to the battle-field or preparing for it. Next week we intend to adduce examples in support of this.[22]

This article, written in Gujarati, is aimed at members of Gandhi's own merchant community. The propaganda contained within it is shocking in its audacity. If Gandhi is to be believed, joining this armed Volunteer Corps will be like an "annual picnic," complete with a pleasing amount of exercise. Tickling the Indian ego, Gandhi assures his community members that everyone will love them if they become soldiers. Then he makes the bizarre claim that military service involves no "greater risk to life" than the average profession.

At this point, let us remind the readers that Gandhi's autobiography claims he "bore no grudge against the Zulus" and was delighted to receive the nonviolent task of nursing wounded Zulus. Yet mere days before deploying to the battlefield, Gandhi told his Gujarati audience that the Volunteer Corps was "much more important" than the Stretcher-Bearer Corps because it is a "permanent body" which will be "issued weapons." He also claims that the "work will be only to carry the wounded," after which the corps will be immediately disbanded. Where is the nursing of Zulus in this scenario? The very definition of "nurse" implies extended medical care, not simply the shuffling around of wounded bodies. Gandhi's aggressive campaign for a stretcher-bearer corps was merely so it could be used as a stepping-stone to a permanent place in the military hierarchy.

The second article, published on June 30, 1906, a few days after Gandhi departed for the battlefield, was titled "Should Indians Volunteer or Not?" This article read:

We commented on this subject in our last issue. Towards the end of that article, we had said that most of us held back only because of fear. There is, however, no cause whatever for fear, as should be evident from the examples we propose to give for the benefit of those who believe that we should be ever ready to participate in war if we want to live happily and respectably in Natal, in South Africa or, for that matter, in any part of the British Empire. The Crimean War caused heavy casualties; yet it has been estimated that fewer men died from bayonet or bullet wounds in that war than through sheer carelessness or perverse living. It was calculated that, on an average, more men died of fever and other diseases during the attack on Ladysmith than by Boer bullets. The experience in every war has been similar.

Moreover, those who can take care of themselves and lead regular lives while at the front can live in health and happiness. The training such men receive cannot be had elsewhere, that is, if they do not go to the front only to prove their valour or quench their thirst for blood. A man going to the battle-front has to train himself to endure severe hardships. He is obliged to cultivate the habit of living in comradeship with large numbers of men. He easily learns to make do with simple food. He is required to keep regular hours. He forms the habit of obeying his superior's orders promptly and without argument. He also learns to discipline the movement of his limbs. And he has also to learn how to live in limited space according to the maxims of health. Instances are known of unruly and wayward men who went to the front and returned reformed and able fully to control both their mind and body.

For the Indian community, going to the battle-field should be an easy matter; for, whether Muslims or Hindus, we are men with profound faith in God. We have a greater sense of duty, and it should therefore be easier for us to volunteer. We are not overcome by fear when hundred of thousands of men die of famine or plague in our country. What is more, when we are told of our duty, we continue to be indifferent, keep our houses dirty, lie hugging our hoarded wealth. Thus, we live a wretched life acquiescing in a long, tormented process ending in death. Why, then, should we fear the death that may perhaps overtake us on the battle-field? We have to learn much from what the whites are doing in Natal. There is hardly any family from which someone has not gone to fight the Kaffir rebels. Following their example, we should steel our hearts and take courage. Now is the time when the leading whites want us to take this step; if we let go this opportunity, we shall repent later.[23]

Gandhi's solution to achieving peace and respectability is to go to war against the blacks. It is peculiar that a man who claims his "heart was with the Zulus" should advocate following the example of those going to "fight the Kaffir rebels." The Father of Nonviolence appears to be channeling Orwell's Big Brother as he preaches that "War is Peace." This interpretation is reinforced by Gandhi's portrayal of military life, which he calls both an "annual picnic" and a facilitator of "health and happiness." According to Gandhi, there is no good thing that cannot come from life on a battlefield, whether friendship, self-discipline, or a fit body. His insistence that Indians must "participate in war if we want to live happily and respectably in Natal" is a classic example of scare tactics.

Religion is the backbone of his closing argument as he insists that Indians, being "men with profound faith in God," must go to the battlefield to help kill blacks. Gandhi's mixture of religion and politics to suit his ideology should be the envy of any serious jihadi or crusader.

Before we move to an examination of Gandhi's few weeks on the Zululand battlefield, let us summarize his lengthy campaign in support of the war effort. Beginning with his first letter on November 18, 1905, Gandhi spent a total of about seven months making his case for uniting with the British against the Zulus.

His first several letters were primarily directed towards the white government and media in an attempt to justify his desire for some sort of Indian corps. While demanding training for "actual warfare" the whole time, Gandhi employs several arguments. His chief argument is that Indians can make quick work of the blacks and will be efficient in "defence of the Colony." He then makes a legal maneuver, resurrecting a dormant law to convince Natal leaders of their legal obligation to recruit Indians for the military. As a last ditch effort, he pleads for Indians to be given an opportunity to do menial fieldwork for the British Army. This demand was, in practicality, granted when he was allowed to raise a stretcher-bearer corps.

After laboring for about four months to justify the war preparations, Gandhi turns his attention to the Indian readers of *Indian Opinion*, particularly the Gujaratis. While challenging their masculinity, he implements propaganda techniques to prevent his community from thinking too deeply about the Zulu struggle. He tells Natal authorities it will be "criminal folly" if they don't accept his proposal for an Indian corps. Not only is it the duty of Indians to enlist, but it is also the duty of Natal authorities to open doors for Indians to enlist. Then Gandhi begins to tickle egos while trying to heighten the gravity of the Zulu revolt by predicting its likely spread.

He frankly tells his Indians readers that they are "fellow-Colonists" with the whites. Once his Indian corps suggestion is accepted, he begins demanding Indians start a fund drive in addition to joining the military. Finally, he offers a series of deceptions about the nature of the battleground: it's good for your health, not at all risky, similar to an annual picnic, a source of pride, a way to become self-controlled, a place to learn discipline; a source of pride, and a source of companionship. Indeed, Gandhi is so adept at spinning propaganda that world militaries having difficulty recruiting might consider asking, "What would Gandhi say?"

Considering the bigger picture of what prompted the war in the first place, which was black anger at harsh colonial policies, we cannot help but wonder why Gandhi desired to war *against* the blacks. In his autobiography, he assures us his "heart was with the Zulus" and he "bore no grudge" against them. If that was the case and the Zulus had "harmed no Indian," why did he dedicate seven months of his life to convincing a profoundly reluctant British government to permit an Indian corps? Of course, Gandhi did say that "the wounded Zulus would have been left uncared for" without the Indian Stretcher-Bearer Corps. Was Gandhi's *Indian Opinion* campaign simply a complicated strategy to get Indians into a position where they could care for wounded Zulus? For that matter, was his heart really with the Zulus?

Once he was appointed a Sergeant Major (see Plates 5 and 6) and completed recruitment of his small Corps, Gandhi was deployed to the battlefield. From there, he regularly forwarded battlefront dispatches to the *Indian Opinion*. It is within these dispatches that we can discover whether Gandhi's "main work was to be the nursing of the wounded Zulus." The first dispatch which concerns us began with the day of June 26, 1906:

> **June 26:** "On the 26th our task was allotted to us. Nine of us were to form a fatigue party to accompany the tank-waggon, which brought water from an adjoining stream. Some of us were detained to disinfect the whole camp, under the superintendence of Dr. Savage, the District Surgeon for Mapumulo, and from three to four of us were to dress the wounds on the backs of several Native rebels, who had received lashes."[24]

Singh & Watson

June 27: "Early on the morning of the 27th, therefore, one-half of the Corps, with two stretchers under Sgt.-Major Gandhi and Sgt. Joshi proceeded to Otimati, where instructions were received to take a stretcher to carry one of the troopers who was dazed. Fortunately, the trooper had recovered before the party reached Thring's Post. But by an unfortunate accident, another trooper, by name Forder, had received a bullet-wound in the thigh from a co-trooper. He, however, pluckily rode to the camp. The stretcher party had to assist Mr. Stokes, of the N. M. C., in treating the wounded trooper, and others, who had received slight injuries through accidents or otherwise, requiring medical help."[25]

June 28: "The stretcher party at Otimati were to take to Mapumulo Private Sutton of the Durban Reserves, whose toe was crushed under a waggon wheel, and Trooper Forder. The latter had to be carried on a stretcher, as his wound was very delicate. The work of carrying Trooper Forder proved to be much heavier than we had thought. The energy of all the available men had to be taxed to the utmost in carrying the wounded men, especially as it meant going uphill all the way. As we were nearing Mapumulo, the Captain of our escort sent word that, if it could be managed, Forder should be placed in the ambulance waggon, as the Natives about the hill might wrongly consider that the rebels had succeeded in wounding at least one of our men. Trooper Forder, on hearing the message, gladly volunteered to go into the waggon. And the fatigued bearers were equally glad to be relieved of the necessity of having to carry their charge up the very steep hill near Mapumulo."[26]

One brief mention of caring for Zulus does appear in Gandhi's account of his first day in the field, which incidental treatment we dwell on later in this chapter. Given the above account we don't know exactly which task among the four listed on June 26 was assigned to Gandhi himself. Regardless, the work assignment soon changed. On June 27, Sgt. Major Gandhi and half of his corps were assigned to transport injured British soldiers. The same task consumed the whole of the following day.

The work at Mapumulo continued for about four days as troops assembled to deliver a crushing blow to the Zulu rebels in the region. The Zulu chiefs were also busy gathering their forces. During the final week of June, there was a mass exodus of Zulu workers from Durban. More than a thousand dock workers, about 500 domestic workers, and around 40 percent of the African Borough Police responded to the call for men to fight the British. The British commanding officer, Colonel McKenzie, gathered about 2500 troops at Thring's Post while he developed a battle-plan for striking the three major bodies of rebel Zulus. Chief Meseni was south on the Umvoti River with the largest force, Chief Matshwili was northeast in the Isinzimba Valley, and Chief Ndlovu was north in the Imati Valley. As tensions rose, Colonel Sparks wrote to the government asking for revolvers to be issued to the Indians for protection, but the action came before he received an answer. Although Sparks wrote the letter, is it possible he did so at Gandhi's urging? In the midst of the conflict, when Gandhi in his autobiography says his heart was already with the Zulus, did he continue his campaign for arms? The reader can no doubt imagine the peculiarity of a similar situation where, for instance, arms might be requested for the Red Cross. Was Gandhi pursing his demand for arms in the midst of war, just as he persistently did before, and as we shall see, after the war?

The Indian corps continued to work at Mapumulo till the morning of July 3:

> **July 3:** "With this brief interruption, then, the whole Corps resumed its former work, with which it had commenced, and continued to do so till the morning of the 3rd July, a day that will ever remain memorable to the members of the Corps.... At daybreak, the movement of the troops became naturally more rapid, and the distance between them and us began to increase. However, there was no prospect before

us except that of running after the troops or of being asse-gaied by the rebels. Probably we had a narrow escape. At 7 o'clock troops were operating at some distance from us. As we were struggling along, we met a Kaffir who did not wear the loyal badge. He was armed with an assegai and was hiding himself. However, we safely rejoined the troops on the further hill, whilst they were sweeping with their carbines the bushes below. Thus, we had to perform what seemed to be a never-ending march."[27]

Strangely, to Gandhi the most memorable moment of the war was a brief encounter with a rebel Zulu. Despite his claim that his "heart was with the Zulus," Gandhi and his fellows were clearly quite frightened by this "Kaffir" who "did not wear the loyal badge." They only considered themselves safe when back amongst the armed colonial soldiers. The next several days were spent simply marching with the army and Gandhi noted "it was a stroke of good luck that there were no casualties or accidents on our side" because they were "dead tired."[28]

July 8: "Transport that was provided for the footsore bearers put us on our feet again, and we were able to respond to the call of duty on the morning of the 8th. Orders were received on Saturday evening that we should follow with our stretchers the guns that were to leave for the Tugela Valley at 3 a.m. the following day. Compared to the work done in the Umvoti Valley, our task was easy, and the march could not have covered more than 16 miles. We returned to camp the same day."[29]

Instead of tending wounded Zulus, the Corps was now assigned to accompany the British cannon. During this time, Col. McKenzie moved against Chief Matshwili's Kraal at Isinzimba. About 550 Africans, including the chief, were killed in the surprise attack at dawn, but Gandhi reported that the Indian corps had a relatively easy day, marching about eight miles out and back. After Col. McKenzie's successful assault on the Zulu camp, one wonders why Gandhi's day was easy. Was it because there were no Zulus left alive to nurse?

The troops rested the following day, which was July 9.

July 10: "We had to proceed to the Otimati Valley with the infantry, and though the work was very difficult, we had by this time become more or less seasoned. We had to take two days' rations with us; the path lay through what would ordinarily be an inaccessible valley. It was impossible for any ambulance to go down, and in parts we had to descend steep precipices. Troopers had to lead their horses, and the route was so long that we never seemed to reach the bottom. However, at about 12 o'clock we finished the day's journey, with no Kaffirs to fight. But an incident happened on the way down the valley which was calculated to test our ability to do stretcher-bearing work. A Kaffir, being a friendly boy, who was guiding a private of the D. L. I., was shot by him, under the belief, it is said, that the Native was misleading him. The Native was badly wounded, and required carrying, which was entrusted to us. Orders were given that we were to take him the same day to Mapumulo, and we were given four friendly Natives to help us, as also to guide us. Three of them, however, as soon as the troops were out of sight, deserted us, and the fourth, though he remained with us, declined flatly to go with us to Mapumulo, as he feared that, without an escort, we might be cut to pieces by the enemy. Fortunately, the troops were yet within reach. The Sergeant-Major, therefore, reported the matter to the proper officer."[30]

This report has the corps caring for a wounded black. However, the injured boy was not a rebel Zulu, as Gandhi's autobiography reports, but a loyal servant of the British Empire. Additionally, Gandhi explicitly says that the boy was cared for on orders. The passage is further marred by the rueful comment that there were "no Kaffirs to fight" and Gandhi's description of his black assistants as faithless and cowardly. Gandhi is quick to report the desertion to the British authorities.

July 11: "The following day we resumed our march with our precious charge, with orders to go to Mapumulo. We were given about 20 Kaffir levies to help us. They did so with much difficulty over part of the way, and then, too, because Doctor Savage happened to be with us. The Natives in our hands proved to be most unreliable and obstinate. Without constant attention, they would as soon have dropped the wounded man as not, and they seemed to bestow no care on their suffering countryman.

"However, the Indian bearers carried him to Mapumulo in splendid style. All our resourcefulness was put to the test during the march. After we had finished the most difficult part of our journey along a narrow and steep pathway, the Japanese stretcher on which we were carrying the patient, who was very bulky, gave way, fortunately without hurting him."[31]

Gandhi does not even have kind words for the "loyal" blacks. He considers them "unreliable" and "obstinate" and so self-centered they don't even care for members of their own race. He decries their "unreliability" and "obstinance" although these traits could easily be considered an exercise of nonviolent noncooperation against the British. Rather than nursing wounded Zulus, Gandhi is cultivating a deep irritation towards his native helpers.

The Indian Corps spent the 12th resting, the 13th returning to Thring's Post, and the 14th waiting in camp. On the 14th, the African chiefs finally surrendered to the British and troop demobilization was begun. The stretcher-bearing corps was officially discharged on Thursday, July 19, while Gandhi claimed his assurance "that the little band is capable of performing any work that may be entrusted to it."[32] He was soon awarded a war medal by the British authorities in recognition of his participation in the war.

What are we to conclude from the above account of Gandhi's activities during the Zulu War? Remember that Gandhi claimed that "our main work was to be the nursing of the wounded Zulus," yet a mere two days of the several weeks in the field were spent caring for wounded blacks. Both times the Indian Corps only did so upon orders and the second time the injured black was not even a rebel Zulu, but a British loyalist. In other words, the sum effect of Gandhi's participation in the war was to assist the British colonials, which he made clear was his goal throughout his activism before the war.

Any doubt about our conclusions thus far concerning Gandhi's actions during the war will soon be erased by Gandhi's July 20, 1906 postwar report. Written from Durban and published by the *Indian Opinion*, the report read:

Thanking the organization on behalf of the Corps, Mr. Gandhi said that what the Corps had done was only its duty. If the Indians really wanted to show their appreciation of the work of the Corps, they should try through the Government to have a permanent Corps set up and should also exert themselves to improve their physique in order to qualify for admission. He said that if, for any reason, the traders could not enlist, other educated Indians as well as the servants and clerks of traders could easily do so. From experience gained during the fighting, he could say that the whites treated the Indians very cordially, and distinctions based on colour had ceased to exist. If a larger Indian Corps was formed on a permanent footing, such fellow-feeling would increase, and it was likely that in the process white prejudice against Indians might altogether disappear. He therefore very strongly recommended the formation of such a Corps.[33]

Gandhi followed this up with a July 31 letter to Col. Hysop, the Principal Medical Officer of the Natal Militia, which was republished in an August issue of the *Indian Opinion*. Gandhi summarized the work of the stretcher-bearers, concluding his letter with a call for weapons:

> Members of the Corps were all untrained and untried men; they were called upon, too, to do responsible and independent work, and to face danger unarmed. If the Government would form a permanent Ambulance Corps, I think that special training is absolutely necessary, and that they should all be armed for self-protection. As one who has been intimately connected with the Indian community for the last thirteen years, I have ventured to place the above views before you for your consideration.[34]

Considering Gandhi's creative retelling of his war activities, his entire account of the Zulu War is suspect. Although he tries to hypnotize unsuspecting readers with his solitary story of accidentally treating Zulu rebels, our discovery of the historical Gandhi will make readers abundantly clear that his intentions for participating in the war had nothing to do with nursing wounded blacks.

The popular belief holds that Gandhi engaged in deep soul-searching during the war, even in the midst of long, hot marches through the Zulu grasslands. This was when he supposedly took the famous *Brahmacharya* vow that would lead him to change the world. However, his reports during and after the war reveal nothing of the kind. His July 20 report, published immediately after the war on blacks, only recommends Indians get in good physical shape so they can qualify for military enlistment and his July 31 letter clamors for weapons. Where is the soul-searching? Why is there no mention of the vow? If this was when the celibate and nonviolent Gandhi was born, why was he so silent about the momentous occasion?

Other questions also remain. Why was Gandhi so desperate to obtain a permanent Indian Volunteer Corps? Why did he consider an armed corps "much more important" than bearing stretchers? If his "heart was with the Zulus" and he wanted to nurse the injured black rebels, why was there any need in the present or future for arming the Indians? If Gandhi had really self-sacrificially nursed the Zulus during the war, would not his reputation have precluded the need for weapons to defend himself from the Zulus? If his participation in the war was truly intended to serve the Zulus and Gandhi's experiences had led him to take his *Brahmacharya* vow, should not Gandhi have considered his mission accomplished when the war ended? Instead, he continued to agitate for a permanent, armed corps.

One of Gandhi's last major defenses of the British war effort came a few weeks after war's end. On August 4, 1906, Gandhi published a piece in the *Indian Opinion* titled "Egypt and Natal – A Comparison: Is This Civilization?" Within this short article he clarified his stance on torture, arguing in the Gujarati language that Egyptian rebels were treated worse than the Zulu rebels, therefore the latter had no justification in complaining about mistreatment. He wrote:

> A controversy is going on in England about what the Natal army did during the Kaffir rebellion. The people there believe that the whites of Natal perpetrated great atrocities on the Kaffirs. In reply to such critics, *The Star* has pointed to the doings of the Imperial army in Egypt. Those among the Egyptian rebels who had been captured were ordered to be flogged. The flogging was continued to the limits of the victims' endurance; it took place in public and was watched by thousands of people. Those sentenced to death were also hanged at the same time. While those sentenced to death were hanging, the flogging of the others was taken up. While the sentences were being executed, the relatives of the victims cried and wept until many of them swooned. If this be true, there is no reason why there should be such an outcry in England against the Natal outrage.[35]

Considering all this evidence and our countless unanswered questions, we should turn to Richard Grenier. In his famous 1983 review of the "Gandhi" film, he wrote:

It is something of an anomaly that Gandhi, held in popular myth to be a pure pacifist (a myth which governments of India have always been at great pains to sustain in the belief that it will reflect credit on India itself, and to which the present movie adheres slavishly), was until fifty not ill-disposed to war at all. As I have already noted, in three wars, no sooner had the bugles sounded than Gandhi not only gave his support, but was clamoring for arms. To form new regiments! To fight! To destroy the enemies of the empire! Regular Indian army units fought in both the Boer War and World War I, but this was not enough for Gandhi. He wanted to raise new troops, even, in the case of the Boer and Kaffir Wars [Editor's Note: This is another name for the Zulu War], from the tiny Indian colony in South Africa. British military authorities thought it not really worth the trouble to train such a small body of Indians as soldiers, and were even resistant to training them as an auxiliary medical corps ("stretcher bearers"), but finally yielded to Gandhi's relentless importuning. As first instructed, the Indian Volunteer Corps was not supposed actually to go into combat, but Gandhi, adamant, led his Indian volunteers into the thick of battle. When the British commanding officer was mortally wounded during an engagement in the Kaffir War, Gandhi - though his corps' deputy commander - carried the officer's stretcher himself from the battlefield and for miles over the sun-baked veldt. The British empire's War Medal did not have its name for nothing, and it was generally earned.[36]

These 100 years later, perhaps we can find some clarity about Gandhi's occupation during the war in the kind words of a letter sent him by the Governor of Natal. Dated August 7, 1906, the letter reads in part:

I cannot allow demobilization to take place without placing on record on behalf of the Government my appreciation of the patriotic movement made by the Indian community of

Natal in providing a Bearer Company for service in the field during the rebellion.

The number of casualties in our forces have been providentially small and the labours of the company have not therefore been so heavy as they would otherwise have been.[37]

Although Gandhi's autobiography deceives the reader in an effort to cover his militaristic tracks, the Natal Governor's words cannot be misunderstood. His praise of Gandhi's patriotism and assertion that low casualty figures can be partially attributed to Gandhi's work clearly reveals that the Stretcher-bearer Corps toiled in support of the British Empire and against the Zulus.

Gandhi's grandson, Arun Gandhi, co-authored *The Forgotten Woman*, a book about his grandfather's wife, Kasturba. Arun gives a lengthy account of his grandfather's participation in the Zulu War, including commentary on why the elder Gandhi chose to participate:

A correspondent commenting in the *Natal Advertiser*, for example, on what he viewed as the absurd idea of enlisting Indian soldiers to help fight Zulus, had slyly suggested that "the Indians, so that they may not run away, should be placed in the front line, and then the fight between them and the Natives will be a sight for the gods." How, Mohandas asked himself, could such venomous racial hatred be eradicated? How could such degrading stereotypes be dispelled? Perhaps he should advise his countrymen to volunteer for combat and ask for frontline duty. Yet, when he contemplated the conflict itself, his only reaction was misery at the thought of so much violence.[38]

Arun also reports that a few days after Gandhi's return from the battlefront, Kasturba prepared a homecoming feast for her husband and several of his friends.

Of course, the letter in which Gandhi responds to *The Natal Advertiser* is the same one in which he bemoans the lack of fire-arms training for Indians. Clearly, Arun Gandhi has read the *Collected Works*, including the many perplexing passages which we have examined throughout this chapter. This causes us to wonder if he is perhaps naïve and completely overlooked his grandfather's demand that Indians be given "the opportunity of a thorough training for actual warfare." Did Arun simply miss the pro-war agenda of Gandhi's letters? Or is he perhaps continuing his grandfather's "experimentation with the truth"?

Researching the origins of the *Brahmacharya* vow would be far easier, except Gandhi claims to have destroyed the bulk of his papers from that era of his life. This destruction, which was likely invented to dissuade overcurious researchers from investigating the ethereal vow of poverty and celibacy, is documented in Gandhi's *Satyagraha in South Africa*. He offers his vow as the excuse for destroying the papers:

> I have thrown away or burnt such things in my life. I destroyed such papers as I felt it was not necessary to preserve them or as the scope of my activities was extended. I am not sorry for this, as to have preserved all of them would have been burdensome and expensive. I should have been compelled to keep cabinets and boxes which would have been an eyesore to one who has taken the vow of poverty.[39]

Yet Pyarelal, Gandhi's longtime secretary, wrote: "Luckily Gandhiji had brought with him from South Africa a boxful of correspondence and other documents relating to his work there.... He had also maintained a systematic and fairly exhaustive record of clippings from contemporary newspapers for the period 1889-1900 in thirteen scrapbooks."[40]

What happened to the paperwork from 1900 onward, in particular the period covering the 1906 Zulu rebellion? Can we safely infer that Gandhi himself destroyed these documents? In another twist, Ananda M. Pandiri says in *A Comprehensive, Annotated Bibliography on Mahatma Gandhi* that upon returning to India in 1915, Gandhi donated around 15,000 of his books to Sheth Maneklal Jethabhai Pustakalya, a library located in Ahmedabad, Guja-rat.[41] If a man destroys papers to fulfill his vow of poverty and avoid the eyesore of many "cabinets and boxes," why would he keep a "systematic and fairly exhaustive record of clippings," let alone 15,000 books?

After this lengthy expose of the events surrounding Gandhi's vow, the reader will no doubt be asking many questions. Is it possible there was no soul-searching or postwar vow? Considering the preponderance of the evidence, we have constructed a possible re-interpretation of the events in Gandhi's life.

Gandhi did no soul-searching during or after the Zulu rebellion of 1906, possibly took a vow of celibacy, and definitely did not take a vow of poverty. He did not destroy documents, but rather in 1915 brought all the paperwork he had with him to India. Upon his arrival, he donated 15,000 books to the library while retaining important documents for his personal records. Sometime between 1921 and 1925, as his name gained worldwide attention, he decided it was time to clean up his past. The easiest way at the time was to destroy documents, particularly those dealing with the 1906 war. Then he rewrote the missing period in his two autobiographical accounts. In other words, he engaged in a cover-up of his past.

We have established using his own writings that Gandhi concocted the racial train incidents to cement his reputation as a humanitarian. During the Zulu War, Gandhi had a chance to perform actual humanitarian work. Instead, he chose to join the British in suppressing the fledgling Zulu revolt against apartheid and then lie about his participation many years later. The relevance of this truth is that it severely damages Gandhi's veracity. Unlike the alleged train incident, Gandhi did not invent his participation in the war. However, that participation illustrates his willingness to experiment with the truth. Not only did he make mistakes that harmed fragile minority groups, but he also refused to own up to those mistakes, instead twisting reality to benefit his public image.

NOTES

[1] CWMG, Vol. 74, p. 275.

[2] Fatima Meer, *Mahatma Gandhi: 125 Year*, ed. B.R. Nanda (New Delhi: Indian Council for Cultural Relations and New Age International Publishers, 1995), pp. 48-49.

[3] D.G. Tendulkar, *Mahatma: Life of Mohandas Karamchand Gandhi* (Bombay: Vithalbhai K. Jhaveri and D.G. Tendulkar, 1951), Vol. 1, pp. 91-92.

[4] Calvin Kytle, *Gandhi, Soldier of Nonviolence: An Introduction*, rev. ed. (Washington, D.C.: Seven Locks Press, 1982), pp. 85-87.

[5] Louis Fischer, *The Life of Mahatma Gandhi* (New York: Harper & Brothers, 1950), pp. 57-58.

[6] Mohandas K. Gandhi, *An Autobiography, or the Story of my Experiments with Truth* (1927, 1929; reprint, Boston: Beacon Press, 1957), p. xii.

[7] Mohandas K. Gandhi, *Satyagraha in South Africa* (1928; reprint, Ahmedabad: Navajivan Publishing House, 1972), pp. 90-91.

[8] CWMG, Vol. 5, p. 11.

[9] Ibid., pp. 32-33.

[10] Ibid., pp. 124-25.

[11] Ibid., p. 146.

[12] Ibid., pp. 179-80.

[13] Ibid., p. 189.

[14] Ibid., pp. 191-92.

[15] Ibid., p. 202.

[16] Ibid., pp. 210-12.

[17] Ibid., p. 238.

[18] Ibid., p. 258.

[19] Ibid., p. 251.

[20] Ibid., pp. 258-59.

[21] Millie G. Polak, *Mr. Gandhi: The Man* (London: George Allen and Unwin, 1931), p. 43.

[22] CWMG, Vol. 5, pp. 268-69.

[23] Ibid., pp. 273-74.

[24] Ibid., p. 277.

[25] Ibid.

[26] Ibid., pp. 277-78.

[27] Ibid., p. 278.

[28] Ibid., p. 279.

[29] Ibid., pp. 279-80.

[30] Ibid., p. 280.

[31] Ibid., pp. 280-81.

[32] Ibid., p. 281.

[33] Ibid., pp. 281-82.

[34] Ibid., p. 286.

[35] Ibid., p. 290.

[36] Richard Grenier, "The Gandhi Nobody Knows," *Commentary* Magazine, March 1983.

[37] R. A. Huttenback, *Gandhi in South Africa: British Imperialism and the Indian Question, 1860-1914* (Ithaca, N.Y.: Cornell University Press, 1971), pp. 125-26.

[38] Arun & Sunanda Gandhi, *The Forgotten Woman: The Untold Story of Kasturba Gandhi, Wife of Mahatma Gandhi* (Huntsville, Ark.: Ozark Mountain Publishers, 1998), pp. 133-134.

[39] Mohandas K. Gandhi, *Satyagraha in South Africa* (Ahmedabad: Navajivan Publishing House, 1972), p. 221.

[40] Pyarelal, *Mahatma Gandhi: The Early Phase* (Ahmedabad: Navajivan Publishing House, 1986), vol. 1, p. xiv.

---

[41] Ananda M. Pandiri, *A Comprehensive, Annotated Bibliography on Mahatma Gandhi* (Westport, Conn.: Greenwood Press, 1995), pp. 320-21.

Ten

Politics of Victimization

~

I am but a seeker after Truth. I claim to have found a way to it. I claim to be making a ceaseless effort to find it. But I admit that I have not yet found it. To find Truth completely is to realize oneself and one's destiny, i.e., to become perfect. I am painfully conscious of my imperfections, and therein lies all the strength I possess, because it is a rare thing for a man to know his own limitations.

~ Mahatma Gandhi
Nov. 17, 1921

G andhi's biographies and autobiographies are probably the most shameless example of exhibitionism since St. Augustine's *Confessions*. No one in history before or since Augustine has so successfully recorded the autobiographical events of his life to win over an audience. In the case of Augustine, the public relations campaign was a different kind of Immaculate Conception. In his case, the personage was sold to the public as a sinner turned saint, an individual sanctified by miraculous intervention. In Gandhi's case, the Immaculate Conception took a different form. In this case, the avatar, prophet, and saint was already fully formed, a self-realized being from birth. All that was missing from the attempt to form a new religion was the miracles. The quintessential political opportunist, Gandhi soon hit on the formula to change all that. The Immaculate Conception was now born in his mind. He would invent a past. He would make himself into a martyr. He would give the world a biography that would show him not as a man of privilege, not as a high caste Hindu sent to the London Bar, but as a victim of persecution, a martyr, one who had endured the worst slights and insults a man can experience only to rise from these humiliations phoenix-like to forgive his enemies. In addition, he portrays himself as Buddha-like in his renunciation of worldly attachments. He is the *sunyasi* par excellence, one whose renunciation could not be more complete or dramatic, one who gives up all the privileges of the legal profession and the bid for higher office for the sake of a higher and nobler cause, *Satyagraha*. No longer will he attire himself as a gentleman of privilege. No longer will he rub shoulders with the elite. It is at this time that the loincloth adorned *sunyasi* is born, relinquishing all the trappings of worldly success and attachment, but for his beloved wife. Had it been politically expedient to dispense with his life's companion, it is doubtful he would have hesitated. However, in the Christian world in which he hoped to win converts, abandoning a wife would not have been a saintly option.

Reverend Doke's book is the first book that detailed Gandhi's historical encounter with the racial train and coach incidents as he was traveling in South Africa in 1893. Nothing pertaining to the incident had ever appeared in print before 1909. This alone makes the biographical account of J. J. Doke highly suspect. Is this to impute opportunistic motives to Rev. Doke? Well, on that account he does rather implicate himself. For as Bishop Mathews has pointed out, Rev. Doke firmly believed that it would serve Indian political cause were Gandhi to be known in England. What was the best method for making him known? In asking him if he is prepared to be a martyr, Doke's question could not be more direct. What the question implies is that the reverend is fully prepared to make a martyr out of Gandhi. All he requires is his permission. This is precisely what Rev. Doke's biography was designed to do - turn Gandhi into a martyr. How did it do so? In the same way all successful biographies of martyrs do and none less so than the New Testament. It highlighted the hardships and persecutions of Gandhi. It invented a fable that would show a martyred saint rising from the cross, not to vanquish his enemies, but to spread a message of peace and non-violence, forgiveness of sins, and a call to love thy neighbor. By making a martyr out of Gandhi, Rev. Doke assures Gandhi of a following in England. By asking Gandhi if he is prepared to be a martyr, Doke is really asking him if he is ready to be portrayed as one. While some might object that the question is of a different import and really asks if Gandhi is prepared to die for a cause, we would argue that the question is subtler. As Bishop Mathews implies in his own Gandhian scholarship, Rev. Doke was looking for a hero for his cause. He selected Gandhi knowing it would help the cause of Indians for the exploits of their hero to be known in England. Doke asks Gandhi if he is prepared to be a martyr because that is precisely what he intends to make of him through his biography. Gandhi will be shown to be a martyr. The political power and influence to be gained from such a reputation will be enormous. What the reverend really desires to know is whether Gandhi is prepared to bear the responsibility. The biographical accounts of the racial train and coach incidents are now hatched as the means of portraying his victimization, persecution, and martyrdom. On this hinges the crucifixion and resurrection of the martyr of the new religion. On the basis of this story the exodus will begin. Only in this instance, it is not the slaves that are forced to leave, but their colonial masters.

Why is it only at this juncture that we learn of the harrowing ordeals Gandhi was forced to endure under the racist apartheid laws of South Africa? Why have we no allusions to this incident prior to 1909? How is it that a man humiliated by the worst form of racial violence could neglect to mention it in any of his writings before 1909? How is it that it does not appear even as a diary entry prior to this date? Could a man suffering from the sting of racial intolerance and injustice simply forget about it for sixteen years? Would it not have won more converts to his cause to reveal the full extent of his hardship and adversity at an earlier date? Was there a political expedient in suppressing the incident? It does not seem likely. What could Gandhi possibly have to gain from suppressing details of his life that would have served as his *causus beli*?

What is more likely is that Rev. Doke's visit provided an opportunity. The 1908 interview would have laid the foundation for Gandhi's martyrdom. This was the meeting that would give the political opportunists the "opportunity" they were looking for. They would make a martyr out of Gandhi to support their cause. All they had to do was make the story more convincing. They would promulgate a new faith, a new religion, a new ideology. To get it off the ground, they required a fable, a story, a miracle. A death and resurrection motif was all that was required. They would have their saint martyred only to rise again from defeat. Their saint would be subjected to the worst forms of humiliation such men of privilege could imagine. He would be denied access to first class travel. He would be forced to move to van compartments. He would be tossed off trains. He would be left to freeze half to death in railway station waiting rooms in the harshest and coldest of winter nights.

As for *Satyagraha in South Africa* and the *Autobiography* accounts, why were they penned at this time? Was it undertaken simply to keep Gandhi occupied while in prison? When one looks at historical figures writing while they are in prison, there is usually a seditious motive behind their writing - the revolutionary is impelled to write out of a desire to be subversive, to undermine the regime, to deprive the ruling caste of its legitimacy, to provide the oppressed with a *causus beli*, and promote themselves as champions of the cause of freedom. Gandhi's motives may have been no different. He certainly has cause for grievance and, unless saintly in his capacity to turn the other cheek, very probably has an axe to grind. It is fascinating to see how the account of the racial train and coach incidents, never before referred to in any of Gandhi's diary notes, personal letters, or other writings, suddenly surfaces. Why now? Well, first the facts suggest that they are fabricated. Therefore, there had to be a generational delay to ensure that those who knew the truth had died off before the lie could be disseminated. The other most obvious motive is that it had never been more politically expedient or timely. Now that he was facing the full brunt of British colonial law, Gandhi could now legitimately refer to the entire history of racial intolerance and injustice that had affected his life in order to show a pattern and to highlight the extreme injustice of his current plight. Under the scrutiny of the international community and press, the British would feel compelled to behave respectably and to appear progressive. Policies would be adopted highlighting their moral superiority to less humane colonial regimes like the one in South Africa. Soon they would be beating themselves at their own game, withdrawing from India of their own volition so as not to lose their standing in the eyes of the world community and among subjects within the British Empire and Commonwealth.

As stated in Chapter Four, Gandhi's *Autobiography* has another strange facet. He himself tells us in the introduction:

> [It] is not my purpose to attempt a real autobiography. I simply want to tell the story of my numerous experiments with truth.... But I should certainly like to narrate my experiments in the spiritual field which are known only to myself, and from which I have derived such power as I possess for working in the political field.

So there, we have it. He is admitting unequivocally that he is not even attempting to undertake a real autobiography, but merely experimenting with the truth, which means that he is free to opportunistically play with the facts in whatever form he chooses in order to produce whatever effect he likes.[1] If anyone has a different interpretation of his words, we invite him to suggest one. The facts could not be plainer. Gandhi admits that he is not giving a factual account of events. In fact, he is not even attempting to do so. By his own admission, he is experimenting with the truth, which at best means that he is not telling the truth and at worst lying. But since he is on record in the introduction admitting that he is making no attempt at a real autobiography but merely experimenting with the truth, we cannot call him a liar since he is an admitted liar. An admitted liar has the virtue of being honest about his lies. Of course we are being facetious and have our tongues firmly planted in our cheeks, but irony is unavoidable on this point. It is simply laughable that the provocative introduction to a work with an even more provocative title could have been overlooked for so long. *An Autobiography: The Story of My Experiments With Truth* is a title selected by a man who is having a good joke at the world's expense. He has chosen the title confident in the knowledge that only a few initiates who are in on the scheme know his true face and have seen behind the mask. And he is equally confident that the rest of the world is so in the dark that they cannot see the face behind the mask even though he has taken the trouble to tell everyone that he is wearing one. *The Story of My Experiments With Truth* is a provocative title that makes it clear to anyone with eyes to see with that he is not revealing his true self in a "real autobiography," but is employing a mask, a façade, a persona in a self-confessed attempt at political opportunism. There is no other way of taking these words than to see his autobiography as an acknowledged fiction. To admit to his reader that he is not attempting to write a real autobiography, but merely experimenting with the truth is tantamount to confessing that his autobiography orients itself toward truth rather as Dostoyevsky's and Dicken's novels do. In short, it is a work of fiction and cannot be seen otherwise because of his own words on the subject. One wonders how such a startling admission could have been overlooked by the previous generation of scholars. But then it is our observation that scholarship itself should come under the microscope of skeptical inquiry, since the scholarly community has found itself in error on a whole plethora of subjects over the centuries.

So what is Gandhi playing at? Does he take us for fools? Is there any reason why he shouldn't? It seems fair in hindsight for him not to expect much inquisitiveness from the scholarly community. There is certainly no reason for him to have had higher expectations. The history of scholarship would have confirmed in his mind that he had nothing to fear from posterity. Their ineptitude and incompetence would leave him unscathed and unmolested. Prior to the release of *Gandhi: Behind the Mask of Divinity*, there was barely an attempt to penetrate the façade. In fact, people took the mask for the real McCoy. In fact, the word "persona," referring to the mask worn by actors upon the stage, is the same as that worn by the consummate actor Mahatma Gandhi, the mask people take for his true face. When are scholars going to wake up to what many among the "uneducated" masses in India already know, that it was all a ruse, a charade, and theatrical revelry of Academy Awards proportions?

Consistency in terms of testimony is vital. If disparate accounts given by the same witness do not match, the natural reaction of any investigator is to question the authenticity and truthfulness of the testimony. We simply wish to let the historical record speak for itself. We believe Gandhi has not been entirely on the level with the world. We believe that the historical record shows this. Gandhi has embellished and sensationalized the events that took place in South Africa a century ago out of political opportunism. It may be that this is justified. It may be that the ends justify the means. It may truly be the case that a white lie in service of a higher and nobler cause is a lie well told. We do not even intend to question this. All that we are attempting to show is that Gandhi is exploiting the politics of victimization to his own advantage, staging his own mini drama as state propaganda in an attempt to instill guilt in the imperialists and self-righteous conviction in the oppressed in hopes of hastening the day of liberation.

It should be clear to the reader by now that Gandhi's testimony does not hold up under cross-examination, and if it does not hold up in a court of law, why should it be allowed to stand unchallenged in an academic court? Subjecting Gandhi's four accounts of the racial train and coach incidents that allegedly took place in South Africa to skeptical inquiry illustrates that they don't pass even the most basic tests of modern skepticism. There is nothing consistent or reliable about any of his testimony. The fact that it has survived this long without being challenged is truly incredible to us and should be equally so to a questioning world. What this points to is the fact that mass media and popular culture decide how popular a figure is going to be. You can't blame the so-called ignorant masses for being duped by the popular image of an individual presented by the media on behalf of the Gandhi propaganda machine, for clearly the academic establishment is just as guilty of perpetuating myths without subjecting them to proper scrutiny. Much of the myth surrounding Gandhi has been perpetuated by academics who are afraid of examining the issue too closely for fear of damaging their reputations or academic standing. They don't want to be accused of maligning a hero or scandalizing a sacred cow. Instead, they embrace the clichés, the purported stories and myths and add to the dung heap of lies till it rises so high, it forms a veritable mountain, which, once erected, is difficult to remove, requiring the bulldozers of a generation of skeptics to reduce it to its proper size once more.

To give an example of the literature that has been overlooked in the case, Edward Donald Campbell was the stationmaster at the Pietermaritzburg station in 1893.[2] In his book, he has recorded a sensational incident that took place in June 1893 at the Pietermaritzburg train station dealing with an engine and its operator.[3] Keep in mind that this is the same year that the purported train incident at the same station was supposed to have occurred. The incident recorded by the stationmaster has nothing to do with Gandhi. This is important. This book was written in 1951 long after Campbell had retired and during the ensuing years after 1893 when Gandhi had become world famous and the train incident at Pietermaritzburg had become well known, and after Gandhi, the greatest leader of the twentieth century, had been assassinated in 1948 - a sequence of events that Campbell could not have possibly missed. Given all this, he failed to mention even a word on the incident that had allegedly taken place at the time when he himself was the stationmaster at Pietermaritzburg. This only means that for Campbell nothing had transpired in June 1893 related to Gandhi of any kind.

Further testimony for the mountain of testimony overlooked by Gandhian scholars of the 20th century is the article by F.E.T. Krause, "Gandhiji in South Africa" which was written after Gandhi's assassination in 1948. In this article, he offered a brief account of his own background, "It was in 1893 that I returned from Europe where I had been studying law, and started practice as an Advocate of the Old High Court of the South African Republic at Pretoria. I had taken a law degree in Holland, and had also been called to the English Bar, having been a student at the Middle Temple, London."[4]

What makes this article so important is that he met Gandhi in 1893:

Singh & Watson

I believe it was in 1893 when I met him in Pretoria. A brother of mine, Dr. A.E.J. Krause, was then the Attorney General of the Republic. The law at that time was that no native was allowed to be at large, especially at night, without being in possession of a pass from a white man. The police had a right to stop any native and to demand his pass and, if he could not produce one, he could be arrested, fined or imprisoned as if he had committed a criminal offence. [Gandhi] was liable to the same restrictive laws and so, to protect him, my brother granted him a Certificate of Exemption. I remember an incident which occurred when my brother had invited him one night to dinner. The natives, serving at the table, protested at being called upon to attend to an Indian, and it was only after it had been explained to them that [Gandhi] was a great man, just like a native chief, that they were prepared to continue their services.[5]

What intrigues us is that Mr. Krause had met Gandhi in 1893 in Pretoria. This had to be within days after Gandhi had landed in Pretoria after allegedly going through a series of racial assaults during his journey to Pretoria. If Gandhi's encounters were factually correct, there is no way that Krause could have possibly been oblivious to the bruises or other objective signs of injury that Gandhi must have sustained on his body. Moreover, if the racial encounters were accurate, Gandhi could not have resisted relating his story to Krause. And Krause would have mentioned it here in this article. Due to his complete silence on these alleged train and coach incidents, there is only one logical conclusion one can reach: The purported racial incidents never took place. Gandhi fabricated the entire story in order to represent himself as a victim of racial violence and discrimination, deriving direct benefit from the politics of victimization. In addition to this rather damning omission, in his brief account, F.E.T. Krause offers his impressions of Gandhi, whom he claims to have met on several occasions. It was in his official capacity as the State Prosecutor at Johannesburg that Mr. Krause came to know him. The nature of their relationship appears to have been strictly one of business and was apparently of an official, legal and political nature. There is no hint of any kind of intimacy or friendship in the account, though it is clear that Mr. Krause appears to have held Mr. Gandhi in high regard and to have respected him deeply. It is clear, however, from his testimony that it is in an official capacity that he came to know Gandhi: "In 1896, I was appointed the State Prosecutor at Johannesburg, and since that time and until the Anglo-Boer War in 1899, I had many opportunities of meeting Gandhi."[6] We are left in no doubt then that this man knows Gandhi personally and counts himself a competent judge of both his political views and his moral character. Having been ushered into Gandhi's company in an official capacity, he has grown familiar enough with his political views to offer his opinion of the man.

Mr. Krause begins his account with the statement "small things often have great repercussions."[7] To be subjected to racial discrimination is hardly a "small thing" as Mr. Krause calls it. Being a white man of privilege and never having tasted the bitterness of such a painful experience, Mr. Krause would of course be inclined to regard racial discrimination as a small matter. What the account given to us by Mr. Krause indicates is that Gandhi is not so much offended by the fact that apartheid laws exist and that people of color are forced to carry security passes, but that these laws applied to Gandhi and his fellow Indians, whom Krause informs us, he apparently viewed as a caste separate and above that of native [black] South Africans. The law that angered Gandhi was a law restricting the freedoms of the South African natives. It is doubtful whether Gandhi would have shown any objection to the law had its jurisdiction not extended to other people of color, which ultimately included himself and other Indians. Mr. Krause, then State Prosecutor of Johannesburg, a clear authority on the law, describes the security law as given above.

It so happens that Mr. Krause's brother was the Attorney General of the Republic. This served Gandhi well apparently as he could gain certain privileges through the association, which were unavailable to people less well connected. Mr. Krause recounts how it was only through the intervention of his brother, Dr. A.E.J.

Singh & Watson

Krause, the Attorney General, that Gandhi was able to obtain a level of immunity from the restrictive laws then in place.

What is clear here is the fact that it is not the law itself that offended Gandhi on moral grounds. What apparently offended Gandhi, according to Krause, is the fact that the apartheid laws applied to him, and by extension, his people:

> The impression I formed was that he resented the fact that his people should be and were placed in the same category as the uncivilized and primitive native, and that they should consequently be subject to the same restrictive laws. I believe the inference is justified that when on his first visit to the Transvaal he found that the civilized and educated Indian, by reason only of the colour of his skin, was looked upon as an inferior human being, that it was this circumstance which was the spark which fired him with that resolution to devote all his life and energy to right the wrongs of his people.[8]

One wonders if the catalyst for Gandhi's civil rights battle was truly humanitarian or whether it was rather the personal injuries and slights he had suffered that became the impetus for his dauntless fight. Indeed, Krause's unintended paradoxical remark perfectly sums up the ironic hypocrisy of Gandhi's own human rights position. It should be clear then, that Mr. Gandhi's motivations were predicated on "selfish" and not "unselfish" motives since he held himself and his people to be superior to the South African natives, as indicated by Krause's own inference and we quote:

> I believe the inference is justified that when on his first visit to the Transvaal he found that the civilized and educated Indian, by reason only of the colour of his skin, was looked upon as an inferior human being, that it was this circumstance which was the spark which fired him with that resolution to devote all his life and energy to right the wrongs of his people.[9]

Gandhi Under Cross-Examination

Before the advent of *Satyagraha in South Africa* and the *Auto-biography* in India, one biography in particular alluded to this series of racial train incidents as follows:

> Journeying to the Transvaal in a railway train, the guard unceremoniously ordered him to quit the first-class compartment, though he had paid for it, and betake himself to the van. Refusing, he was brutally dragged out with his luggage. And the train at once steamed off. All this was on British soil! In the Transvaal itself things were even worse. As he was sitting on the box of a coach on the way to Pretoria, the guard asked him to dismount because he wanted to smoke there. A refusal brought two consecutive blows in quick succession.[10]

Based on the weight of evidence and proper and due analysis, we can say that the racial incidents on board the trains and coaches did not take place. These lies had their inception in the face-to-face meetings that took place between Doke and Gandhi in 1908, meetings through which the first seed of "martyrdom" was laid in Gandhi's mind. From there, the building of the "martyrdom complex" within Gandhi continued to grow and shape itself in conformity to the surrounding political situation in British India. What Gandhi has left us is the composite story of his racial incidents concocted circumspectly over the years. That the individual attains martyrdom means that the individual has died for the cause. However, in Gandhi's case, the word was ingeniously applied to mean martyrdom through suffering. In other words, martyrdom without actual death! We have been able to reconstruct the different steps of Gandhi's composite story from the following:

After Rev. Doke planted the "martyr" idea in Gandhi's mind and he accepted it, he looked back into the past to see what racial incidents had actually transpired in South Africa. He remembered the incident of Tyab Mohamed who faced racism when forced to move from his compartment three times in a single night's train journey in November 1893.[11] Gandhi took that incident and transposed it into his own life in June 1893. The three humiliations of

Tyab Mohamed were converted into the three humiliations of Mahatma Gandhi, incidents he purportedly faced on his three-day journey from Durban to Pretoria as evident in the 1909 account of the biography authored by Doke. To this inventively transposed story, he added the assault of 1908 that occurred at the hands of a Pathan, replacing this burly Pathan with the burly Dutchman:

(1) Eviction from the train at the Pietermaritzburg train station.
(2) Facing racism on the stagecoach only to be followed by the assault of the Dutchman.
(3) Experiencing racial discrimination at the Grand National Hotel.

The first stage of the composite story had begun. The victim who went by the name Tyab Mohamed had his name and identity changed to M. K. Gandhi. Next, the assailant who went by the name of Mir Alam (the Pathan) had his name and identity changed to the unnamed Dutchman. This first stage of the story could have remained intact and functional as long as no one in South Africa found out about it. It should not surprise us that Gandhi did not promote Doke's book in South Africa lest it should jeopardize the "martyr complex" of his own invention. You can see there were very good reasons for this. Keep in mind that at this stage of the political agenda, Gandhi is embroiled in the Satyagraha war against the white minority government, and as a consequence, he and his associates faced a minor racial incident in September of 1913. Because of this minor incident, Gandhi wrote a letter of complaint to the General Manager of the railways. This 1909 stage of the composite story remained intact for the rest of Gandhi's time in South Africa until 1914 when he left for India via England.

In India, in 1919, Gandhi turned against the British colonial government. The politics resulted from that required that the "martyr complex" of 1909 composite story be readapted to a new set of political circumstances - requiring an entirely new embellishment. Therefore, the idea of martyrdom took on a whole new scope for Gandhi in light of the fight against British colonial rule. From that point, he decided to add to the composite stories already enshrined in the *Satyagraha in South Africa* and in the *Autobiography* and seduce an entire generation with his bag of tricks.

To concoct this new fabrication, he added the incident of September 1913 to the original 1909 composite story. Thus, in the accounts of *Satyagraha in South Africa* and the *Autobiography*, we see the new additions of "General Manager" and "Indians." The letter that Gandhi actually sent to the General Manager in September 1913 was transposed to June 1893 and appeared in both the *Satyagraha in South Africa* and *Autobiography* accounts. The company of Indians who were with him on the railway platform in September 1913 was transported in the time machine back to the alleged incident of June 1893. Their presence is thereby felt in both the *Satyagraha* and *Autobiography* accounts and they are seen facing discrimination routinely. For the benefit of his religiously induced readers both in India and abroad, he made the *Autobiography* account considerably longer and more complicated by bringing in new actors strategically placed to render the story of heartbreaking racism more dramatic and believable. This account had the desired impact: An appreciation in the minds of the readers of Gandhi's "martyr complex."

It appears that Gandhi never paid attention to the fact that his new additions to the composite story are inconsistent and some downright contradictory with his earlier account given in the 1909 story or perhaps he simply didn't care. Or he knew that the religious nature of his *Autobiography* would have such a profound effect on the consciousness of the world that no one would question the accuracy nor the veracity of his claims. As it turned out, Gandhi assumed rightly. There must have been another factor lurking in the back of his mind, and that was that those persons who had been in South Africa and had known the true Gandhi, had died by the time the *Satyagraha in South Africa* and the *Autobiography* accounts surfaced. So it seems Gandhi was safe from anyone in South Africa who could refute the composite stories that gave credence to the "martyr complex" he wished to cultivate.

As this composite story assumes larger proportions in the *Autobiography* account, this brings us to 1938 when Reverend John

Mott interviewed Gandhi.[12] Perhaps being unprepared and put on the spot, Gandhi couldn't remember all the details of the complex composite story. Or perhaps he did not want to leave exposed the intricate web of stories that he had established earlier. Whatever the actual case may be, he added another twist to the story by camouflaging his previous embellishments by limiting the story given in response to Mott's question on the train and coach incidents to a mere three acts, namely, eviction from the train, a confrontation with a white man in the room, and an assault by a coachman. As a result of this new racial twist and because of Rev. Mott and his popularity within the Christian churches, this 1938 account received more notoriety among the clergy. Unfortunately, no one within the ranks of the clergy ever set out to verify the validity of these incidents. In fact, in Gandhi's mind, this 1938 account was evidently meant to arouse the guilty conscience of the white man, who at the time was generally presumed to be perpetuating racial hatred against people of color.

We are the first people in history to have questioned the racial train and coach incidents. However, we are not the first in history to recognize Gandhi's ability to stretch the truth. Gandhi's propensity to concoct fables is mentioned in at least two other places.[13] [14] Given the lack of evidence for the purported racial incidents that took place on the trains and coaches, we must ask another difficult question: Did Gandhi travel by train and coach from Durban to Pretoria in June 1893? Mr. Mahadevan, a reputable Gandhian scholar believes that Gandhi traveled to Pretoria not in June but sometime later.[15] Athalye, who authored the book, *The Life of Mahatma Gandhi*, one of the first biographies of Gandhi following his return to India in 1915, reported that Gandhi boarded the train at Pietermaritzburg (instead of at Durban) and that is at this time that the racial incident ensued.[16] Athalye's book was published before both Gandhi's *Satyagraha in South Africa* and the *Autobiography*. Given the nature and the extent of Gandhi's "experiments with the truth" we need to ask ourselves: Is it possible now to write an accurate biography? Given the lapse of time and confounded by the real possibility of more lies scattered throughout the Gandhi accounts - all well guarded by the Gandhi propaganda machine - the task of writing an accurate biography of Gandhi will certainly be challenging for the next generation of scholars.[17] This task has only been further complicated by Gandhi's already well-oiled propaganda machine, which has turned out the most remarkable products, consistent with his own experiments with the truth. The comment of Bernard Aluwihari is perhaps the best example of this. The complexities of the scholarly task of putting Gandhi's life to rights has only been made more monumental by the glorifications and deifications of the counterfeit saint by Aluwihari, one of Gandhi's team to personally assist and serve him in England while attending the Round Table Conference in 1931. It was this particular member of Gandhi's public relations team who would engage in the shameless task of deifying and beatifying every letter in Gandhi's name with a childish acronym, the exercise of an adolescent mind whose dispensation is on a par with the simple-minded flock of people that soak up such drivel like a sponge. Just read Aluwihari's acronym yourself and reflect on the sheer banality of the exercise, which is as childish and simple-minded a version of the man and his life as you could hope to find:[18]

G for God
A for Ass
N for Noodle
D for Devil
H for Hell
I for Idiot

It would be comforting if only schoolteachers and their impressionable young pupils embraced these quaint and innocent nursery rhyme versions of history, but it is with the very same simple-mindedness that so many university professors accept this baby formula and lap it up. It is they who repeat the slogans like those of Einstein, "Generations to come will scarce believe that such a one as this walked the earth in flesh and blood" as though it were a mantra for endowing one with enlightenment as opposed to a slogan for programming the mind. To repeat Goebbels, "Repeat a lie often enough and people will believe it."

NOTES

[1] For example while inquiring into the incident at Johnston's Family Hotel in Pretoria, as recorded in Gandhi's Autobiography, we found that Gandhi has misrepresented the facts once again. L.W. Ritch, one of the white associates of Gandhi in South Africa states that he first met Gandhi in 1895, and some considerable time after that, he himself helped Gandhi to find lodgings at a hotel owned by Heath - a well known hotel owner in Johannesburg. The details of Ritch's account are remarkably similar to those described by Gandhi in his account of what allegedly transpired at Johnston's Family Hotel in 1893. See *Incidents of Gandhiji's Life*, edited by Chandrashankar Shukla, Vora and Co. Pub., Bombay, 1949, pp. 287-91.

[2] Burnett Britton. *Gandhi Arrives in South Africa.* Canton, Maine: Greenleaf Books, 1999, page 20. In a personal communication the author has confirmed of Mr. Campbell as the station-master of Pietermaritzburg railway station in 1893 and provided a book reference of *Who's Who in Natal* (1906).

[3] Edward D. Campbell. *The Birth and Development of the Natal Railways.* Pietermaritzburg: Shuter and Shooter, 1951, p. 132.

[4] Quoted in *Reminiscences of Gandhiji*, edited by Chandrashanker Shukla. Vora and Co. Pub., Bombay, 1951, p. 157.

[5] Ibid., pp.159-60.

[6] Ibid., p. 160.

[7] Ibid., p. 160.

[8] Ibid., p. 160.

[9] Ibid., p. 160.

[10] Taken from *Mahatma Gandhi: His Life, Writings, and Speeches*, Ganesh & Co. Madras 1921, page 13. The chapter is titled "Mohandas Karamchand Gandhi: A Sketch of his life and Career." Natesan and his associates in south India most probably wrote this book. Whether Gandhi was consulted and approved it is not known to date.

[11] CWMG 1, #106, p. 420. On a different note, in a thesis at the University of Natal (2002), titled, "Turbans and Top Hats: Indian Interpreters in the Colony of Natal 1880-1910," Prinisha Badassy, the author, mentioned the case of an Indian, named David Vinden (1859-1919), who encountered a racial incident on the Natal railway on October 19, 1906. Badassy observed that this incident was

strikingly reminiscent of the incident Mahatma Gandhi purportedly suffered as shown in the film "Gandhi." We find that the case of Vinden has no commonality with the case of Gandhi whether in the movie or otherwise.

[12] It is clear from reading Reverend John Mott's biography that in spite of some of his reservations about Gandhi's stand on Christianity and its missionary activities, he never knew about the lies pertaining to the 1893 racial incidents that Gandhi had communicated to him.

[13] Harry F. Field. *After Mother India*. London: Jonathan Cape and Company, 1929.

[14] T.K. Mahadevan. *The Year of the Phoenix: Gandhi's Pivotal Year in South Africa, 1893-1894*. Chicago: World Without War Publishers, 1982.

[15] Ibid., p. 35.

[16] D.V. Athalye. *The Life of Mahatma Gandhi*. Poona, India: Swadeshi Publishing Company, 1923 (1st edition); 2nd edition in 1926.

[17] Another example worth reading is that of Rev. Martin Luther King, Jr. who delivered a Palm Sunday Sermon on March 22, 1959 at the Dexter Avenue Baptist Church just days after he had returned from India. This is the only sermon in which King referred in some detail to the events of Gandhi's life, including the racial train incident: "And one day he [Gandhi] was taking a train to Pretoria, and he had first-class accommodations on that train. And when they came to took up the tickets they noticed that he was an Indian, that he had a brown face, and they told him to get out and move on to the third-class accommodation, that he wasn't supposed to be there.... And Gandhi that day refused to move, and they threw him off the train. And there, in that cold station that night, he stayed all night, and he started meditating on his plight and the plight of his people. And he decided from that point on that he would never submit himself to injustice, or to exploitation.... As he started organizing his forces in South Africa, he read the Sermon on the Mount...." [The Papers of Martin Luther King, Jr. Volume 5: *Threshold of a New Decade, January 1959-December 1960*. Berkeley: University of California Press, 2005, pp. 145-157]

[18] Horace Alexander. *Gandhi Through Western Eyes*. Philadelphia, PA: New Society Publishers, 1984, page 84 fn. With respect to Aluwihari's acronym, Agatha Harrison believes that "N" stands for "No one." Bernard Aluwihari had accompanied Gandhi from India and returned to India with Gandhi and his accompanying entourage. [*The Americanization of Gandhi*, pp. 268-69]

Conclusion

Modern Echoes

~

M ayawati Kumari is the Chief Minister of Uttar Pradesh, India's most populous state. Although she is from the lowest caste, once called "Untouchables," she has been successful enough to be counted by *Forbes* magazine in 2008 as 59th out of the 100th most powerful women in the world.[1] Mayawati is a profound exception in India, where the vast majority of Untouchables and other lower castes live in extreme poverty. In 2007, she had hard words for Gandhi, blaming him for planting the seeds of division within India: "It was he (Gandhi) who gave the name *Harijan* to people from lower castes and weaker sections of society. He divided Indian society into two categories - the weaker sections and upper castes."[2] [Editor's note: See Appendix V for an explanation of *Harijan*.]

On the other hand, there is Narendra Modi, the upper-caste Chief Minister of Gujarat, Gandhi's home state. In 2007, he claimed: "We Gujaratis are followers of Mahatma Gandhi. We are peace loving people."[3] Jewish-American journalist Robert Kaplan profiled Narendra Modi "India's New Face," an April 2009 article published in *The Atlantic* magazine. Kaplan described Modi as "the brightest star in the Hindu-chauvinist Bharatiya Janata Party," saying:

"Under Modi, Gujarat has become an economic dynamo. But he also presided over India's worst communal riots in decades, a 2002 slaughter that left almost 2,000 Muslims dead. Exploiting the insecurities and tensions stoked by India's opening to the world, Modi has turned his state into a stronghold of Hindu extremism, shredding Gandhi's vision of secular coexistence in the process. One day, he could be governing the world's largest democracy."[4]

Modi has been denied a visa twice by the U.S. State Department because of his unquestionable complicity in the 2002 Hindu pogrom in Gujarat. Yet he is poised to possibly become Prime Minister of India. This gets at the core issue of how India can produce a leader who is simultaneously a staunch proponent of Hindu extremism and yet claims to be a follower of Gandhi. Are politicians like Modi actually adhering to the mythical image of Gandhi or are they simply perpetuating the Gandhian experimentation with the truth?

Whatever the answer, Modi's case is one example of how nuclear India, despite being an emerging world power, remains deeply divided along caste and religious lines. After reading this book, one can certainly sympathize with Mayawati's belief that Gandhi's racial views harmed the Dalits. As Mayawati asserted, Gandhi bears much responsibility for the strife in India, which is why we need an in-depth analysis of his myth.

Gandhi has clearly divided prominent Indian leaders of varying castes. This is the way throughout much of India, where those who invoke Gandhi generally do so to justify actions contrary to his mythical image. A good example is the former prime minister, Indira Gandhi (no relation to Mohandas). In 1984, on Indira Gandhi's orders, the Indian Army attacked the early 17th century Golden Temple in Amritsar, resulting in the deaths of thousands of Sikhs. In an interview with *Time* magazine about the attack, Indira Gandhi deepened the debate on Gandhi when she said: "Mahatma Gandhi, in his time, accepted that necessity."[5] This comment appears specifically crafted to justify the bloody attack while pacifying the Western mind by masking the violence with the peaceful image of Gandhi.

To see just how Gandhi influenced Indian society, we need only look at the condition of the country today. Although Modi claims Gujaratis are "peace loving people," the reality is that Gujarat, like the rest of India, is wracked by anti-minority violence. Whether Buddhist, Christian, Dalit, Muslim, or Sikh, every Indian minority is threatened by consistent and frequent persecution and state-sponsored Hindu pogroms. Amnesty International, Human Rights Watch, and other groups have published thousands of pages documenting the endemic persecution of Indian minorities. We will present a few examples of the violence, which has gone practically unchecked since 1947.

In March 2009, two Dalit men were hacked to death for attempting to worship at a Hindu temple.[6] Fundamentalist Hindus brutalized the Christian community of Orissa in the summer of 2008, raping, torturing, and murdering Christians while burning thousands of their homes and churches.[7] The 2002 Gujarat pogrom resulted in the murder of up to 2000 Muslims, many of whom were gang raped or burned alive by Hindu fundamentalists.[8] In 1992, a huge mob of Bharatiya Janata Party members and other Hindu nationalists destroyed Babri Masjid, a 16th century [Muslim] mosque in Uttar Pradesh.[9] There are many more such examples we could offer, but for reasons of brevity we will end here.

Gandhi is considered the Father of Nonviolence. He is also honored within India as *Rashtrapita* or "Father of the Nation." Yet India is torn by ongoing anti-minority violence, which sparks a question. Why is India, of which Gandhi is the *Rashtrapita*, so violent? Perhaps if India placed any real value on the myth of Gandhi, the world would see an actual transformation of India into an internally peaceful nation. Instead, we are left with an India which reflects the real (and disturbingly racist) Gandhi far more accurately than the mythical Gandhi.

The constitution of India is heavily influenced by the "Father of the Nation's" ideology. Indeed, he helped to lay the framework for a constitutionally mandated anti-minority policy. On December 4, 1947, Gandhi explained his expansionist ideal for Hinduism, saying: "It cannot be said that Sikhism, Hinduism, Buddhism and Jainism are separate religions. All these four faiths and their offshoots are one. Hinduism is an ocean into which all the rivers run. It can absorb Islam and Christianity and all the other religions and only then can it become an ocean. Otherwise it remains merely a stream along which large ships cannot ply."[10]

This philosophy was enshrined in Article 25 of India's Constitution, which reads:

25. Freedom of conscience and free profession, practice and propagation of religion.-

(1) Subject to public order, morality and health and to the other provisions of this Part, all persons are equally entitled to freedom of conscience and the right freely to profess, practise and propagate religion.

(2) Nothing in this article shall affect the operation of any existing law or prevent the State from making any law-

(a) regulating or restricting any economic, financial, political or other secular activity which may be associated with religious practice;

(b) providing for social welfare and reform or the throwing open of Hindu religious institutions of a public character to all classes and sections of Hindus.

Explanation I.- The wearing and carrying of kirpans shall be deemed to be included in the profession of the Sikh religion.

Explanation II.- In sub-clause (b) of clause (2), *the reference to Hindus shall be construed as including a reference to persons professing the Sikh, Jaina or Buddhist religion, and the reference to Hindu religious institutions shall be construed accordingly* [emphasis added].

When one reflects on Article 25, it is clearly tantamount to a bloodless genocide against India's minorities. With the stroke of a pen, it seeks to forcibly convert the listed minorities to Hinduism.

Those minorities who challenge their classification as "Hindus" face harsh rebuke by the military might of the nuclear Indian state. Considering the underlying Gandhian philosophy of Article 25, the forced identification of even Muslims and Christians as "Hindus" is not off the charts. If Gandhi was truly a civil rights model who loved unity, why does his philosophy as written into the Indian Constitution seek to force non-Hindus to adopt his religion?

Gandhi's fast and loose handling of the truth, which he called "experimentation," has gone unchallenged for too long. Gandhi produced such a potent experiment that it caused his victims to consider their victimizer a hero while many others sing his praises. Now we must ask whether the experimentation with the truth has stopped? Is the laboratory where Gandhi mixed his potions of truth, half-truth, and lies closed? Or do others toil in that same laboratory to carry on his work with greater potency?

Many who accept the reality of Gandhi's racism in South Africa also frequently ask if he changed later in life. They suggest that perhaps at some point Gandhi repented of his ways, made amends, and altered his behavior from then on. However, Mayawati's observations are based on actions years later in India, far from the shores of South Africa. Furthermore, Gandhi's writings nowhere contain anything even remotely resembling an apology for or repudiation of his actions in South Africa. He was consistent in his racial and religious views from Africa to India, advocating an Indo-Aryan purity of race ideology the entire time. A sampling of that consistency can be seen in Appendix V. Furthermore, even at the height of his popularity as a messiah of nonviolence, Gandhi toyed with violence, as documented in Appendix VI.

Blacks throughout the world have been twice victimized by Gandhi: first by Gandhi himself and then by his "propagandhi." Even after helping lay the foundation for apartheid in South Africa, Gandhi found a way to do more harm by then rewriting history and casting himself as a champion of black civil rights. Sentletse Diakanyo, a young, black South African columnist for the Mail & Guardian online, reflected on this suggestion in a 2008 article. He wrote:

> The greatest injustice against the struggle for liberation of black people was the projection of Mahatma Gandhi as committed to a cause against segregation. It is a fallacy that Gandhi in his struggles had any interests of black people at heart. His was a selfish cause to advance interests of Indians while encouraging continuing subjugation of black people.... To continue to honour and celebrate this man is to insult humanity![11]

Can society continue to view Gandhi as the great Mahatma found in his myths? So far, we have proved that Gandhi fabricated the train incident, promoted racism and segregation in South Africa, fought in a war to suppress blacks, and may have even lied about the *Brahmacharya* vow. Despite that, he is continually propagated as a hero for the black community and portrayed as a Great Soul (Mahatma). At this point we have no choice but to ask: is it possible that Gandhi was no Mahatma?

Indeed, we must ask many hard questions. Are blacks today made to feel an unresolved debt for Gandhi's mythical sacrifices? Who benefits from continued propagation of Gandhi? Who funded the "Gandhi" film, which was the single most influential tool in spreading the Gandhi myth? Who pays for the hundreds of Gandhi statues which dot our globe (see Plate 7). Academics, politicians, civil rights activists, black leaders and religious figures need to seek answers to these questions. Furthermore, the world must address the issue of Gandhi and confront his proponents, who deceptively cultivate African gratitude (see Plate 8) with the modern-day toys and trinkets of the Gandhi myth.

In June 2007, the United Nations passed a resolution declaring October 2, Gandhi's birthday, an "International Day of Non-Violence." India sponsored the resolution and Anand Sharma, India's Minister of State for External Affairs at the time, introduced it to the U.N. General Assembly. In his remarks, Sharma said Gandhi pursued "a just and equitable world where people live with dignity and in peace and harmony with each other in diverse and pluralistic societies."[12] This resolution is yet another trophy on the shelf for those propagating Gandhi, demanding a study of how his proponents benefit from this propagation? Do his proponents sincerely believe they can continue Gandhi's experiment without addressing his historical past?

Many people insist that the Gandhi myth has inspired much good in this world and should therefore be allowed to remain intact. Why ruin a good story, even if it's not true? In fact, if Gandhians practiced what they preached, there might be little reason to expose Gandhi. However, we all too frequently find Gandhi's proponents emulating his tactic of preaching peace with his mouth while practicing violence and prejudice with his hands. Like countless other nations which bear no allegiance to Gandhi, India remains torn by violence and racial strife. Gandhi's proponents consistently use his "Father of Nonviolence" image to conceal their underlying exercises of violence and prejudice. This is evidenced by everyone from Narendra Modi to Indira Gandhi, who employ Gandhi's faux persona to mask the ongoing persecution of minorities within India.

The peace movement in particular needs to seriously reexamine Gandhi. No other figure has earned a higher place within that movement than Mohandas Gandhi, who is unfortunately essentially credited as the founding father of modern day peace activism. Sadly, this means the movement's ideological foundations lie over deadly fault lines. As more and more people become aware of the historical Gandhi, the peace movement risks global skepticism of its noble cause because of its close association with the man.

Justice for those harmed by Gandhi's anti-black activism demands that the truth be told. According to Sentletse Diakanyo, promoting Gandhi as a civil rights hero is "the greatest injustice against the struggle for liberation of black people." Considering all this, we are reminded of Dr. Martin Luther King, Jr.'s words, when he wrote: "Injustice anywhere is a threat to justice everywhere." Exposing the truth about Gandhi, therefore, should be done not only to prevent people from using his image to mask their questionable activities, but also simply for the sake of justice.

Dr. King fought and died to give civil rights to American blacks, boldly standing in the path of racism. His efforts benefited millions, inspiring civil rights struggles for minorities in America and around the world. People particularly remember Dr. King's famous speech, in which he said: "I have a dream that my four little children will one day live in a nation where they will not be judged by the color of their skin but by the content of their character."

In 1905, ten years after his post office segregation victory, Gandhi expressed his own dream. He wrote to the Minister of Education to complain about a decision to integrate Indian and black schoolchildren, saying: "The decision to open the school for all Coloured children is unjust to the Indian community, and is a departure from the assurance given... that the school will be reserved for Indian children only."[13]

The paths charted by King and Gandhi were starkly divergent, never to meet. King's path leads to a belief in all men being created equal, while Gandhi's path teaches that all men are forever unequal. We should celebrate men like Dr. King, who spoke, believed, and lived his nonviolent message of racial justice and a color-blind society, not men like Gandhi who spent decades promoting racial segregation and fought to suppress minority rights.

Gandhi's myth warrants serious academic investigation. Rather than accepting the myth as a "good story," our civilization has a moral obligation to own up to the truth about Gandhi. Simultaneously, we must also decry the unacceptable propagation of Gandhi. If we refuse to do so, we risk becoming willing participants in the ongoing experimentation with truth and its consequences. Perpetuating the myth merely displaces past heroes and those yet to come who truly deserve to be honored.

Gandhi has been placed on a pedestal as the champion of nonviolence, peace, diversity and pluralism. Yet whomever our civilization chooses to place on that pedestal is a reflection of what we believe. When we honor and even bow down to the person on that pedestal, we are implicitly agreeing with their actions and beliefs. This fact should inspire a call for deeper examination of Gandhi, who has been so frequently equated with Jesus, Buddha, and Mohammed. Does he deserve to be on that pedestal? This is a verdict our civilization must make as we progress and evolve.

NOTES

[1] Mary Ellen Egan and Chana R. Schoenberger, "The World's 100 Most Powerful Women," *Forbes*, August 27, 2008.

[2] "Mahatma Gandhi divided India on caste lines: Mayawati," eNews.com, October 27, 2007.

[3] Nagendar Sharma, "Modi invokes the Mahatma," *Hindustan Times*, December 8, 2007.

[4] Robert D. Kaplan, "India's New Face," *The Atlantic*, April 2009.

[5] "The Roots of Violence," *Time*, July 2, 1984.

[6] "Two Dalits hacked to death," *The Hindu*, March 7, 2009.

[7] U.S. Department of State, "2008 Human Rights Reports: India," February 25, 2009.

[8] Human Rights Watch, "We Have No Orders To Save You: State Participation and Complicity in Communal Violence in Gujarat," April 2002.

[9] Mark Tully, "Tearing down the Babri Masjid," BBC News, December 5, 2002.

[10] CWMG, Vol. 97, p. 465.

[11] Sentletse Diakanyo, "On Mahatma Gandhi, his pathetic racism and advancement of segregation of black people," *Mail & Guardian Online's Thought Leader*, October 17, 2008.

[12] "Introduction of the Draft Resolution on 'International Day of Non-Violence'," Anand Sharma, United Nations General Assembly, June 15, 2007.

[13] CWMG, Vol. 4, p. 402.

Glossary

~

Ahimsa: "Nonviolence."

Avatar: A god incarnated in a human form.

British Raj: British colonial rule.

Brahmin: The highest of the four caste groups.

Brahmacharya: Observance of chastity.

Caste: Color. The top three castes are collectively referred to as "upper castes." Those of the Shudra caste are called "lower caste."

Coolie: An unskilled laborer or a porter.

Dalit: The modern term for "Untouchable."

Gujarat: A state in western India and Gandhi's birthplace.

Gujarati: A language of the people of the state of Gujarat. Also, any person with a background from Gujarat is referred to as Gujarati.

Kaffir: A derogatory term for the black people of South Africa. Use of the word is equivalent to the term "nigger" and is considered hate speech in modern day South Africa.

Ji: An honorific suffix used to show reverence, as in "Mahatmaji" or "Gandhiji."

Mahatma: Great soul.

Pathan: A resident of the Northwest Frontier territory of Pakistan and adjoining Afghanistan.

Sannyasi (or Sunyasi): A wandering recluse.

Satyagraha: Nonviolent resistance.

Satyagrahi: One who practices Satyagraha.

Shudra: The lowest of the main caste groups. Shudras are essentially serfs.

Swaraj: Self-rule or independence.

Untouchable: The lowest, outcaste group.

Varna: A Hindu term for "caste."

NOTE: Some words in this book are spelled differently from the standard American usage. These words spelled by Gandhi (for example "colour" rather than "color") are grammatically accurate using the British English system of spelling.

Appendix I

Gandhi Timeline

~

Mohandas K. Gandhi lived to be seventy-nine years old (1869-1948) and his life was extremely complex. There are so many rooms in the mansion of his life it is bewildering to even the most adept researcher. To fully comprehend Gandhi's encounters on the trains and coaches, it is important to understand his life timeline, which spanned the continents of Asia, Africa, and Europe.

Before South Africa

DATE	DESCRIPTION
1869	Gandhi born in Porbandar.
1880	Enters Kathiawar High School.
1882	Marries Kasturba.
1888	
Spring	Birth of his first son, Harilal.
Sept.	Sails for England to study law.
Nov.	Admitted into the Inner Temple.
1891	
June 10	Called to the Bar.

June 12   Sails for India.

1892
May   Fails to establish law practice.
Spring   Birth of his second son, Manilal.

1893
Apr.   Sails for South Africa, alone, to take up a job as a
                   legal advisor.

South Africa (1893-1914)

1893
May   Gandhi visits the Durban courthouse.
June   While traveling, he is supposedly ordered off the
                   train at Pietermaritzburg railway station. While
                   traveling, he is supposedly assaulted on the coach.

1894
Aug.   Natal Indian Congress is established.

1896
June 5   Sails to India.
Nov. 30   Sails for South Africa along with his family.
Dec. 12   Gandhi reaches Durban.

1897
Jan. 13   Gandhi attacked by mob upon leaving the ship.
May   Birth of his third son, Ramdas.

1899
Dec.   Left for the Boer War - Indian Ambulance Corps.

1900
Jan.   Corps is active in the Boer War.
May 22   Birth of his fourth son, Devadas.

1901
Oct.   Gandhi leaves South Africa for India.

1902
Dec.   Returns without his family to South Africa after failing to establish a legal practice in India.

1903
Feb.   Opens a law office in Johannesburg. British Indian Association is established.

1904
Feb.   Plague breaks out in Indian Location in Johannesburg.
Nov-Dec   Phoenix Settlement established.
Dec. 24   First volume of *Indian Opinion* issued from Phoenix Settlement.

1905
Aug.   Natal Legislative Council passes poll tax bill. Gandhi calls for revision of the bill.

1906
Jan. 1   Poll tax enforced on Indians over the age of 18.
Mar. 17   Gandhi begins to organize against the Zulu Rebellion.
June-July   Gandhi participates in war against Blacks.
Sept. 11   Calls for withdrawal of Asiatics. Registration Bill in Johannesburg.
Oct. 3   Sails for U.K. to seek redress from the British government. Returns to South Africa on Dec. 18.

1907
July 31   General strike after a mass meeting.

1908

Jan. 10	Sentenced to two months imprisonment; released on Jan. 30. In South Africa, he goes to prison three more times.
February	Gandhi is assaulted by a Pathan. Gandhi and Rev. J. J. Doke's friendship grows.

1909

June 23	Gandhi sails for England.
Oct. 29	His first biography "*M. K. Gandhi: An Indian Patriot in South Africa*" is published.
Nov. 23	Gandhi writes *Hind Swaraj* on his journey back to South Africa.

1910

May 30	At Tolstoy Farm for passive resisters, the struggle continues.

1914

Jan. 13	Gandhi and General Smuts begin negotiations, resulting in a compromise.
July 18	Gandhi sails for England, never to return to South Africa again.
Aug. 4	World War I starts.
Aug.	Gandhi forms Indian Volunteer Corps, but falls ill with pleurisy and is unable to continue command task.
Dec. 19	Sails for India, reaches Bombay on Jan. 9, 1915. Awarded *Kaiser-i-Hind* medal.

India 1915-1948

1916	Gandhi starts participating in Indian politics. He takes on other non-political causes dealing with religion, "human rights," etc.
1918	Gandhi starts to participate actively in promoting military activities for World War I.

Singh & Watson

Apr. 30	Promotes his past military leadership roles in South Africa to achieve present goals of recruiting more Indians for the war. He continues to act as recruiting sergeant for the British government. World War I ends.
1919	Gandhi turns against the government. First nation-wide civil disobedience campaign. Campaign against the Rowlatt Bills in April fails. Tragedy at Jallianwala Bagh in Amritsar, and other events.
May 7	*Young India** starts from Bombay.
Sept. 7	First issue of *Navajivan** in Gujarati.
Oct. 8	*Young India* moves to Ahmedabad, Gujarat. Gandhi assumes editorship of *Young India*. * Both newspapers existed before Gandhi assumed control of them.
1920	Gandhi writes his "The Doctrine of the Sword."
1921	His second nationwide non-cooperation movement fails. He decides to write an autobiography.
Nov. 17	Gandhi writes "Why Did I Assist In War."
Nov. 19	City of Bombay experiences riots.
1922	
Mar. 10	Gandhi is arrested and sentenced to six years in jail at Yeravda Prison.
1923	
Nov. 26	He begins writing *Satyagraha in South Africa*.
1924	
Feb. 4	Released from jail.
1925	
Dec. 3	Weekly installments of his A*utobiography* appear in *Young India*.

1926

Apr. 5 — *Unity* begins to publish his *Autobiography* on a weekly basis until Nov. 25, 1929.

1929

Mar. — Interviews with foreign visitors.

July — "To the American Negro: A Message from Mahatma Gandhi" is published in *Crisis.*

1930

Jan. — Indian Declaration of Independence Proclamation.

Mar. 12 — Begins Salt March

Apr. 6 — Breaks salt law on the beach at Dandi.

1931

Sept. 12 — Gandhi attends Round Table conference in London.

Dec. 14 — Meets Romain Rolland in Switzerland.

1932

Aug. 17 — Prime Minister Ramsay MacDonald hands down the Communal Award.

Sept. 20 — Gandhi begins a fast unto death in protest of separate electorates for Untouchables.

Sept. 24 — Poona Pact signed.

Oct. 26 — Organizes *Harijan Sevak Sangh.*

1933

Feb. 11 — First issue of a weekly paper, *Harijan,* in English.

Feb. 23 — First issue of *Harijan Sevak* in Hindi.

Mar. 12 — First issue of *Harijanbandhu* released from Poona in Gujarati language.

1936

Feb. 21 — Interview with American Negro delegation.

1937

| Jan. | Meeting with Dr. Benjamin E. Mays. Meeting with Dr. Tobias. |

1938
Dec.   Interview with John R. Mott.

1939
Jan. 1   Interview with Chinese delegation. Interview with Reverend S.S. Tema.

1942
May 16   Interview with the press.
June 4   Interview with Louis Fischer.
June 10   Interview with Preston Grover.
July 1   Letter to Franklin D. Roosevelt.

1945
May 30   Interview with Denton J. Brooks, Jr.

1946
Jan.   Talk with Indonesian sailors. Discussion with Black soldiers.

Mar. 24   Statement to the press regarding South Africa's "Land and Franchise Bill."
Apr.   Interview with South African delegation.
July 17   Interview with Louis Fischer.

1947
Aug. 15   The British leave India. The colony is divided into Pakistan and India.
Aug.   Meeting with Dr. William Stuart Nelson.

1948
Jan. 30   Gandhi is assassinated.

After Gandhi's Death

1948   Beginning of apartheid laws in South Africa.

1950s-1990   Institutionalization and implementation of various apartheid laws in South Africa.

1958-1994   *The Collected Works of Mahatma Gandhi* is published as a project of the government of India in 100 volumes, about 50,000 pages. Also published is *Sampurna Gandhi Vangmaya*, the Hindi translation of *Collected Works*. A translation in the Gujarati language is near completion. In 2000, a revised sixth edition of Collected Works is published.

1964
June   Nelson Mandela is convicted of sabotage and treason and sentenced to life in prison.

1982   *Gandhi* movie is released.

1990   President FW de Klerk reforms the apartheid laws and Nelson Mandela is released.

1993
June   Gandhi statue is set up in Pietermaritzburg, South Africa. Mandela and de Klerk are awarded the Nobel Peace Prize.

1994
Apr.   Nelson Mandela is elected president in the first multi-racial democratic elections in South Africa.

1997
Apr.   Conferral of the "Freedom of Pietermaritzburg" award on Mahatma Gandhi.

1997

Oct.	Nelson Mandela refuses to rename the Pietermaritz-burg railway station in honor of Mahatma Gandhi.
1999	Nelson Mandela steps down as president of South Africa.
2002 Oct.	Participants of Miss India Worldwide pageant ceremoniously follow historic trail of Mahatma Gandhi by train in South Africa, including Maritz-burg.
2003 Feb.	Indian cricket team boards the Gandhi memorial train and reenacts Mahatma Gandhi's train journey of 1893 up to Piermaritzburg.
2003 Oct.	City of Johannesburg set up a statue showing Gandhi as a young lawyer at the Gandhi Square in central Johannesburg, South Africa.

Appendix II

Lapses in the Account

~

Mr. Hassim Seedat, a lawyer in Durban, is the one responsible for selecting June 7, 1893 as the date of Gandhi's alleged racial assault at the Maritzburg train station. Mr. Seedat has also selected May 23, 1893 as the date of Gandhi's alleged arrival in Durban. In his autobiography, Gandhi stated that he reached Durban "towards the close of May," and after a stay of only a few days - "on the seventh or eighth day after my arrival" - he boarded the train in which he was to have the racial encounter at the train station. Mr. Seedat has thus far failed to respond to our inquiry as to how he was able to arrive at these exact dates. In commenting on the Pietermaritzburg experience that was alleged to have occurred in 1893, Seedat has noted the inconsistency between the 1938 account by Dr. John R. Mott and earlier accounts. After quoting the biographical account of the Maritzburg incident as recorded by Rev. Mott in an interview, Seedat undertakes a defense of Gandhi's shoddy memory:

> The event Gandhi described had taken place nearly forty-six years before, on the night of 7 June 1893. It is not surprising that after all that time there should have been some errors in Gandhi's recollection. He had arrived in Durban from India earlier than he remembered, on 23 May 1893, and it was not the railway guard that had turned him off the train at Pietermaritzburg station. In fact, the guard had summoned the aid of a police constable when Gandhi had

refused to budge from his seat, and the constable had cere-
moniously pushed him out of the compartment and pitched
his luggage after him (Memorial Edition, p. 20, 1993). This
paper also appeared in *The Pietermaritzburg Experience"
in Pietermaritzburg 1838-1988: A New Portrait of an African City* on page 210.

What is clear from Hassim Seedat's apology for Gandhi recorded above is that he is anxious to explain away Gandhi's mistakes as apparent lapses of memory. The justification for this is
that the events described occurred forty-six years before the interview, and without the aid of diary notes referring to the incident,
Gandhi is to be forgiven for his faulty memory. However, we are
not as forgiving on that account. To be subjected to racial assault is
one of the most humiliating experiences in life. As for Seedat's
reference to Gandhi's confusion over the exact date of his arrival,
insisting that he arrived in Durban earlier than he had recalled, in
no way inoculates Gandhi against other criticisms that can be
brought to bear on his flawed memory.

To reiterate a point mentioned earlier, in the 1925 autobiographical account, Gandhi refers to the waiting room at Pieter-
maritzberg Station being empty when he first entered it and that it
was not until midnight that he was joined by another passenger.
Yet, in the 1938 account, Gandhi insists that the waiting room was
already occupied by a white man upon his arrival, and that he was
afraid of this stranger. Given the timeframe when Gandhi issued
this 1938 statement, we believe it was pure political opportunism
that caused him to fabricate this story after the fact. Seeing as it
was precisely his aim to shame the white man into relinquishing
the "Jewel in the Crown," it was only natural that he should seek to
make of the white man the greatest boogeyman that ever lived.
One further point has to be made on this score. Differences between the 1924 and 1925 accounts of what took place at Pieter-
maritzberg are more dramatic than those found in the 1925 and
1938 accounts and these accounts are only a year apart. Blaming
discrepancies in the 1938 account on the lapse of many years is not
a sufficient defense. Indeed, the entire Gandhi myth hinges on

Singh & Watson

these incidents alleged to have taken place in South Africa in 1893. It is these incidents that Gandhi claimed launched his career in non-violent resistance.

With respect to June 3, 1893 as a date to the alleged racial incident, please see the following reference: Fatima Meer, ed. *The South African Gandhi: An Abstract of the Speeches and Writings of M. K. Gandhi 1893-1914.* Durban, South Africa: Madiba Publishers, 1996, page 32.

Appendix III

Gandhi and His Brother

~

The situation arose when Gandhi decided to take his brother's part in a contentious matter that placed his brother's career prospects in jeopardy. The situation involved an accusation hanging over his brother's head that he had provided false advice when employed in the office of secretary and advisor to the late Ranasaheb (head of the princely state) of Porbandar. The matter had been referred to the Political Agent (a British White official) and had placed Gandhi's brother in a very compromising situation. As Mohandas Gandhi was acquainted with the Political Agent, whom he had known in London, his brother appealed to Mohandas to talk to the Agent (referred to by the name sahib) in order to disabuse him of the prejudice and antipathy he felt toward him. While reluctant to curry favor in this way, Mohandas appears to have felt pressured by filial loyalty to take his brother's part in the affair, a forgivable sin in its own right. Approaching the white-sahib of his acquaintance to appeal for clemency on his brother's behalf, Mohandas reluctantly brought the matter to his attention. Putting the case before him, Mohandas could see that the white-sahib was displeased and could not be budged on the matter. If anything Gandhi's intervention appeared to do more harm than good, since it seemed to only confirm the white-sahib in his opinion that Gandhi's brother was a schemer and an opportunist. We find no irony in this, since after all the two Gandhis are brothers. The white-sahib's words leave no room for doubt on his position. He is as firm and unbending as a Roman column:

> Your brother is an intriguer. I want to hear no more from you. I have no time. If your brother has anything to say, let him apply through the proper channel.... You must go now. (The Autobiography, p. 98)

When Gandhi appealed to the white-sahib to hear him out, this only incensed the gentleman more. It was this further affront that caused him to summon his peon, whom he instructed to show Gandhi the door. Displaying further reluctance to leave, Gandhi was then manhandled by the peon, who took him by the shoulders and showed him out bodily. Gandhi was so outraged by this quite minor and arguably even justifiable conduct on the part of the white-sahib that he presented the sahib shortly thereafter with a letter demanding an apology, the absence of which would provoke legal action. Gandhi's letter read as follows: "You have insulted me. You have assaulted me through your peon. If you make no amends, I shall have to proceed against you." (Ibid, p. 98) This clearly shows that Gandhi is not in the habit of pocketing insults, particularly those involving physical force. His letter to the white-sahib shows how strongly he felt over a rather minor physical altercation, which is a justifiable action taken against trespassing persons displaying an apparent unwillingness to leave private property. The white-sahib's response to Gandhi's letter presents a viable defense of his actions:

> You were rude to me. I asked you to go and you would not. I had no option but to order my peon to show you the door. Even after he asked you to leave the office, you did not do so. He therefore had to use just enough force to send you out. You are at liberty to proceed as you wish. (Ibid, p. 98-99)

It happened that a highly esteemed barrister by the name of Sir Pherozeshah Mehta was in the city of Rajkot at the time of this altercation. Gandhi recounts how he sought the barrister's counsel on the strength of his case against the white-sahib. It appears that Gandhi was duly advised to call off his dogs as he was unlikely to get very far with a public official of such high office, such that far from standing any chance of winning as plaintiff, he was far more likely to ruin his career and prospects by being disbarred from the legal profession.

Appendix IV

Gandhi and Freemasonry

~

Proving that Gandhi is associated with Freemasonry is no easy task. We have Gandhi to thank for revealing that fact in his own diary. The overwhelming majority of scholars have a tendency to take everything literally, especially from a man whose word they consider to be as good as gold, this notwithstanding the fact that he openly admits to being experimental with the truth. Did Gandhi write the passage about to be discussed in Masonic code? Should the passage in question be taken figuratively rather than literally? It seems rather odd not to have given it something more than a cursory read since it exhibits a particularly uncharacteristic lack of clarity and sense, when Gandhi is very coherent, concise and succinct when he chooses to be.

The following passage is taken from Gandhi's *London Diary* dated November 12, 1888, purportedly at a time just before he leaves for London. What Gandhi is describing here has escaped examination by scholars. If read today, it would be interpreted by the less discerning as a literal account of a series of accidents that befell him while journeying from place to place. This would not be a correct interpretation. What Gandhi is in fact describing in coded language, which can be understood by higher degree initiates of Freemasonry or by researchers of the Craft, is his probable initiation into Freemasonry:

Amidst thoughts, I came unconsciously in contact with a carriage. I received some injury. Yet I did not take the help of anybody in walking. I think I was quite dizzy. Then we entered the house of Maghjibhai. There I again came in contact with a stone unknowingly and received injury. I was quite senseless. From that time I did not know what took place, and after that, I am told by them, I fell flat on the ground after some steps. I was not myself for 5 minutes. They considered I was dead. But fortunately for myself the ground on which I fell was quite smooth. I came to my senses at last and all of them were quite joyful. The mother was sent for. She was very sorry for me, and this caused my delay though I told them that I was quite well. But none would allow me to go, though I afterwards came to know that my bold and dearest mother would have allowed me to go. But she feared the calumny of other people.... (CWMG 1, pp. 4-5)

The *London Diary*, which Gandhi began writing within six weeks of his arrival in London, must be evaluated carefully. The editors of CWMG confess that this diary was originally about 120 pages in length. Accordingly, Gandhi handed over this diary to Chhaganlal Gandhi, his cousin, in South Africa, who was also going to London in 1909. Only 20 pages of this diary are available in the CWMG. The rest are unaccounted for. Mr. T. K. Mahadevan, a long time Gandhian scholar is also mystified by the disappearance of so many pages from the *London Diary*. It would not be mystifying at all if the diary were recognized for what it is. We believe that this *London Diary* may in fact be Gandhi's Freemason diary. Quite possibly the diary is in fact a coded account of Gandhi's initiation through the various degrees of Freemasonry. In his book *The Year of the Phoenix*, Mahadevan brings us an update that Chhaganlal entrusted the *London Diary* to Mahadev Desai, Gandhi's chief secretary in India in 1920. The diary subsequently disappeared from view thereafter and has not been seen since. Is it possible that the *London Diary* contained such compromising information, i.e. his possible close association or even initiation into the various degrees of Freemasonry, that Gandhi and his close associates decided to destroy it or put it in safe hiding during the early 1920s? What else could have been in that diary that Gandhi deemed unsuitable for the public at large? On the surface, after all, its contents ostensibly consist of nothing more than insignificant diary notes of a young man attending law school in London.

The preceding passage describing a plain account of a mishap occurring during a coach journey has never been discussed openly. We believe it is possible that, what Gandhi is in fact describing, is his initiation to Freemasonry. It is based on the Masonic legend of the murder of Hiram Abif, the alleged architect of King Solomon's Temple. For details read *The Hiram Key* by Christopher Knight and Robert Lomas, London: Arrow Books. Ltd., 1977, p. 175.

It seems that Gandhi's diary account of what took place that day in Rajkot (in India) is written in Masonic code. The two blows he describes receiving were more likely in fact blows to the head, which rendered him senseless. Regarding the first blow, he states, "I came unconsciously in contact with a carriage." He certainly would be unconscious of such a fate if he were blindfolded, which of course all initiates to the Third Degree of Freemasonry are. After the first blow, we are told that he entered the "house of Maghjibhai." It is in this house that he tells us, "There I again came in contact with a stone unknowingly and received injury." Again, he uses the word "unknowingly" quite inexplicably unless we decode the Masonic language and the intended allusions made. He would quite naturally "unknowingly" come in contact with the stone maul or hammer that administered the ritual deathblow inside the temple if he were blindfolded, and he is clearly inside a building structure he describes as the "house of Maghjibhai." He then tells us that he was out for the space of five minutes and that "they" thought he was dead. The "they" he is likely referring to are his fellow Masons, who would regard him as dead after receiving the ritual blow to the head, a reenactment of the final fatal blow that killed Hiram Abif in the Temple. But Gandhi tells us that he did not sustain injury because he landed on a smooth surface, "But fortunately for myself the ground on which I fell was quite smooth." So it would have been if he landed on the smooth surface of solid Masonry, which forms the floor of all Masonic Temples. He then tells us that he came to, "I came to my senses at last and all of them were quite joyful." The Third Degree of Freemasonry concludes with the Worshipful Master leading the candidate to his burial shroud to behold the skull and crossbones, thereby confronting his own death ritualistically. Following the ceremony, the initiate rises to receive cheers and rejoicing from his fellow Masons. This accounts for the joy experienced by Gandhi's brethren on this occasion. We are then informed that, "The mother was sent for." An interesting and unmistakable meaning is here implied. He does not say, "My mother was sent for." He explicitly states, "The mother was sent for." While some might argue that this is an easy mistake for a non-native speaker of English to make, we have to remember that Gandhi was a master of the English language and was not given to making mistakes with articles such as "the." "The mother" is a pointed reference to Hiram Abif's mother, who Masons refer to as "The Widow." Hiram Abif is in fact referred to as "the widow's son" in Freemasonry. And Masons themselves often refer to themselves as "the sons of the widow." Gandhi then tells us that she, the Widow, was quite sorry for him and that she "feared the calumny of other people." This is a clear and explicit reference to the villainy of the "three unworthy craftsmen" known as the "three Juwes" and their kind.

We believe that Gandhi, while openly confessing to being Hindu, is also associated with Masonry. The fact that he is describing an incident that allegedly took place in India in a diary entry made in London on November 12, 1888 reveals a great deal. The Indian setting is a cover for an initiation that took place in London's Temple Bar contemporaneously with the diary entry and not the record of a biographical event from some years earlier as is implied. Higher Degree initiates of Freemasonry would not be fooled by the references, while uninitiated scholars and researchers, or those lacking research knowledge on Freemasonry, would naively overlook the hidden import of the diary entry. More recently, Professor Elizabeth De Michelis (from the University of Cambridge) in her book "*A History of Modern Yoga*" on page 69 mentioned that, "by 1920 there were 183 lodges in the three presidencies."

This is interesting in the sense that Gandhi's longtime place of residence was located within the Bombay Presidency, one of the three presidencies in question. De Michelis has reported that by the early 1880s "it was the fashion with the Indians to become members of the Freemasonry." Therefore, it is quite plausible that Gandhi had contacts or even membership within Freemasonry before going to London in 1888 when his law education commenced. How easy or difficult it is to investigate this relationship in a scholarly fashion will be left to the scholars of the future. The following information might be of benefit to future scholars, who might wish to dig into this mystery further:

In 1905, while in South Africa, under the auspices of the Johannesburg Theosophical Lodge, Gandhi delivered a series of lectures on Hinduism at the Masonic Temple located at Plein Street. The current website hosted by the Grand Lodge of India acknowledges the names of Motilal Nehru (prominent lawyer of the early part of the 20th century British-India), Rajendra Prasad (first president of the Republic of India), S. Radhakrishnan (a reputable Hindu philosopher, and second president of Republic of India), and C. Rajagopalachari (former governor-general of India) as noteworthy members of Freemasonry. Incidentally, these men were also close disciples of Gandhi while Gandhi lived in India.

In 1969, while celebrating Gandhi's birth century, the Grand Lodge of India (GLI) volunteered to put into writing an account explaining the mystery surrounding Gandhi's name. Grand Master K. Gopalswami acknowledged in 1969 Gandhi as a "true Freemason" and made it clear that "Mahatma Gandhi was a great Freemason, although he was not a regular member of the Craft." In other words, GLI is saying that on a superficial account, Gandhi doesn't hold the membership. But on a deeper level, Gandhi is a true Mason. This is no different from the views put forth by the Theosophists regarding his membership in the Theosophical Society. They too considered Gandhi as a true Theosophist and not as one of its card-carrying members. The Theosophical Society is known to have close associations with Freemasonry. It is clear Gandhi exhibited a combined "Freemasonry-Theosophy" complex. A good example of this complex had surfaced earlier in a 1932 book titled,

"The Phoenix: An Illustrated Review of Occultism and Philosophy" by Manly P. Hall (1901-1990). Hall, himself a 33-degree Freemason and a prolific writer of Freemasonry books and its other related typologies clearly depicted Gandhi as one with a "Freemasonry-Theosophy" complex very much of a Hindu orientation and something of an amalgam of the three. This was discussed under the chapter titled, **"The Tenth Avatar"** on pp. 69-72.

Appendix V

Gandhi's Racial Views

~

In 1921-22, Gandhi published his views on the Hindu caste system in a newspaper called *Navajivan*. This monthly newspaper was published by Gandhi in Gujarati and eventually Hindi. The following selection of comments are taken from articles written by Gandhi in the Gujarati language:

(1) I believe that if Hindu society has been able to stand, it is because it is founded on the caste system.

(2) The seeds of *Swaraj* are to be founded in the caste system. Different castes are like different sections of military division. Each division is working for the good of the whole.

(3) Caste has a ready-made means for spreading primary education. Each caste can take the responsibility for the education of the children of the caste. Caste has a political basis. It can work as an electorate for a representative body. Caste can perform judicial functions by electing persons to act as judges to decide disputes among members of the same caste. With castes it is easy to raise a defense force by requiring each caste to raise a brigade.

(4) I believe that interdining or intermarriage is not neces-

sary for promoting national unity. That dining together creates friendship is contrary to experience. If this were true there would have been no war in Europe.

(5) In India children of brothers do not intermarry. Do they cease to love because they do not intermarry? Among the *Vaishnavas* many women are so orthodox that they will not eat with members of the family nor will they drink from a common water pot. Have they no love? The caste system cannot be said to be bad because it does not allow interdining or intermarriage between different castes.

(6) Caste is another name for control. Caste puts a limit on enjoyment. Caste does not allow a person to transgress caste limits in pursuit of his enjoyment. That is the meaning of such caste restrictions as interdining and intermarriage.

(7) To destroy caste system and adopt Western European social system means that Hindus must give up the principle of hereditary occupation, which is the soul of the caste system. Hereditary principle is an eternal principle. To change it is to create disorder. I have no use for a *Brahmin* if I cannot call him a *Brahmin* for my life. It will be chaos, if every day a *Brahmin* is to be changed into a *Shudra* and a *Shudra* is to be changed into a *Brahmin*.

(8) The caste system is a natural order of society. In India it has been given a religious coating. Other countries not having understood the utility of the caste system, it existed only in a loose condition and consequently those countries have not derived from caste system the same degree of advantage, which India has derived.

(9) These being my views I am opposed to all those who are out to destroy the caste system.

Gandhi coined the term *"Harijan,"* meaning "Children of

God," as a new name for the Untouchable community. In conjunction with this, he propagated himself as a hero who held nothing but the deepest love for the Untouchables. The Dalits, however, have utterly rejected this term in favor of the self-applied "Dalit." The community views Gandhi's *"Harijan"* term as a derogatory and deceptive word designed so he could publicly convey sympathy for the community without actually doing anything of substance to improve their situation.

Dr. B. R. Ambedkar, a Dalit leader and the most revered figure in his community, was a contemporary of Gandhi. Ambedkar was born into the Untouchable community, but by a stroke of luck and the compassionate sponsorship of a Maharaja, he became one of the rare Untouchables to receive a university education. After completing his education in London, he became increasingly wary of Hinduism. His mistrust of the religion flourished to the point where, in protest of the Hindu caste system, he publicly burned one of the sacred Hindu texts. Having heard and rejected the calls of both Hinduism and Gandhism, Ambedkar eventually converted to Buddhism to escape the oppression of caste.

Like Mayawati, Ambedkar blamed Gandhi for entrenching the pathetic situation of low-caste Indians. Ambedkar had a twenty year working relationship with Gandhi, during which he had a chance to discover and comprehend the man's character. Gauging by what Ambedkar wrote about his experiences, he believed Gandhi damaged the Dalits and other minorities, saying: "If a man with God's name on his tongue and a sword under his armpit deserved the appellation of a Mahatma, then Mohandas Karamchand Gandhi was a Mahatma!" (B. R. Ambedkar, *Gandhi and Gandhism*)

Gandhi was thoroughly consistent in his obsession with race. We remind the reader of his comment equating Indian and Anglo-Saxon ethnic ancestry, saying: "Both the Anglo-Saxon and the Indian races belong to the same stock... both the races have sprung from the same Aryan stock, or rather the Indo-European as many call it." The consistency of Gandhi's Indo-Aryan ideology was reflected in his correspondence with Hitler. Although we will briefly discuss that correspondence, it is obviously not the topic of the book. Yet considering Gandhi's questionable guidance for India on

Hitler and the sharp spike of sales of *Mein Kampf* in India today, the issue of Gandhi's interaction with Hitler deserves a study all its own.

Gandhi frequently wrote about Hitler in his articles and letters. On May 15, 1940, he wrote: "I do not consider Hitler to be as bad as he is depicted. He is showing an ability that is amazing and *he seems to be gaining his victories without much bloodshed* [emphasis added]." (CWMG, Vol. 78, p. 219) Gandhi's comment that Hitler's victories came "without much bloodshed" was made barely seven months after the invasion of Poland, which saw 66,000 Polish killed in approximately five weeks. In fact, the Battle of the Netherlands, which resulted in the death of over 2,300 Dutch, ended on May 14, 1940, only one day before Gandhi made this comment. On May 26, 1940, while the German assault on Norway and Denmark was still in progress, Gandhi said, "I do not believe Herr Hitler to be as bad as he is portrayed. He might even have been a friendly power as he may still be." (Ibid., p. 253) The campaign against Norway and Denmark caused the deaths of approximately 6,100 Allied troops.

On December 24, 1940, Gandhi wrote a lengthy letter to Adolf Hitler, telling him: "We have no doubt about your bravery or devotion to your fatherland, nor do we believe that you are the monster described by your opponents." Like his other letters to Hitler, Gandhi addressed this one to his "dear friend," going out of his way to assure Hitler "that I address you as a friend is no formality." (CWMG, Vol. 79, pp. 453-56)

Considering Gandhi's lack of clarity on the problem of Hitler, it is a strange twist of fate that the Führer's *Mein Kampf* has become a modern-day bestseller in Gandhi's India, flying off the shelves to land in the hands of Indian college students. Although India is an emerging power which hopes to take a larger position of leadership in the world, countless students are using Hitler's manifesto as a business primer for self-improvement and management education. However, others argue the book is popular for political reasons. Dr. J. Kuruvachira, a professor of philosophy at Salesian College in Nagaland, said: "While it could be the case that management students are buying the book, my feeling is that it has more likely influenced some of the fascist organisations operating in India." (Monty Munford, "Indian business students snap up copies of Mein Kampf," *The Daily Telegraph*, April 20, 2009).

Appendix VI

The Doherty Murder

~

In 1921, Gandhi helped to cover up the murder of an American citizen by Gandhians who were rioting during the second Satyagraha movement. The murdered man, William Francis Doherty, was an engineer working in Bombay. In 1929, his wife dictated a sworn statement to a Los Angeles notary concerning events after her husband's death.

The viciousness of the attack on her husband, who had his eyes gouged out, is a trademark of Hindu extremist assaults and state-sponsored pogroms against Indian minorities today.

Mrs. Doherty's Sworn Statement

State of California County of Los Angeles

ANNETTE H. DOHERTY, being first duly sworn oath, deposes and says:

My deceased husband, William Francis Doherty, an American citizen, was a mechanical and electrical engineer and business associate of Mr. Richard J. Brenchley, engaged in sand extraction at Mumbra, adjacent to Bombay, India.

On November 19th, 1921, as he was quietly proceeding to

the Bombay Improvement Trust work-shops, he was set upon, his eyes were gouged out and eventually he was beaten to death by a group of rioters in a public street of Byculla, a suburb of Bombay.

This was during the visit of the Prince of Wales to India, when Gandhi was at the height of his popularity as a saint and political leader, and had, through his violent speeches against the British, worked his followers into a frenzy of race hatred. My husband was probably mistaken for a Britisher when he was murdered by Gandhi's followers.

Within three days following this killing of my husband, word was brought me from Gandhi that he greatly desired an interview with me, begging me to set a time when I would receive him. I was then stopping with an American family in Bombay. Gandhi's emissary was Mrs. Sarojini Naidu, the Indian poetess and politician.

Mrs. Naidu was greatly agitated, and made many statements to me that I feel she would now like to unsay. Her chief concern, however, was that the American public should never be allowed to hear of this outrage committed upon my husband; and she very frankly asked me my price for refraining from ever discussing or advertising the affair in America and from myself returning to America. Under no condition, said Mrs. Naidu, would they be willing that the American public should learn that they were killing people so promiscuously that even a white face cost a man's life.

As to Gandhi's request for an interview with me:

At that time he was going about so unclothed that Mrs. Naidu suggested I call upon him rather than that he come to the American home where I was stopping - inasmuch as this latter might prove embarrassing. It was therefore determined that I should see him at his own headquarters in Bombay, which I did, a motor car having been sent by him to fetch me.

Upon this occasion of my visit with Gandhi he repeated to me in substance what Mrs. Naidu had said, but even more emphatically stressed the point that Americans, because they were so much in sympathy with him in his political views, must on no account learn the details of the murder of my husband lest it hurt the success of his movement in America and prejudice our people against him.

ANNETTE HELEN DOHERTY.

Subscribed and sworn to before me this 4th day of January, 1929,

W.J. SCHISEL Notary Public in and for the County of Los Angeles, State of California. My commission expires Jan. 18, 1931.

Bibliography

~

Alexander, Horace. *Gandhi Through Western Eyes*. Philadelphia, PA: New Society Publishers, 1984.

Athalye, D.V. *The Life of Mahatma Gandhi*. Poona, India: Swadeshi Publishing Company, 1923 (1st edition); 2nd edition in 1926.

Bowles, Chester. *The Conscience of a Liberal: Selected writings and speeches*. New York: Harper & Row, 1962.

Briley, John. *Gandhi: The Screenplay*. New York: Grove Press, 1982.

Britton, Burnett. *Gandhi Arrives in South Africa*. Canton, Maine: Greenleaf Books, 1999.

Brown, Judith M. and Martin Prezesky, eds. *Gandhi and South Africa: Principles and Politics*, Pietermaritzburg: University of Natal Press, 1996.

Campbell, Edward Donald. *The Birth and Development of the Natal Railways*. Pietermaritzburg: Shuter and Shooter, 1951.

Chatfield, Charles, ed. *The Americanization of Gandhi: Images of the Mahatma*. New York: Garland Publishing, Inc., 1976.

Cooper, Robert. *Around The World With Mark Twain*. New York: Arcade Publishing, 2000.

De Bertodano, Teresa. *Soul Searchers: An Anthology of Spiritual Journeys*. Grand Rapids, Michigan: William B. Eerdmans Publishing Company, 2002.

Devanesen, Chandran D.S. *The Making of the Mahatma*. New Delhi: Orient Longmans Ltd., 1969.

Doke, Joseph J. *M. K. Gandhi: An Indian Patriot in South Africa*. London: Indian Chronicle, 1909.

Duminy, Andrew and Bill Guest, ed. *"Natal and Zululand: From Earliest Times to 1910 A new History"* Pietermaritzburg: University of Natal Press, 1989.

Field, Harry F. *After Mother India*. London: Jonathan Cape and Company, 1929.

Fisher, Frederick B. *That Strange Little Brown Man Gandhi*. New Delhi: Orient Longmans Ltd., 1970 (reprint).

Gandhi, Arun and Sunanda. *The Forgotten Woman: The Untold Story of Kastur, Wife of Mahatma Gandhi*. Hunstville, Arkansas: Ozark Mountain Publishers, 1998.

Gandhi, M. K. *Mahatma Gandhi: His Life, Writings, and Speeches*, Ganesh & Co. Madras 1921.

Gandhi, Mohandas K. *Satyagraha in South Africa*. 1928; reprint, Navajivan Publishing House, 1972.

Gandhi, Mohandas K. *An Autobiography or The Story of My Experiments With Truth*. (1927, 1929); reprint, Boston: Beacon Press, 1957.

Gandhi, Mohandas K. *Collected Works of Mahatma Gandhi*. Government of India, 2000 (6th edition).

Hoyland, John S. *They Saw Gandhi.* New York: Fellowship Publications, 1947. 2nd edition published by National Education Association of the United States, 1953.

Hunt, James D. *Gandhi and the Nonconformists: Encounters in South Africa.* New Delhi: Promilla & Co. Publishers, 1986.

Kurtz, Paul. *The New Skepticism: Inquiry and Reliable Knowledge.* Buffalo, N.Y.: Prometheus Books, 1992.

Laband, J. and R. Haswell, eds. *Pietermaritzburg 1838-1988: A New Portrait of an African City,* Pietermaritzburg: University of Natal Press and Shuter & Shooter, 1988.

Mahadevan, T.K. *The Year of the Phoenix: Gandhi's Pivotal Year, 1893-1894.* Chicago: World Without War Publications, 1982.

Mathews, James K. *The Matchless Weapon: Satyagraha.* Bombay: Bharatiya Vidya Bhavan, 1989.

Mehta, P.J. *M. K. Gandhi and the South African Indian Problem.* Madras: G.A. Natesan & Company, [1912?]

Meer, Fatima, ed. *The South African Gandhi: An Abstract of the Speeches and Writings of M. K. Gandhi 1893-1914.* Natal: Madiba Publishers, 1996.

Nayar, Sushila. *Mahatma Gandhi: Satyagraha at Work* (Vol. 4). Ahmedabad, India: Navajivan Publishing House, 1989.

Nietzsche, Friedrich. *The Genealogy of Morals*, ed. and trans. Oscar Levy, London: Foulis Ltd, 1913.

Polak, Henry S.L., H.N. Brailsford, and Lord Pethick-Lawrence. *Mahatma Gandhi.* London: Odhams Press Ltd, 1949.

Polak, Henry S.L. *M. K. Gandhi: A Sketch of His Life and Work*. Madras: G.A. Natesan & Co. 1910. Subsequent editions after 1922 were published under the title, *Mahatma Gandhi: The Man and His Mission*.

Pyarelal, Mahatma Gandhi: *The Early Phase*, Volume 1. Ahmedabad: Navajivan Publishing House, 1965.

Pyarelal and Sushila Nayar. *In Gandhiji's Mirror*. Delhi: Oxford University Press, 1991.

Singh, G. B. *Gandhi: Behind the Mask of Divinity*. Amherst, N.Y.: Prometheus Books, 2004.

Sparks, Allister. *The Mind of South Africa*. New York: Alfred A. Knopf, 1990.

Shukla, Chandrashanker, ed. *Incidents of Gandhiji's Life*. Vora & Co. Pub., Bombay, 1949.

Shukla, Chandrashanker, ed. Reminiscences of Gandhiji. Vora and Co. Pub., Bombay, 1951.

Tendulkar, D.G. *Mahatma: Life of Mohandas Karamchand Gandhi*. New Delhi: The Publications Division, Government of India, 1952.

Xavier, N.S. *Two Faces of Religion: A Psychiatrist's View*. Tuscaloosa, Alabama: Portals Press, 1987.

Index

~

About the Authors

~

Col. G. B. Singh (ret.) served in the U.S. Army. He is a professional student of Indian politics, world religions and their true historical values and political impacts, and the life and teachings of Gandhi. He lives in Tennessee, USA.

Dr. Tim Watson gained his higher education in Europe and taught for several years in East Asia. He currently teaches philosophy and communications in Toronto, Canada, and hosts a weekly radio show at thatradio.com.